The New Politics of

# Sage Politics Texts

SAGE Politics Texts offer authoritative and accessible analyses of core issues in contemporary political science and international relations. Each text combines a comprehensive overview of key debates and concepts with fresh and original insights. By extending across all main areas of the discipline, SAGE Politics Texts constitute a comprehensive body of contemporary analysis. They are ideal for use on advanced courses and in research.

# The New Politics of Welfare

*Social Justice in a Global Context*

Bill Jordan

SAGE Publications
London • Thousand Oaks • New Delhi

SAGE Publications Ltd
6 Bonhill Street
London EC2A 4PU

SAGE Publications Inc.
2455 Teller Road
Thousand Oaks, California 91320

SAGE Publications India Pvt Ltd
32, M-Block Market
Greater Kailash – I
New Delhi 110 048

**British Library Cataloguing in Publication data**

A catalogue record for this book is available
from the British Library

ISBN 0 7619 6021 X
ISBN 0 7619 6022 8 (pbk)

**Library of Congress catalog card number 98–61178**

Typeset by Mayhew Typesetting, Rhayader, Powys
Printed in Great Britain by The Cromwell Press Ltd,
Trowbridge, Wiltshire

# Summary of Contents

# Contents

# List of Figures

# List of Tables

# Acknowledgements

I am very grateful to a number of friends and colleagues who read the first draft of this book, and made helpful criticisms and suggestions, especially Hartley Dean (whose detailed comments and overall perspectives were especially valuable), Michael Breuer, Mita Castle-Kanerová and Ian Holliday; and also to the anonymous readers of my original proposal for the book. I have tried to do justice to all their suggestions, but inevitably fallen short in some respects.

Gill Watson has worked extremely hard and efficiently to turn my early-morning handwriting into electronic text, and I am very much indebted to her for her expertise and support.

Thanks also to Lucy Robinson at Sage Publications for her advice and encouragement, and to all my colleagues in Exeter, Huddersfield, Bremen, Bratislava and Budapest for what I have learned from them recently.

# 1

# Introduction: Social Justice in a Global Context

This book is an analysis of the emerging orthodoxy on social welfare in the United Kingdom and the United States of America. Tony Blair and Bill Clinton agree on many aspects of social policy, and the reforms they have implemented are similar in many features. Their programmes are a positive and proactive response by nation states to the phenomena of globalization.

The new politics of welfare is far more than a plan to reform the social services. It takes the moral high ground, and mobilizes citizens in a thrust for national regeneration. It deals in ethical principles, and appeals to civic responsibility and the common good. Above all, it bids to recreate a cohesive community, through the values of self-discipline, family solidarity and respect for lawful authority.

Yet it does so at a time when national governments seem most ineffectual in the face of global market forces. If postwar welfare states appeared to have made workers less dependent on competing in the labour market, globalization now puts the wage relation back at the heart of the political struggle. Instead of resisting this, the new social politics reinforces it, by promising to 'put the work ethic back at the centre of the welfare state'. It drives citizens into the waiting arms of a revitalized global capital, exhorting them to intensify their competitive efforts for the sake of greater productivity and growth.

In doing so, it claims to be acting as much for social justice as for economic efficiency, and to build new links between the two.[1] It insists that the greatest wrongs are now being done by those who rely too much on collective provision, not those who exploit the skills and energies of their employees. It uses the authority of the state to ensure that there is no shortage in the supply of capable staff to meet the demands of 'flexible' labour markets.

This book focuses on three features of the new politics of welfare. The first is its appeal to *national renewal* through a strong work ethic and high rates of participation in the formal economy. The Blair–Clinton orthodoxy asserts the claims of the national polity over individual egoism and international opportunism alike. Its version of social justice chooses to ignore transnational issues that greatly complicate both the ethical and the economic analysis of situations facing First World governments. In this and the final chapter I shall highlight the dangers hidden by its rhetoric of national mobilization.

The second is its claim of *moral authority* in the implementation of measures to restrict the payment of benefits and put stronger conditions around eligibility for social protection. Part of this claim is derived from the resounding electoral victory achieved by Tony Blair, and the high job-competence ratings given to Bill Clinton – despite personal scandals – in opinion polls. But a stronger element is the appeal to values drawn from the family, the association and the traditional community – to reciprocity, responsibility and mutuality, and the obligations these imply. I shall question whether it is possible to give a coherent account of social justice in a large society based on impersonal interactions, in terms of principles derived from these quite different spheres.

The third is its *denial of the continuing relevance of class and exploitation*, as factors in the analysis of social justice. The new Blair–Clinton ortho-doxy emphasizes employability and equality of opportunity, in a popu-lation treated as competing for commensurable rewards. Its version of distributive justice deals in the resources individuals need to gain the advantages they merit in such competition. This book is not a reassertion of the primacy of class struggle in social relations, and anyone looking for such an analysis will be sadly disappointed in it. But it does point to the weaknesses of a policy programme that neglects the problem of exploitation in labour markets, and ignores fundamental differences in power and resources between groups interacting in the economy.

The book puts forward a critique of the new politics of welfare from the standpoint of liberal democratic theory (in its broadest sense), and an alternative policy programme. It reasserts aspects of liberal demo-cratic theory that have been neglected since the advent of the New Right. The alternative programme accepts the goals of the Blair–Clinton approach (better access to employment for all, fairer sharing of the work that is to be done, and better targeting of those in greatest need) but argues that they can be far more reliably achieved by a radically different set of measures. This alternative approach recognizes the insecurities of the middle classes and the impoverishment of less skilled workers, but also that the informal economic activities of poor people can be the basis for the regeneration of their districts and the improvement of their quality of life. This alternative programme is set out in Chapter 5.

The book's other objective is to compare the new orthodoxy in the UK and the USA with the dilemmas facing the more conservative regimes of Europe, and especially Germany. As the rising tide of unemployment and the escalation of on-wage social costs threaten to become a vicious circle, and the economic stagnation of Germany spreads pessimism over the whole European project, I shall analyse the prospects for European social policy. In particular, I shall consider the relationship between the debates about 'the social question' and the prospects for economic and political integration. This will include an analysis of the trajectories of the former communist countries of Central and Eastern Europe – both those set to join the European Union in the first wave, and those who must continue to wait before the gates. This discussion is drawn together in Chapter 6.


## Scope and methods of the book


The new politics of welfare draws on two repertoires to explain the need for reform and mobilize electorates in support of its response to globalization. Tony Blair and Bill Clinton[2] use economic arguments to snow that past arrangements are now outdated, and that reforms are necessary for the sake of economic efficiency, prosperity and growth, to improve the welfare of all citizens. They also use a rhetoric of social justice – normative arguments to justify changes that redistribute roles and resources, and alter the conditions under which benefits and services are given.

In my analysis in this book I shall also draw on two theoretical literatures that address these issues, and seek to combine them in a coherent way. The first is the literature of the *public choice* school, that applies economic methods to political decision making.[3] In this theoretical tradition, political choices and institutions are explained in terms of the actions of individuals who are rational maximizers of their own utility. Politics is concerned with rules and systems for efficient allocations of goods which markets undersupply, because they are too costly to divide up among exclusive owners and exchange for a price. Yet rational-egoistic individual agents can reach collective agreements about such goods, because each benefits from cooperation and restraint. The same theoretical demonstration of the benefits of orderly market exchange (under rules against violence, fraud and theft) also explains the advantages of collective procedures for providing law and order and defence, environmental protection and basic education. Because people live together, and some decisions affect them all, they must take collective action to supply these goods.[4]

However, some collective choices (such as those listed above) benefit all members of a community, and other choices benefit only some, while hurting others. It is the latter decisions that concern distributive or social justice, and it is to these that *normative theory* applies. Theories of justice have been part of the mainstream of political thought since the Classical Greek philosophers, and the methods of analysis that are characteristic of this tradition will be used. For example, in Chapter 3 I shall explain and criticize the new Blair–Clinton orthodoxy's claims about how the principles of equality, merit and need can be reconciled through its reforms of welfare institutions.

At first sight this combination of two theoretical approaches may seem ambitious. Yet these two methodologies are not as separate as they might seem. In most of the literature of public choice, collective decisions about the allocation of resources are made under rules that are seen as built into the constitutional principles of the polity. These rules reflect values that are supposed to enter the public choice process through a (fictitious, hypothetical) 'social contract' between individuals who come together and voluntarily form themselves into a political unit. This consensual basis for political arrangements can, of course, be traced to theorists such as Hobbes and Rousseau, and is most promi-nent in the work of the modern author John Rawls.[5] In his theory of justice, therefore, we can recognize an example of an analysis which is both individualistic and contractarian in the public choice tradition, and normative in the tradition of moral and political philosophy. Rawls' citizens agree unanimously and for all time on certain principles (equal liberty for all, and the equal distribution of opportunity, income, wealth and self-respect, unless an unequal distribution of any or all of these values is for everyone's advantage), and these normative commitments then become the constitutional basis for all their political arrangements. Rawls' theory will be further discussed on pp. 85–6.

Because most public choice analyses[6] assume a 'social contract' such as Rawls', they then go on to discuss allocations that will be given unanimous consent by citizens, because they cannot make one person better off without making another worse off (the so-called Pareto criterion of allocative efficiency). If individuals are assumed to have the option of joining or leaving a political association, then unanimity is required,[7] and under assumptions of rational egoism individuals will only endorse decisions that are Pareto-efficient. Hence equity is built into the theoretical basis of the model.

But in the real world – as all public choice theorists readily concede – there are several facts that complicate such assumptions. The main difficulty is that political units of many different sizes exist, and individuals' interests as members of their local authority (city or state) are not necessarily the same as those as citizens of the national polity. It makes a difference whether we see the 'social contract' as between members of a city or a nation state, and (if the former) whether we treat national political arrangements as a kind of federation of local ones. So – even if the assumptions that justify Pareto-efficient allocations are accepted – there may be differences in optimal decisions according to one's perspective on this dimension.

This difficulty is greatly magnified if we look at choices from the perspective of the whole world's welfare. Globalization increases the scope for individuals to move between nation states, and choose which one to live and work in (not necessarily the same for both). It also increases the necessity for transnational regimes of collective regulation and decision making. But there is a majority of citizens of every state who are not mobile, yet whose welfare is directly affected by others' mobility, and by transnational decisions. Hence the assumption of unanimous consent to allocative choices is far from realistic, and the notion that reallocations that promote *global* efficiency necessarily benefit the citizens of every state is quite misleading. These issues will be further explored in Chapter 6.

The contractarian assumptions of mainstream public choice analyses imply that there is a consensus over values that is reflected in the constitution and decision procedures (such as voting). Normative theory in the tradition of moral and political philosophy (like other schools of welfare economics)[8] assumes that rules and even constitutions can be changed, and presents arguments for changing them. The new Blair–Clinton orthodoxy follows this tradition in arguing for something like a 'new social contract' (or New Covenant), which in the UK includes important changes in the constitutional status of Scotland, Wales and now also Northern Ireland, and in the voting systems there and for the European Parliament. In this sense, the new politics of welfare is radical, and concerns fundamental change.

However, in so far as capitalists and skilled workers do have scope to treat the whole world as if it is just one place, and all the rest of the population does not, the leaders of the new orthodoxy on welfare face many constraints on their reforms. They cannot afford to make changes that will work to the disadvantage of mobile global actors, or those whose life chances depend directly on them. Hence they are driven towards choices that may run against the interests of the poorest and least advantaged minorities among their citizens. In Chapter 2, I seek to explain decisions over cutting benefits for lone parents, and imposing coercive conditions around support for long-term unemployed people, in terms of the interaction between these factors.

In principle, the process of globalization is easy to understand. As barriers to free exchange of goods and services of all kinds, and also of mobility of people and information across borders, are gradually weakened, so those factors which are mobile seek more efficient and profitable uses in other parts of the world, because they are no longer tied into the regulations that restrained competition through domestic institutional structures. As returns to security and stability under systems of national economic management have declined, those to mobility and innovation have grown, and factors that can move do so. In addition to capital (e.g., a factory owner selling his plant in the industrial town of Telford in the English Midlands, and reopening his production of the same goods in one of the new economic regions of China),[9] this includes skilled labour – especially workers in those information industries and communications systems which sustain the global economy.

This example of the outcomes of global market forces can be seen as an increase in efficiency. Under the assumptions of the public choice theory, it is therefore *ipso facto* equitable. The large welfare gains to previously underemployed rural workers in developing countries such as China are greater than the losses to redundant, immobile workers in the First World, and global income is increased, by the move. In principle, the gainers could afford to compensate the losers, so everyone would be no worse off than before, and some (very poor) people considerably better off. But of course there is no mechanism of world government through which the Chinese who benefit can give compensation (e.g. welfare benefits or retraining) to the citizens of Telford who are the losers. And Tony Blair's government must decide how to set levels and conditions of unemployment benefit in the light of his goal of attracting and keeping international investment, from corporations in South East Asia, the USA and elsewhere in the world.

For these reasons, there is clearly an important distinction to be made between the *economic* equity that is assumed to be built into Pareto-efficient resource allocations, and the redistributions that would be made under principles of social justice, applied to all members of a community. The tension between these two perspectives is an integral feature of the new politics of welfare, and my analysis, relying on these two quite different but interlinked methodologies, will seek to illustrate the paradoxes and contradictions in the new orthodoxy that arise from the interactions between them.

## The constraints of globalization

The new politics of welfare draws on both liberal-contractarian analyses of economic rights and equity, and reformist versions of social rights and justice within a solidaristic framework. In this way it is able to emphasize the constraints imposed by globalization (the requirements of competitive efficiency in world markets), and the moral demands of communal values. Two distinctive political repertoires[10] are thus combined, in order to justify redistributive limits, along with ethical principles of giving and sharing.

In the liberal-contractarian tradition, economic freedom and personal autonomy are guaranteed through constitutions – as in the USA – which define individual rights under agreed rules (see previous section). In T.H. Marshall's famous analysis of the emergence of democratic citizenship, civil rights of this kind were established first (in the eighteenth century), then the political rights of democratic govern-ment (in the nineteenth), and finally the social rights of twentieth century citizens[11] (see pp. 77–8). But in the solidaristic tradition of Continental European conservatism, and of socialism, social cohesion was achieved by various systems of social protection before liberty and democracy were established. Catholic social philosophy and corporatist institutions appeal to values of social harmony, integration and inclu-sion for their versions of social citizenship.

The new Blair–Clinton orthodoxy relies on ideas of economic justice from the contractarian repertoire to insist on global market constraints to redistributive allocations for the sake of competitive efficiency. But it also insists on the moral bonds of membership between citizens, and especially on their obligations to work and contribute for the sake of solidarity and social justice.

The new politics of welfare seeks a programme that can manage and reverse the losses to immobile (unable or unwilling to retrain or relo-cate) labour in First World countries, and the disruption to whole communities caused by rapid change. It acknowledges that the 'golden age' of welfare states is past,[12] and that nation states must now compete with each other for shares of transnational investment and trade in goods and services.

The new orthodoxy also aims to provide a model (the 'Third Way') for those who suffer far more extreme examples of these phenomena in the Second World, post-communist countries of Central and Eastern Europe. Their special situation, as an example of a system of economic management and social protection that has been swept away by global market forces, will be another whole theme of this book. At a time when the first of these are hoping to join the EU in the next five years, the new politics of welfare are highly relevant to their immediate futures.

The post-communist countries of Central and Eastern Europe are still struggling to manage the effects of price competition and private ownership on a previously centralized command system, with political allocation of all resources. What we see is the distributive outcomes when previously subsidised groups are suddenly put at the mercy of world markets, and when governments cannot afford to offer them any

shelter. This is most dramatic in the case of single-industry towns and
state farms. Here the whole formal economy has collapsed, and
exchange is organized between and through informal networks, among
exclusive groups (or 'families') who control particular resources.[13]
Moreover, even social assistance comes to be constituted in rights
derived from interactions between groups of social workers and their
clients, excluding the poorest from relief, while conflicts between local
villagers and 'outsiders' who settled on state farms and now find
themselves without work prospects can result in the disqualification of
the latter from assistance.[14] Some whole economies have sunk from
urban, industrial production into re-ruralization; for instance, in the
Ukraine, the production of vegetables, fruit and livestock in the cities
has expanded as manufacturing has declined, and the majority of
national income is now generated in the rural economy. The outcome is
that 90 per cent of the Ukrainian population now live below the level of
the 10 per cent who were poor under communism, and national income
per head is now officially recorded as lower than that in India, Sri
Lanka, Indonesia or even Papua New Guinea.[15]

In the dominant view of the situation in the 1990s, national governments are strictly limited in their scope for combating the effects of
these processes on their citizens. If they try to 'capture' or 'channel'
capital into national production (through various kinds of social
contract) they risk losing the benefits associated with international
flows, both in terms of opportunities for more profitable returns for
'national' capital abroad, and in terms of access to more efficiently
produced goods from other countries. In the end, the inefficiencies and
costs of such a strategy defeat its purposes, as the Mitterand government discovered in the early 1980s, the Scandinavian countries
recognized in the mid-1980s and the whole Soviet bloc acknowledged
in 1989. Furthermore, the attempt to compensate immobile factors by
taxing mobile gainers from the globalization process is self-defeating,
because the latter simply move their resources abroad, or organize
political resistance that is likely to be decisive in a democratic system,
especially if the economy is not prospering.

Some authors question whether globalization has really progressed as
far as this analysis suggests, and whether it really constrains national
policies so radically. For instance, Hirst and Thompson[16] devote a whole
book to questioning many of the claims of those who see the rise of
international corporations and the growth of trade as the outstanding
characteristic of the current period. At best, there has been uneven
development among the First World countries in their involvement in
these processes, and the success of the South East Asian 'tiger' economies
may lie as much in their subtle resistance to import penetration as in
their capture of a growing share of global export markets. Indeed, this
'success' is itself called into question by recent recessions in that region,
and especially the collapse of the South Korean economy. All the

phenomena of the globalization hypothesis – the movement of the terms of trade towards the newly industrializing countries, the mobility of skilled labour and the decline in wage rates to international low levels – have been sceptically analysed by writers on the left including Gordon[17] and Ruigrok and Van Tulder,[18] leading to doubts about the extent to which they really constrain government social policy.

It is a very important question whether there are real limits for social policy and redistributive justice, and whether national economies can still be understood in terms of traditional international trade theory, or whether some new analysis and different assumptions are required (see pp. 211–12). Unfortunately the evidence is still inconclusive, and the question still contested, although (as in the case of global warming) there is increasing consensus around a paradigm change. What counts for current politics is the growing belief that such constraints exist, and the fear that programmes to combat poverty and unemployment through higher public expenditures will trigger speculation against the national currency, or disinvestment by foreign firms. In this context, the idea of a global market is probably even more powerful than global economic forces themselves; governments believe that they are competing for prizes in budgetary rectitude before a panel of international financial institutions, and this affects their actions. In Europe, all these constraints have been strongly reinforced by the requirement to limit government borrowing in the period leading up to European Monetary Union.

On this account, the period after the Second World War provided exceptionally favourable conditions for the establishment of welfare states. Because of economic protectionism in the prewar period, and the blockades and disruptions of the war itself, the volume of world trade was extremely low, in comparison with the period before the First World War. Exchange controls and other barriers to capital mobility, along with the division of the world into mutually hostile power blocks, further inhibited the development of the global market. In this environment, nation states were able to establish institutions for sharing the benefits of rapid postwar growth between organized capital and organized labour, under settlements which gave all citizens new forms of social protection. Because each First World country's economy was dominated by a number of large national firms, and each enjoyed a protected domestic market and a regional or wider segment of the markets in the developing world, these settlements could guarantee to both the 'social partners' considerable returns to the restraint of competition between them, and thus avoid the suboptimal stalemates of the interwar years.

From a global perspective, the institutions of First World welfare states can be viewed as barriers to the optimal allocation of resources worldwide. For instance, Olson[19] saw all such arrangements as 'distributional coalitions' between the collective actors (large industrial cartels, trade unions, government bureaucracies) for capturing the 'rents' associated with a form of protectionism. In a free market, capital should flow to those productive sites where it can be most efficiently combined with labour power to produce goods and services at the lowest possible costs. This usually implies that it will move towards less developed regions of the national and the global economies, and hence improve the productivity and wages of hitherto unorganized workers, whose full potential is yet to be realized. But agreements such as those between the 'peak organizations' of capital and labour in the First World countries tied capital to national economies, through complex corporate institutions, including interdependencies between banks and large industrial firms – an institutional system most developed in Germany and Japan, which contributed to their exceptional success at this time.

In this way, capitalists and workers were paid more, in profits and wages, than the competitive return on capital and labour should have warranted. The 'rent' (i.e. the difference between the returns that would have been available in free markets, and the ones generated by these agreements) that they thus enjoyed, by restraining competition and restricting output, was at the expense of producers and consumers in the developing economies, who were forced to take their prices for manufactured goods, and depended on them for purchase of raw materials. Welfare recipients in First World countries benefited indirectly from these 'distortions' in productive allocations, just as poor people in the developing countries suffered from them.

On this analysis, welfare states (including health and social services in kind) were reliant on particular conditions and institutional restraints which have progressively eroded or disintegrated since the late 1960s, initially because full employment policies upset the balance of power between capital and labour, and allowed wage earners to claim a disproportionate share of the fruits of this arrangement, and profits to fall too low.[20] As world trade grew, and barriers to capital transfers were dismantled, international corporations developed new institutions for escaping the restraints of these agreements. As a result, there emerged a new international division of labour, with manufacturing production resited in newly industrializing countries in Southern Europe, the Middle East, Latin America and especially South East Asia. Above all, the evidence of much faster growth in these economies, and the rapid expansion of their manufacturing sectors, contrasted with the relative stagnation of the US and European economies in the 1970s, and the decline in industrial employment – most spectacularly in the United Kingdom and Belgium, where it fell from over 40 to under 30 per cent of all employment in that decade.[21]

The 1980s can be seen as a period when some First World countries struggled fairly successfully to preserve the institutional structures of welfare states, while others voluntarily embarked on radical reforms to open up their economies to global market forces. In the former group, Germany, Sweden and Austria were all held out as examples of successful corporatist systems,[22] with very low rates of unemployment and satisfactory growth. In the latter, the United Kingdom, the USA and New Zealand were taken as instances of market-minded radicalism, with high unemployment and polarization leading to social division and political conflict.

Yet the situation in the 1990s can be recognized as far more fluid than this. What Esping-Andersen[23] described as the 'three worlds of welfare capitalism' (distinguishing between the social democratic regimes of Scandinavia, the Christian Democratic regimes of Continental Europe, and the liberal regimes of the Anglo-Saxon countries) can now be seen as 'strategies', none of which can claim consistent success.[24] The Scandinavian countries – and especially Sweden – have suffered a decline in their relative prosperity, and a rapid growth in unemployment and social assistance claims (especially in Finland). The Continental European countries now suffer from high and persistent unemployment, and rising contribution rates for social benefits and services. The Anglo-Saxon countries have the highest rates of poverty and inequality, and insecurity of employment, along with evidence of social conflict (such as rising expenditure on criminal enforcement). Furthermore, even the success of the 'tiger' economies of South East Asia, with their rapid growth of incomes and their dramatic expansion of manufacturing and share in world trade, is now called into question. In 1997 the collapse of the Thai and South Korean economies, and of sections of the financial sector in Japan, indicated that much of this success was founded on the availability of artificially cheap capital, rather than some novel and enduring solution to the problems of sustainable economic development and social stability.

## Social justice, poverty and exclusion

In the postwar period, welfare states seemed to have settled fundamental issues of social justice between citizens of First World polities through institutions linking labour-market participation by working-age men to various forms of social protection. These institutions varied considerably in extent to which they actually redistributed incomes between groups, or produced equality of outcome. Indeed, one whole cluster of welfare regimes, the Christian Democratic states of Continental Europe, used social insurance systems to maintain differentials of income between a hierarchy of social status groups during their retirements; these welfare states structured and integrated interdependent but unequal income groups, redistributing across the life cycle of each rather than between them. In liberal, Anglo-Saxon countries, low rates of social insurance benefits meant that public assistance continued to play an important role in social policy, and that poor people were therefore an identifiable segment of society, qualifying by means tests for limited transfers, financed out of general taxation.

During the 1970s, a number of critical voices were raised against the version of social justice institutionalized in these settlements. First, feminists pointed out that they reinforced patriarchal domestic rela- tions, by linking benefits (and – in the case of Continental European regimes – health care insurance) to men's employment.[25] Along with income taxation systems, they therefore structured welfare provision according to a 'breadwinner model'[26] of contributions and eligibility, with women formally classified as dependants. Indeed, this can be seen as an essential characteristic of the restrained competition that charac- terized postwar social citizenship. Women who had been active as workers during wartime mobilization, were henceforth to be confined to the household economy, and hence to become labour-market outsiders, competing only with each other, and with some other excluded groups, for subordinate, lower-paid, less skilled and specially segmented jobs.[27]

As women participated more in public economic life, campaigns for equal opportunity (especially in the USA and the UK) spilled over into action for equal treatment in the welfare state.[28] Only in Scandinavia – and especially Sweden – did women achieve something close to this status, and then by a double-edged development. The rapid expansion of services for child care, family, youth and community support in the 1970s provided relatively well-paid public sector employment for women, but tended to confine them in this sector – as specialist welfare state workers, involved in social reproduction, rather than the primary processes of the productive economy.

The other criticism of these settlements was their protection of First World nationals against the claims of immigrants and would-be immigrants from the developing world. As we have already seen (pp. 9–10), welfare states could be analysed as systems for distributing the 'rents' for restrained competition between collective actors in these countries, gained at the expense of Third World citizens, who would have benefited from unregulated global markets to these extents. But even more, they represented barriers to inward migration to these countries, and justified immigration controls and limits. Social citizen- ship was a status that privileged white Europeans, and justified discrimination against black and Asian immigrants, even when post- colonial changes promised them access to European states.[29] Neo-fascist and other racist groups used defence of 'their' benefits and services as justifications for violence against foreigners and non-white residents.

Yet welfare states created niches for immigrant workers, because their protections (minimum wages and conditions, unemployment benefits) made citizens into rather expensive employees, and gave them scope for refusing exploitative contracts.[30] Hence a perpetual tension was created between social citizens and these outsiders, with battles for access to full membership, to labour markets and to easier entry built into the politics of all First World countries – albeit in very different forms.[31]

In the 1990s, it has become clear that these criticisms point towards a more fundamental problem about social justice and welfare states. The idea of citizenship as full membership of a political community implies a closed, exclusive system of cooperation, in which members contribute to the common good and refrain from mutually harmful conflict. The ideal polity of the republican tradition – that of Aristotle, Rousseau and de Tocqueville[32] – is made up of active citizens, sharing a commitment to a high quality of life, within institutions that bind them to common interests and purposes. In this tradition, issues of justice arise between members only in a context of shared resources, mutual benefits and agreed goals. The exclusivity of such an association is closely linked with the principles of contribution and collective responsibility; those who offer public service (e.g., standing for political office, or serving in the defence forces) qualify to make decisions about the distribution of resources and the duties of membership.

Liberalism recognized that – in the mass industrialized societies of the nineteenth century – aristocratic (or even democratic) versions or republicanism needed to be adapted to make room for more anony-mous contributions, indirect participation and plural political cultures. The idea of *rights*[33] implied that polities were not like voluntary associ-ations; citizens did not choose to join them, but were born into them, and could not easily move from one to another. Hence each individual needed a protected space for his or her own projects and commitments, and associations themselves needed freedom to grow and flourish. Above all, the state should not be allowed to coerce citizens, either individually or collectively, in the public interest. So the characteristic duties of membership – paying taxes, voting at elections, giving military service in times of war – did not much interfere in citizens' conduct of their lives, and left them free for economic activities and the plural cultural life of civil society.

But social rights stretched the tenuous connections between the responsibilities of membership and the freedoms of the individual still further. The contributory principle of social insurance, common to the Bismarckian systems of the European Continent and the Beveridgian ones of the United Kingdom, seemed to provide a rationale consistent with the liberal tradition. But it did so only for fully employed males; hence the critique that women were not included as proper social citizens. On the other hand, to expand non-contributory benefits of various kinds (for instance, disability and carers' benefits, and social assistance for lone parents) was to break the link between contributions and redistri-butive measures, and to weaken the moral bonds of membership. And assistance for the long-term unemployed (a category supposedly abolished by Keynesian economic management) provoked still further questions about the limits of redistribution and the obligations of its beneficiaries.

Much of the appeal of communitarianism[34] in the new politics of welfare lies in its assertion of the need to re-establish the connections between individual choice and collective responsibility. It recalls the model of the small association, based on reciprocal exchanges of voluntary labour, and the contribution of small membership dues; it revives memories of the rural village and the close-knit working-class community, as well as the more grandiose visions of past ages of political virtue.[35] It is especially in relation to issues of poverty, family breakup, disorder and criminality that the appeal to past standards of public-spirited cooperation, and to participation (compulsory if necessary) in the common good, have the strongest resonances.

Yet this nostalgia fits badly with the other feature of public life promoted by liberalism – the development of free markets on a global scale, resulting in the enormous expansion of exchanges of all kinds across borders.[36] As Marx foresaw, and Polanyi[37] demonstrated, unregulated capitalism destroys communities and their social institutions, leaving individuals isolated and dependent on its processes. The history of the world since the sixteenth century is of the relentless penetration of capitalist production and market exchange into previously traditional, tribal or peasant communities, where economic relations were embedded in customs of inclusion, sharing and mutual protection. Just as the global forces of commercialization have created almost limitless opportunities for prosperity and economic growth, so they have also created the apparent inevitability of mass poverty and starvation, and the phenomenon of marginal groups living in squalor on the outskirts of the megopoles of the Third World.

As was shown in the previous section, there are strong arguments for free markets as the best long-term route to creating prosperous societies in the poorest regions of the world. But these arguments can be extended to include the abolition of barriers to free exchange of *all* kinds, including border controls and passports.[38] A consistent case for globalized economic development might point to the free movement of people as well as money, goods, services, information and culture across borders. If global economic welfare demands that investment should be allowed to flow to the developing world from the developed, and that bargain-hunters should be able to make deals anywhere about anything, this must include the mobility of labour as well as capital. The issue of self-selecting groups for supplying and consuming welfare goods is analysed in Chapter 4; that of migration, and its relation to collective goods, in Chapter 6.

Thus we can see that notions of justice that focus on the terms of membership of an exclusive association (where membership is limited to those who contribute and share collective responsibility) and those that focus on the potential of the invisible hand to steer individuals towards the fullest realization of their preferences and projects may pull in opposite directions. Liberal conceptions of justice try to straddle the divide between these rival conceptions; they insist that communitarian and republican visions of high political participation, strong mutual ties, shared resources and tough accountability[39] are softened by personal and property rights, and the civic freedoms of the classical bourgeois polity. But the atomism and stateless energy of global capitalism must somehow be anchored in associations and activities for the common good; and the potentially infinite plurality of interest groups, cultural bodies, religious movements, recreational tastes and crazy fanaticism welded together into a democratic process of collective decision-making. Universally triumphant in 1989, liberalism now finds itself universally besieged, trying to suppress conflicts and reconcile differences without stifling the creative destruction that is the essential feature of the global capitalist order.[40]

## Social justice in political thought

The tensions between the two strands of modern political liberalism – free-market economic individualism on the one side, and democratic collective responsibility on the other – have recently entered the theoretical analysis of social justice. On the one hand, neo-conservative versions of the social obligations of citizenship[41] have influenced the discussion of what has emerged as an important topic for social theory.[42] The attempt to define the rights and responsibilities of citizens has pushed liberalism away from the notion of unconditional entitlements and guarantees for human flourishing, and towards limitations and duties, especially for those receiving public services.[43] On the other, in political thought the communitarian turn of the 1980s[44] has shifted attention towards the virtues of active democratic citizenship, and the qualities of a sustainable culture of collective responsibility.[45]

But it is one thing to prescribe participation in the common good through inclusive democratic practices, and quite another to develop a policy programme for the reintegration of the poor,[46] the regeneration of a community spirit[47] or the reinvention of civil society.[48] These are the issues which have confronted the Clinton administration in the USA (for instance, in trying to instigate a national health insurance system, or reform the administration of social assistance) and which currently preoccupy the new Labour government in Britain. Less directly, they underly the dilemmas of the French and German governments, faced with massive burdens of public spending, rising contribution rates for social protection, high and rigid costs associated with the employment of labour power, and a stagnant pool of mass unemployment.

This book will be disproportionately focused on the British situation, because the new Labour government has put forward a bold programme to combat social exclusion and promote social justice through increased labour-market participation and opportunities for lifelong learning.[49] In a radical break with its previous commitments to the welfare state, the Labour administration has chosen to limit or even reduce benefits,[50] and go instead for educational, vocational and employment-orientated policies. In doing so, it grasps the nettle of 1990s social policy dilemmas, and opts firmly for an authoritarian, communitarian route to social justice, paying a high price in terms of traditional liberal rights and social protections.

Furthermore, the British government's spokespersons have been very clear about the philosophical bases of their programme. They have made strong claims about social justice, and the capacities of their policies to combat poverty and social exclusion. Hence the theoretical debates which underpin the politics of welfare in the 1990s can be particularly clearly illustrated by reference to the British case.

This section will address the theoretical origins of the notions of social justice put forward by Tony Blair and his ministers (especially Gordon Brown and Frank Field) – their historical roots, how they relate to current issues over globalization and the future of welfare states, and how these issues will be analysed in subsequent chapters of the book. The following section will consider how social justice as a theoretical topic in current political thought is linked with other debates, on liberal impartiality, on political integration and on multicultural theory. The common themes in the remaining sections of this introduction are the fragmentation of the national solidarities of welfare states, and the increasing heterogeneity of political communities.

Social justice is a reformist project, and its theoretical roots are typically liberal rather than revolutionary socialist. While Marx and Engels scoffed at the concept as an absurdly bourgeois one, the British Social Liberals and neo-Hegelians, and the progressive Catholics of the Continental European countries, simultaneously developed arguments for softening and embedding capitalism.[51] But schemes for social justice typically presuppose *both* political institutions through which market outcomes can be democratically modified, *and* a political community which corresponds with an economic system for production and distribution. In these circumstances it is possible to redistribute roles and resources, and to do so in the name of justice among members of a community engaged in economic cooperation.

Tony Blair's vision of social justice appeals to exactly this philosophical tradition, but in circumstances that scarcely correspond with these requirements. The crisis of the welfare state that justifies a new politics of welfare is – on his own analysis – largely a result of global economic change. As national boundaries become less relevant in economic terms, and political communities become more culturally diverse, neither of the conditions for social justice seems to apply. States are less able to alter distributions, and citizens less able to agree about how to apply principles of justice to the complex social phenomena of our age. Against this background, the new Labour government's ministers strongly assert that there is a set of ethical principles that should govern the distributive allocations, and that there is a reform programme that can establish an institutional framework that can bring about that distribution.

In this they appeal to a long tradition of theory about the moral ideals that should rule the social world, and a notion of distributive justice that can be traced to Aristotle and Aquinas.[52] The concept of social justice first appeared in late nineteenth-century political economy and social ethics, in the writings of J.S. Mill, Leslie Stephen and Henry Sidgwick, and (through followers of T.H. Green)[53] eventually in the work of the New Liberals[54] in the first decade of this century. When Tony Blair speaks of social justice he is certainly referring to the Christian Socialism of William Morris, the Social Liberalism of L.T. Hobhouse[55] and others, and to the traditions of R.H. Tawney, G.D.H. Cole and R.M. Titmuss.[56] Bill Clinton was probably also influenced by these authors through his political studies at Oxford University. He is known to be advised by liberals such as William Galston, civic republicans like Benjamin Barber, the philosopher Richard Rorty, and the communitarians Michael Sandel and Amitai Etzioni. He quotes the progressive movement of reform associated with Theodore Roosevelt's presidency.[57]

What these thinkers had in common was an idea of society as a kind of organism, made up of interdependent parts, with each member's life chances affected by the actions of every other. Such a society was clearly bounded, both territorially and in terms of membership. Within this closed system of cooperation, it made sense to ask of economic processes whether they gave justice in the distribution of burdens and benefits, and to expect political institutions to apply a single system of rules to all members.

As I shall argue in Chapter 2, the new orthodoxy in welfare reform chooses to ignore the fact that today's First World citizens' life chances depend on global markets and the decisions of foreigners, and their economic exchanges are increasingly transnational. In this, the new orthodoxy is following liberal political theory, which has characteristically failed to address transnational distributive issues. On the one hand, liberalism has no theory of political boundaries.[58] It rejects blood and soil nationalism, but has no alternative justification for membership or territoriality. On the other, liberal theory of justice treats political units as unproblematic; for instance, Rawls (see pp. 85–6) assumes that societies are self-contained national communities, that members enter at birth and leave at death, and that institutions can be designed with predictable distributive outcomes for such systems.[59] Hence the Blair–Clinton orthodoxy is in line with liberal tradition in arguing as if the basic structure of social institutions – the political constitution and the main economic and social structures – can determine citizens' opportunities and constraints, and hence set ethical parameters around their roles and responsibilities.

A democratic conception of social justice requires collective decisions to carry out these ethically informed redistributions, and an agency capable of achieving this task. Hence citizens must be rationally persuaded to accept these principles, and to cooperate with the institutions that implement them. But if the inequalities that social justice addresses are not located in a single set of economic and social relations, governed by a territorial nation state, then perhaps the conditions for liberal social justice do not obtain. There are two sources of difficulty here – the transnational interactions of the global market, and the shifting, complex dynamic of group membership, identity and community within and between states. If states try to shape outcomes they may well provoke strategic relocations and regroupings, including new markets in collective goods (see Chapter 4). Both migration and transnational allegiance to ethnic or religious groups make it hard to reach consensus on distributive justice.[60]

According to the new orthodoxy on welfare reform, nation states can reconcile economic efficiency and social justice in this global environment. The focus is the labour market (see Chapter 2). The aim is to design the social institutions that will provide a culture of opportunity and employability for citizens, and will be attractive for these same reasons to international investors. What is good from the standpoint of justice – fair opportunities for all, a responsible sense of membership, an ethic of hard work and equal liberty – is also good for efficiency.

The new orthodoxy reorders the priorities given in postwar welfare states to the three classic elements in distributive justice – equality, merits and needs – and it reinterprets their implications for public policy (see Chapter 3). It emphasizes equality of *opportunity* rather than outcome, and rights to education and training rather than benefits. It wants meritocratic access to positions of power and economic advantage, and it allows the rewards for these to be more unequal than in the regimes for social justice that prevailed in the 1970s. And it provides for 'genuine' needs to be met, with far stricter testing for the authenticity of the claims from unemployment and disability, and probably also of the means of applicants. Its emphasis on self-responsibility and the scope for private welfare provision will be discussed in Chapter 4.

Hence – despite the seemingly unfavourable circumstances of the new global economic environment – the new Blair–Clinton orthodoxy reshapes older liberal ideas about social justice, and mounts a robust defence of the potential of nation states to accomplish ethical distributions among their populations. It insists that popular beliefs on justice can be reconciled, and that a consensus on the principles at stake can be mobilized in carrying through a programme of reform. Despite initial revulsion at his government's measures to cut lone parents' benefits, Tony Blair has embarked on a personal crusade in favour of welfare reform, to win support for his radical approach. And Bill Clinton, having incorporated right-wing moral disapproval into his measures for limiting the welfare provision available to lone parents, and for 'resocializing' them through moral education, has survived a sex scandal at the time of writing, and emerged as the most popular second-term president in US history.

This confidence in the capacities of states to accomplish 'national renewal' in the name of justice makes light of two sets of interlocking theoretical and policy problems. The first concerns issues of transnational distributive justice – how ethical principles apply to inequalities in economic development and incomes per head between countries, and to the attempts by people to move between them in response to such inequalities. These issues will be addressed in detail in Chapter 6. The second is how to achieve agreement on principles of social justice in a complex, diverse, multiethnic and multicultural society. These issues will be introduced in the next section.

## Social justice, political integration and multiculturalism

The new orthodoxy's confident assertion that a single set of principles for social justice can apply to all members of present-day societies is challenged by diversity and the claims of minority groups. Two sets of problems arise for those who advocate a universal rule over distributive shares. The first is whether there can be common values and standards that are acceptable to all groups within a highly differentiated culture. This implies that conflicts will arise between the non-commensurable claims of women and men, of majority and minority ethnic groups and of gays and heterosexuals. The second is whether (even if there can be principles that transcend different cultural values) potential conflicts between groups can be overcome and sufficient social cohesion to ensure compliance with rules can be achieved. Conflicts may be about the distribution of goods that are valued by all,[61] and reflect a struggle for positional advantage[62] – good jobs, good houses, places at good schools, or in good hospitals – or else reflect 'tragic choices', where the winner takes all, and the loser suffers long-term disadvantage.[63] Even if some cultural differences are recognized and respected, the government may have difficulty in achieving sufficient political integration into the framework of society's institutions, and acceptance of the authority of official agencies.

The liberal tradition from which the Blair–Clinton orthodoxy on social justice springs is committed to impartial, universal principles that apply equally to all citizens. In recent years, the multicultural critique of liberalism – that it imposes the standards of the indigenous European majority on minority ethnic groups, and that this is not true equality of treatment because it has a differential impact on those with other beliefs and practices – has gained ground. Liberal theory has been required to accommodate diversity within unity; it has come to recognize both common and differentiated forms of citizenship, with special rights for minorities to protect their cultural identities.[64]

In this way, group rights and a politics of identity[65] have become philosophically respectable, but a basic problem remains over social cohesion and civic unity. Even if societies are divided along lines of culture, religion and ethnic origins, they must reconcile their separate claims for respect and recognition with the political imperatives of restraint and public reasonableness, democratic decision-making and the order and peace from which all benefit. Liberalism still requires a common set of freedoms, while allowing citizens to maintain and adapt a variety of civic associations. All must accept the constitutional settlement that guarantees their freedoms, and the neutrality of the impartial state, keeping their particular differences for the private realm.

There are obvious difficulties here about what constitute the distinctive minority cultures and practices that are to be given the status of group rights, to be recognized and respected. In the field of social justice and welfare provision, these questions surface in issues about the power of official agencies to require conformity to various obligations and conditions for receiving benefits and services. In so far as the new Blair–Clinton orthodoxy introduces moral criteria into the administration of these systems (such as the power of government agencies to enforce 'chastity' standards on teenage lone parents in the USA[66]), these problems become more overt, and the government's welfare regime more contested. In the USA, this is particularly the case, because such policy programmes address themselves especially to the culture of young black mothers, and are influenced by the pressure of fundamentalist Christian groups who seek to moralize welfare systems.

Some liberals argue that immigrants are attracted to First World societies by job opportunities, and do not seek to create a distinctive way of life for themselves and their communities, still less a parallel economy and educational system. It is equal opportunities that are relevant for their life chances, and especially access to upward job mobility through education for the second generation. If a rule that applies to a society is justifiable, then it should apply equally to all. Almost all laws have differential impacts, in that they inconvenience some more than others. So long as there are sufficiently good reasons for having uniform laws, then they must necessarily fall more heavily on certain groups, and arguments from multiculturalism fail to make a case for group exemptions and exceptions.[67]

Against this, it can be argued that multiculturalism merely seeks to extend both the reasons for granting exemptions and the cases regarded as exceptional. Some exemptions and exceptions are normally built into liberal rules (for instance, that ambulances and fire engines do not have to observe speed limits, and that retired people pay tax at a different rate from people of working age).[68] Cultural identity as a source for self-respect must be affirmed, valued and honoured, and this can only be made possible by protecting it from rules enforcing public uniformity.[69] Recent feminist and pluralist thought emphasizes the need for equality among diverse groups who mutually affirm each others' identities,[70] and by debates about institutional (including constitutional) change, that involve mutual recognition in diversity.[71]

These objections only partly overcome the difficulties in the view of political liberalism as justified impartiality. The dominant culture in a liberal state is the official culture of the state and its institutions. Individuals are incorporated as citizens, but not as groups or peoples. The civic integration required by democracy and liberty must injure some people's self-respect (a basic good in liberal societies) because it does not give equal recognition to all identities, and ignores or fails to celebrate some of these. Thus some people's lives (especially those of immigrants and religious minorities) are not validated. Nation states – even those that do not claim a strong national cultural specificity – do privilege national identities, and protect national ways of life. Minority identities are permitted and tolerated as aspects of society's pluralism, but civic integration requires them to be modified for the sake of public reasonableness and political compromise.[72]

The new politics of welfare raises these issues in quite specific ways. For example, by promoting participation in the formal economy, and seeking to formalize and regulate communal or minority ethnic informal production, it privileges a particular view of the proper economic contributions required of citizens, and the appropriate organizational frameworks in which these should be made. These issues will be discussed, among others, in Chapter 5. More worryingly, it deals with problems of political integration and social cohesion by appeals to national renewal for the sake of social justice and prosperity. This could become an authoritarian or even nationalist defence against the ineffectiveness of territorial states against global economic forces, and the fear that immigration will cause congestion and damaging competition over collective goods. In this way, the new orthodoxy on welfare reform could contribute to intolerance against immigrants and minorities, and restrictive policies over migration and asylum. These issues will be tackled in Chapter 6.

## Conclusions and plan of the book

Welfare reform is high on the agenda of the Blair and Clinton governments. The new politics of welfare has been successful so far in the USA and the UK. Even as he was besieged by a sex scandal, Bill Clinton's State of the Union speech for 1998 focused on reforms in education, health and welfare provision. It helped to earn him even higher ratings than his already record job approval polls. Tony Blair has suffered a setback after the first stage in his reform programme. The rebellion by a group of Labour MPs clearly stung the Prime Minister, and he decided to take the battle to the country in a series of party meetings emphasizing the need for reform. He would scarcely have personally taken on this task, or devoted so much priority to it in his schedule, if he did not believe that it was a potential source of strong electoral support for his government.

The goals of welfare reform are simple to explain in ways that allow voters to be mobilized in their support. Equal opportunity for lifetime learning, greater employability and the chance to break out of poverty and social exclusion are the positive elements in this attractive package. The obligation to contribute to national prosperity, to plan responsibly to provide for oneself and one's family, and the state's duty to protect taxpayers' money from unfair exploitation by free-riders, all command popular support, especially from those just above the income levels that qualify for state benefits. Finally, the insistence on conformity to rules and standards, and the tough line on crime (increased imprisonment and 'zero tolerance'), also contribute to a new commitment to reward honesty, industry and thrift, and punish laziness and deviance. The ethical justification for all these principles seems self-evident; together with the guarantee to protect those in 'genuine need', they appear to constitute a set of policies for social justice.

Yet the best programme to implement these measures is far from easy to determine or to execute. In Tony Blair's speeches, popular mobilization for welfare reform starts from facts and figures about how much is spent on income maintenance (nearly £100 billion), and how many remain in poverty despite these rising costs. Between 1979 and 1990/91, average income in the UK rose by 35 per cent, but the poorest 10 per cent had a one per cent decline in real income, while the richest tenth had an increase of 58 per cent. If housing costs are taken into account, the real incomes of the poorest fell by 14 per cent, and those of the richest rose by 62 per cent.[73] But it is not obvious from these statistics whether he is arguing that too much is being spent, or that it is being spent in the wrong ways, and should be more focused on the poor. On the first point, the UK's expenditure on income maintenance, expressed as a percentage of GDP, is one of the lowest in the European Union. It stands at 21.5 per cent, compared with 37.6 per cent for

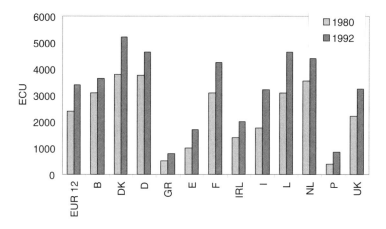

FIGURE 1.1 *Per capita social protection expenditure, 1980 and 1992 (at 1985 prices) (Eurostat, Social Portrait of Europe, 1996, p. 131)*

Sweden, and higher only than Portugal, Spain, Greece and Ireland (for comparative per capita spending, see Figure 1.1).

On the second point, the problem is how to get more money to poor people without harming them in other ways, or being more unjust to others. If the goal is to remove the disincentives and traps built into present systems, then the aim should be to reduce means testing, and the complex administrative processes it involves. Frank Field argued for this approach.[74] Gordon Brown's proposals for the integration of the tax-benefits system, and the introduction of earned income tax credits (on the American model) would certainly reduce administrative complexity, but not necessarily make the poor better off. And the proposed measures to get long-term unemployed people and lone parents back into the labour market involve either tough measures to disqualify some from any entitlement, or cuts in levels of benefits for claimants who are among the very poorest in the country (almost 60 per cent of lone parent families have incomes of less than half the national household average, see Figure 1.2).

The new politics of welfare threatens large sections of the population who are not among the very poorest, and who have a stake in the welfare state. The obvious way to target benefits on those in greatest need is to means test more of the £24 billion that goes on disability payments, or the basic state retirement pension itself, which makes up the single largest element in social security spending. But this would penalize elderly and vulnerable people, and give disincentives to work for those able to enter the labour market. Even the 'affluence tests' mentioned by Harriet Harman during the debate on reform would alarm the large part of the electorate who stand to gain

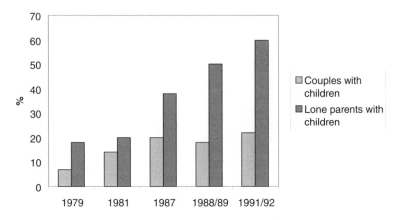

FIGURE 1.2   *Child poverty by family type, 1979-1991/92: percentage in households with below half-average income (Department of Social Security, Households Below Average Income, 1994)*

occasionally or marginally from the system, and have contributed substantially to it.

The strongest appeal of the new politics of welfare is to a set of ethical principles that will reconcile social justice with efficiency. Even if the policy programme involves 'hard choices', as Tony Blair so often repeats, the sacrifices and struggles are worthwhile, because the prize is a society that combines prosperity and fairness. The explicit appeal is to a set of values – hard work, thrift, community, family solidarity and respect for authority – that underpinned the rapid rise of the South East Asian 'tiger' economies. It is ironic that, at exactly the moment that this programme is being so energetically canvassed, these same economies are suffering an economic crisis that casts doubt about the sustainability of their institutional model.

This introductory chapter has tried to put the problems facing the new Labour government in Britain in its quest for welfare reform into the context of the global economic system, and to trace its philosophical roots in European political thought, and especially in the tradition of liberalism. The rest of the book seeks to analyse the implications of this global context for the political principles at stake in welfare reform, and consider the alternatives facing governments that seek to modernize their welfare states to meet the challenges of the next century (and millennium).

In Chapter 2, I shall analyse labour markets as the keys to social justice in the new Blair–Clinton orthodoxy on welfare. I shall consider the case for increasing formal economic participation by improving education and training, and making benefits more conditional, and question whether an approach to social justice that treats the national economy as a unitary system of cooperation can provide a coherent account of the responsibilities of citizenship. In particular, I shall examine the concept of work obligations, as they apply to men and women, and members of majority and minority groups, and how these can be understood within the tradition of liberalism.

In Chapter 3, I analyse the reworking of the relationship between the elements in social justice – equality, merit and need – in the new politics of welfare. I examine the notions of equality of opportunity and 'genuine' need which are central to the new orthodoxy. But the main focus of the analysis is on the attempt to moralize the economy by using principles derived from the social relations of family, neighbourhood and community. I draw attention to the contradictions and confusions of trying to apply codes from personal and informal systems of relationships to impersonal and formal systems, and conclude that the policy programme generated by the new orthodoxy is inconsistent with political liberalism.

In Chapter 4, I address the scope for personal responsibility and private provision in the new politics of welfare. In the new orthodoxy, active citizenship includes an element of managing one's own risks, and seeking to secure one's own protection. I analyse the collective consequences of millions of citizens interacting in search of bundles of collective goods, and forming groups for risk-pooling within welfare states. I argue that much of this activity can be understood in terms of a search for positional advantage, and that welfare reform must take account of the positional nature of many of the goods at stake in these interactions. The goals of policy should include the minimization of costly and welfare-reducing collective outcomes from individually rational strategies.

Throughout these early chapters, my critique of the new orthodoxy points towards an alternative policy programme for social justice. In Chapter 5 I set out such a programme, that accepts the aims of the new orthodoxy, but seeks a way of implementing them that is more consistent with the political traditions of liberal democracy. This programme supplements a universal and unconditional income guarantee by policies at the local level that go with the flow of informal economic activity, and try to support poor people's measures to improve their quality of life, rather than suppressing them.

In the final chapter, I return to the themes of this opening one, and address the complexities of transnational social justice in a globalized economy. In particular, I show how issues of migration and asylum challenge both the Blair–Clinton orthodoxy and the alternative that I have developed in Chapter 5. I argue that these questions cast doubt on the concept of citizenship as an adequate basis for social justice, and address the development of social policy in the European Union as a possible basis for transnational justice.

Throughout the book, I shall take the new orthodoxy on welfare reform as my starting point, because it is the most dynamic element in an emerging politics of welfare. But I shall compare the political forces at work, and the institutional setting for their activity in the UK and USA with those in Continental Europe, and especially in Germany, which holds the key to many EU developments. In the final chapter I shall address the issue of whether the new politics of welfare in the UK and the USA can successfully challenge and transform the German 'social state', and thus the distinctive institutions of the European social policy tradition, and the prospects for social justice in the former communist countries.

## Notes and references

1 P. Van Parijs, 'The Second Marriage of Justice and Efficiency', in P. Van Parijs (Ed.), *Arguing for Basic Income: Ethical Foundations for a Radical Reform*, London: Verso, 1992, pp. 215–40.

2 A. Waddan, *The Politics of Social Welfare: The Collapse of the Centre and the Rise of the Right*, Cheltenham: Edward Elgar, 1997.

3 B. Jordan, *A Theory of Poverty and Social Exclusion*, Cambridge: Polity, 1996.

4 D.C. Mueller, *Public Choice*, Cambridge: Cambridge University Press, 1979, chs 1 and 2.

5 J. Rawls, *A Theory of Justice*, Oxford: Oxford University Press, 1971.

6 For example, J.M. Buchanan, *Public Finance in a Democratic Process*, Chapel Hill, NC: University of North Carolina Press, 1967; G. Tullock, *Towards a Mathematics of Politics*, Ann Arbor, MI: University of Michigan Press, 1967; R.A. Musgrave, *The Theory of Public Finance*, New York: McGraw-Hill, 1959.

7 K. Wicksell, 'A New Principle of Just Taxation', *Finanztheoretische Untersuchen*, Jena, 1896.

8 A.K. Sen, *Collective Choice and Social Welfare*, San Francisco: Holden–Day, 1970; K. Arrow, *Social Choice and Individual Values*, New York: Wiley, 1951.

9 S. Hoggart, 'Is China Trading Places? Why are our plastic bags produced in China and not Telford?', *Guardian*, 28 September 1996.

10 H. Dean and M. Melrose, *Poverty, Riches and Social Citizenship*, Basingstoke: Macmillan, 1998.

11 T.H. Marshall, *Citizenship and Social Class*, Cambridge: Cambridge University Press, 1950.

12 G. Esping-Andersen, 'After the Golden Age: Welfare State Dilemmas in a Global Economy', in G. Esping-Andersen (Ed.), *Welfare States in Transisition: National Adaptations in Global Economies*, London: Sage, 1996, pp. 1–31.

13 K. Frieske, 'In Search of Social Problems: Poverty, Dependency or Social Marginality', paper given at the Third International Conference on Social

Problems, Social History of Poverty in Central Europe, Lodz, Poland, 3–6 December 1997.

14 O. Danglovà, 'In the Trap of Poverty: Analysis of Poverty-Stricken Communities in Southern Slovakia', paper given at the Third International Conference on Social Problems.

15 A. Revenko, 'Poor Strata of Population in Ukraine', paper given at the Third International Conference on Social Problems.

16 P. Hirst and G. Thompson, *Globalization in Question: The International Economy and the Possibilities of Governance*, Cambridge: Polity, 1996.

17 D. Gordon, 'The Global Economy: New Edifice or Crumbling Foundations?', *New Left Review*, 168, 1988, pp. 24–65.

18 W. Ruigrok and T. Van Tulder, *The Logic of International Restructuring*, London: Lawrence and Wishart, 1995.

19 M. Olson, *The Rise and Decline of Nations: Economic Growth, Stagflation and Social Rigidities*, New Haven, CT: Yale University Press, 1982.

20 C. Kindleberger, *Europe's Postwar Growth: The Role of Labour Supply*, Cambridge, MA: Harvard University Press, 1967.

21 B. Jordan, *Rethinking Welfare*, Oxford: Blackwell, 1987, ch. 8.

22 R. Mishra, *The Welfare States in Crisis: Social Thought and Social Change*, Brighton: Harvester, 1984.

23 G. Esping-Andersen, *The Three Worlds of Welfare Capitalism*, Cambridge: Polity, 1990.

24 Esping-Andersen, 'After the Golden Age'.

25 E. Wilson, *Women and the Welfare State*, London: Tavistock, 1977.

26 J. Lewis, 'Gender and the Development of Welfare Regimes', *Journal of European Social Policy*, 2 (3), 1992, pp. 159–71.

27 S. Dex, *The Sexual Division of Work*, Oxford: Blackwell, 1988.

28 F. Williams, *Social Policy: A Critical Introduction: Issues of Race, Gender and Class*, Cambridge: Polity, 1989.

29 Ibid.

30 G.P. Freeman, 'Migration and the Political Economy of the Welfare State', *Annals of the American Academy of Political and Social Science*, 485, 1986, pp. 51–63.

31 T. Faist, 'How to Define a Foreigner? The Symbolic Politics of Immigration in German Partisan Discourse', *West European Politics*, 17 (2), 1994, pp. 50–71.

32 B. Jordan, *The Common Good: Citizenship, Morality and Self-Interest*, Oxford, Blackwell, 1989, ch. 5; A. Oldfield, *Citizenship and Community: Civic Republicanism in the Modern World*, London: Routledge, 1990.

33 M. Freeden, *Rights*, Milton Keynes: Open University Press, 1993.

34 A. MacIntyre, *After Virtue: An Essay in Moral Theory*, London: Duckworth, 1981; A. Etzioni, *The Spirit of Community: The Reinvention of American Society*, New York: Touchstone, 1993.

35 D. Green, *Reinventing Civil Society: The Rediscovery of Welfare Without Politics*, London: Institute for Economic Affairs, 1993.

36 D. Held and A. McGrew, 'Globalization and the Liberal Democratic State', *Government and Opposition*, 28 (2), 1994, pp. 261–85.

37 K. Polanyi, *The Great Transformation: The Political and Economic Origins of Our Time*, Boston, MA: Beacon Press, 1944.

38 J.H. Carens, 'Aliens and Citzens: The Case for Open Borders', *Review of Politics*, 49 (2), 1987, pp. 251–73.

39 B. Barber, *Strong Democracy: Participating Politics for a New Age*, Berkeley, CA: University of California Press, 1984.
40 J. Schumpeter, *Capitalism, Socialism and Democracy* (1943), London: Allen and Unwin, 1947.
41 L.M. Mead, *Beyond Entitlement: The Social Obligations of Citizenship*, New York: Free Press, 1989.
42 M. Roche, 'Citizenship and Modernity', *British Journal of Sociology*, 46 (4), 1995, pp. 715–33; B. Turner, *Citizenship and Social Theory*, London: Sage, 1993.
43 R. Plant, 'Citizenship, Employability and the Labour Market', *Citizen's Income Bulletin*, 24 (July), 1997, pp. 2–3.
44 M. Sandel, *Liberalism and the Limits of Justice*, Cambridge: Cambridge University Press, 1982; MacIntyre, *After Virtue*; C. Taylor, *The Sources of Self*, Cambridge: Cambridge University Press, 1989.
45 W. Kymlicka and W. Norman, 'Return of the Citizen: A Survey of Recent Work on Citizenship Theory', *Ethics*, 104 (2), 1994, pp. 352–81.
46 Commission on Social Justice, *Social Justice: Strategies for National Renewal*, London: Vintage, 1994.
47 Etzioni, *Spirit of Community*.
48 Green, *Reinventing Civil Society*.
49 H. Young, 'Vision for Our Future', interview with Tony Blair, *Guardian*, 17 January 1998.
50 D. Brindle, 'Quest for Benefits Fit for 21st Century', *Guardian*, 16 January 1998.
51 D. Miller, 'Prospects for Social Justice', paper given to the Oxford Political Thought Conference, St Catherine's College, 8 January 1998.
52 Miller, 'Prospects for Social Justice'.
53 Westall Willoughby, *Social Justice*, New York: Knopf, 1900.
54 A. Vincent and R. Plant, *Philosophy, Politics and Citizenship: The Life and Thought of the British Idealists*, Oxford: Blackwell, 1984.
55 L.T. Hobhouse, *The Elements of Social Justice*, London: Allen and Unwin, 1922.
56 E. Durbin, *New Jerusalems: The Labour Party and the Economics of Democratic Socialism*, London: Routledge, 1985.
57 M. Kettle, 'White House Wise Guys', *Guardian*, 19 January 1998.
58 B. Barry, 'Liberalism and Multiculturalism', paper given at the Oxford Political Thought Conference, 8 January 1998.
59 Rawls, *Theory of Justice*.
60 Miller, 'Prospects for Social Justice'.
61 Barry, 'Liberalism and Multiculturalism'.
62 F. Hirsch, *Social Limits to Growth*, London: Routledge and Kegan Paul, 1977.
63 G. Calabresi and P. Bobbit, *Tragic Choices*, New York: Norton, 1978.
64 A. Ingram, 'Models of Integration in Liberal Democracies', paper given at the Oxford Political Thought Conference, 9 January 1998.
65 A. Giddens, *Modernity and Self-Identity: Self and Society in the Late Modern Age*, Cambridge: Polity, 1991.
66 Waddan, *Politics of Social Welfare*, pp. 161–3.
67 Barry, 'Liberalism and Multiculturalism'.
68 T. Modood, question to Brian Barry on the above paper.
69 Ingram, 'Models of Integration'.
70 I.M. Young, *Justice and the Politics of Difference*, Princeton, NJ: Princeton University Press, 1990.

71  J. Tully, *Strange Multiplicity*, Cambridge: Cambridge University Press, 1997.
72  Ingram, 'Models of Integration'.
73  D. Donnison, *Politics for a Just Society*, Basingstoke: Macmillan, 1998, pp. 13–14.
74  F. Field, *The Reform of Welfare*, London: Social Market Foundation, 1997.

# 2

# The Labour Market as the Key to Social Justice

It may seem strange to start the analysis of social justice issues in present-day societies with the specific topic of the labour market. A more logical structure for the book might appear to require a preliminary review of theories of social justice, and how their principles apply to current economic circumstances.

However, so powerful is the influence of the new Blair–Clinton orthodoxy on the politics of welfare that it is far easier to come at general questions of social justice through an analysis of its central theses. For reasons which will be made clear in this chapter, the notions that work contributions give the only sustainable claims to welfare shares, that the worst kind of injustice takes the form of free-riding on the efforts of others; and that all social rights imply obligations to labour for the good of other members of the polity, all exert a mesmeric hold upon contemporary minds. The Blair–Clinton orthodoxy appeals to these moral intuitions very directly, and until they are more closely scrutinized it is pointless to try to move towards a more general consideration of principles of justice.

The first reason why these three theses carry such conviction is that the processes of globalization analysed in the first chapter have placed the wage relation back at the centre of politics. The work of T.H. Marshall (see p. 7 above and pp. 77–8 below) was seminal for the analysis of social justice in the postwar period, because he argued that the welfare state would supersede class as an organizing principle for collective action. Even as late as 1990, Gøsta Esping-Andersen's celebrated account of *The Three Worlds of Welfare Capitalism* was framed in terms of the 'decommodification of labour power' – the eradication of poverty, and of complete reliance upon the labour market.[1] Wage earners in the market are compelled to compete as isolated individuals, dependent on decisions beyond their control. The social rights of citizenship in a universalistic welfare state gave them the resources to mobilize collectively, and resist exploitation.

> If social rights are given the legal and practical status of property rights, if they are inviolable, and if they are granted on the basis of citizenship rather than performance, they will entail a decommodification of the status of individuals *vis-à-vis* the market. But the concept of social citizenship also involves social stratification: one's status as citizen will compete with, or even replace, one's class position.[2]

I shall argue that the transformation of capitalism that was achieved between the late 1960s and the present decade has restored much of the insecurity of unemployment, poverty and wage dependence. The international ascendancy of capital has led to weakening of the social protection that allowed 'decommodification' of welfare states. The Blair–Clinton orthodoxy is persuasive because it asserts what everyone now experiences – that global labour markets are the key determinants of their life chances, though sometimes in circuitous and indirect ways. Yet it simultaneously denies the relevance of class, and the necessity for class mobilization.

The second reason why these theses seem so persuasive is that they reflect the morality of the family, the friendship group, the small association and the close community. They remind us of the lessons on our duties to others that we learnt at our parents' knees, in the school playground, and among our kin and neighbours. Hence they take us 'back to basics' in a nostalgic, emotional and direct way, that seems almost beyond intellectual criticism. Who can dispute the values of reciprocity, care and self-reliance that underpin such durable institutions as the family and the village community?

Thus the three theses appeal to the economic 'realism' of a world transformed by global market forces, and to the moral intuitions of social relations before the welfare state. They look back to 'Victorian values' and community for guidance about how to organize in the face of insecurity and social division. Above all, they apply the morality of our first-line defences against these risks and threats to the politics of social welfare issues.

But I shall argue that there are grave dangers in trying to extrapolate from the principles that regulate these informal associations to the large-scale anonymous interactions of the economy and the polity. In a surprising way, during the decade that followed liberal democracy's triumph (in the collapse of the Soviet Union and its satelites, and of totalitarian rule in much of Asia, Africa and Latin America), most of the fundamental tenets of liberalism have come to be questioned, bypassed or neglected. Among the most important of these is the idea that all citizens should enjoy maximum feasible protection from being coerced for the good of others. However desirable it may be that all should work hard for the common interest, forcing them to do so is a breach of liberal principles.

Another basic liberal tenet is the priority of the right over the good. In a plural society, with very different beliefs and cultural practices co-existing side by side, it is dangerous for one group to impose its conception of the good on others. For this reason, all should enjoy the opportunities and means to develop their versions of the good life, with minimum interference from the public power. Yet in the 1990s, this principle offends the moral susceptibilities of many mainstream bourgeois voters, especially in the UK and the USA. It is not just readers of the *Sun* and *Daily Mail* who feel uncomfortable about the idea of women who have never married bringing up children on state benefits, while living in council houses, or those with invisible disabilities driving round in new cars bought from public funds. Hence the pressure to line up social rights and responsibilities with the moral intuitions of the home and hearth, and the ethical judgements of the local pub.

I shall argue that these intuitions are misleading guides to public policy in a large and plural polity, and have become dangerously unreliable in the context of a global economy. The unquestionable wisdoms of the informal group – that all must do their bit and pull their weight – can draw us into costly mistakes in social policy. It was, after all, the obviously unquestionable moral rule that fathers should contribute to the upbringing of their children that inspired the Major government to create the Child Support Agency in the UK. The fact that it had a sound basis in family morality did not prevent the CSA causing more distress, chaos and injustice than existed before it came into being, or save it from being discredited in 1996 (see below, p. 194).

The plan of this chapter is to set out the background and context for the Blair–Clinton orthodoxy first, then expound its three main theses, and then analyse them in detail. Only after this – in Chapter 3 – will I turn to the main principles of social justice, to show how these can be applied to the puzzling paradoxes revealed in the shortcomings of the new orthodoxy under present-day circumstances.

## Background and context of the new orthodoxy

After a decade in which mass unemployment reappeared in First World countries, it is understandable that the labour market should come to be viewed as the key to social justice. From the perspective of the 1990s, the impact of global economic forces on employment in the advanced industrialized countries could be seen to depend on the structure of labour markets, and their interactions with tax and welfare systems. The United States had achieved sustained growth of employment (albeit much of it very low paid) since the mid-1980s; the United Kingdom had reduced its levels of unemployed, especially since 1992 (though most of the male claimants had somehow 'disappeared' rather than found jobs, and 2.2 million people are still looking for work according to government surveys[3]). The conclusion drawn by the Blair–Clinton orthodoxy was that the persistent high unemployment in Continental Europe was due to rigidities in wages and high social contributions falling on employment. 'Flexible' labour markets and employment-friendly benefits were therefore the most important institutional means of achieving social justice.

Yet the division of labour in present-day advanced economies gives rise to far more complex issues of fairness than this simple summary suggests. It is obvious that in any society social justice must deal in questions about who shoulders the burdens of producing resources for investment and consumption, and of reproducing the social system that sustains the population. The division of labour in the advanced industrialized countries has always been organized through a mixture of labour markets, based on nominally 'free' exchanges between labour power and capital, and the 'moral economy' of households, religious movements, voluntary associations, ethnic groups and community networks, structured by traditional norms and the practices of particular cultures.

The relationship between these two 'spheres' of justice[4] is sensitive; over the centuries, the market economy of employment has gradually replaced the moral economy of extended family and community – hunting tribes, peasant agriculture, village communes, working-class cooperatives and associations – in the Great Transformation of the modern age.[5] But the older system has survived, providing many of the welfare goods enjoyed by prosperous societies through the domestic economy of care, and the efforts of charities and other voluntary bodies. And social policy has often intervened in the moral economy – especially in the family – to try to promote particular patterns of obligation, to regulate informal care, or to reinforce parental responsibility.[6] Bill Clinton's Personal Responsibility Act (1996) is a clear example of this.

With the growing power of international capital since the 1970s, the ability of national governments to provide 'full employment' for adult male citizens through Keynesian and corporatist economic management has been first weakened, then destroyed. Countries like Germany and Japan, Austria and Sweden, which sustained high levels of industrial employment throughout the 1980s, have since suffered much the same

TABLE 2.1 *Unemployment: selected countries, February 1996*

| | OECD standardized rate (%): seasonally adjusted |
|---|---|
| EU average | 11.2 |
| Major 7 nations (G7) | 6.9 |
| UK | 8.4 |
| Finland | 16.5 |
| France | 12.2 |
| Germany (FR) | 8.9 |
| Japan | 3.3 |
| Netherlands | 6.5 |
| Sweden | 9.7 |
| USA | 5.5 |

*Source:* Department for Education and Employment, *Labour Market Trends*, 104 (12), December 1997, table 2.18

structural changes as Britain and Belgium, with the rise in unemployment particularly marked in Germany in the 1990s (see Table 2.1). This has caused some commentators to question the future of the 'employment society', and remind us that in past times most workers were either independent producers for markets, or parts of family units engaged in subsistence-orientated activities.[7] In the Ukraine since 1989, the socialist system of industrial employment has collapsed so dramatically that most of the country's GDP now takes the form of food production, with cities largely re-ruralized, and every available space used for breeding animals or growing fruit and vegetables.[8] Other authors see the change mainly in terms of a breakup of the post-Industrial Revolution norm of employment in a single organization or occupation from school to retirement; instead, work will tend to become more varied, with a periphery of casual short-term contracts, and a core consisting of consultancies, self-employment and telework, as much as in the monolithic structures of factories and offices.[9] Workers must expect to retrain frequently, and to hold a 'portfolio' of several different contracts with a variety of organizations.

In such an environment, regular jobs, with prospects of promotion, incremental salary increases, pensions, perks and other benefits, are clearly valuable assets; those who hold them are labour market 'insiders', whose advantages over 'outsiders' are protected by a variety of professional associations and trade unions. 'Outsiders' tend to be less organized, and hence less powerful, and seldom willing to enter into direct conflict with these interest groups.[10] 'Insiders' in turn may be ready to make some sacrifices to protect their special status and privileges. In Russia and the Ukraine in recent years, up to 20 per cent of jobholders remain unpaid for several months, yet continue to go to work regularly.[11] This confirms that jobs should be regarded as assets rather than burdens in discussions about justice in the division of labour.[12]

On the other hand, the insecure and low-paid work on the fringes of the formal economy is far from being attractive, or a protected niche. As wages for unskilled work have fallen, and working conditions have deteriorated, the incentives for taking such employment have declined. In the UK, the preponderance of part-time work taken by women, and the high rate of employment of wives of men in full-time work, suggest that this segment of the labour market is well suited to secondary earners who are partners of men with job assets as 'insiders'.[13] Conversely, the very high number (almost 3.4 million) of working-age households without any member in employment suggests that these posts do not draw primary earners into formal labour markets readily.

Because of this latter structural factor, the Blair–Clinton orthodoxy has come to rely on semi-coercive measures (cuts in benefits rates and more conditional eligibility) to drive claimants of social assistance into formal employment, or various kinds of training and resocialization for work. The justification for these measures has been that most claimants want to work, and that those who do not are shirking their responsibilities to their fellow citizens and families, and should therefore learn their duties. But it is questionable whether the shift into the labour market of large numbers previously engaged (as lone parents especially) in the moral economy of child care and other unpaid work can be sustained, or whether it is a step towards social justice.

For example, as part of a programme for 'reintegrating' the 17 per cent of the workforce who are currently unemployed in Finland, households that employ cleaners, nannies and cooks are now allowed to be exempt from all social insurance contributions, which affords them a large rebate on the normal costs of such employment.[14] A job-creation programme is thus being used to subsidize the re-establishment of a formal labour market in domestic service, a type of employment which had all but disappeared in an egalitarian, social democratic country with an extensive welfare state. Better-off Finnish families had absorbed all these tasks into the moral economy of the household, and less skilled workers had been redeployed in various kinds of public or private sector service occupations. It seems very questionable whether social justice is well served by recreating the social relations of a nineteenth-century market in services which make workers depend directly on the goodwill of a specific couple for their working conditions, as well as supplying very limited earnings.

In the United Kingdom, such a labour market has been expanding throughout the past 15 years, but its growth is likely to be given a further boost by the abolition of lone parent benefit (and lone parent premium for income support) by the new Labour government in 1997 – though modifications were later made through the Budget. Ostensibly to pay for better child care and training measures, this cut represents an attempt to alter the balance of incentives between formal employment and the moral economy of the household (specifically child care). If the government had been primarily concerned with social justice and the welfare of one million lone parents and their two million children, these measures would have been far more carefully phased in, at least. Instead of being introduced before the child care and other services were in place, the government would have waited to see how effectively these operated. Instead of imposing the cuts indiscriminately on all new lone parent claimants, they would have introduced them first for those with children over 11 years of age, and much later for those with several children under 5. Since a fairly small proportion of lone parents can realistically expect to sustain employment at wages that will support them at rates above the poverty line, this was a transparent attempt to cut public expenditure, in order to keep rash promises on tax rates.

From this example, it becomes clear that the workings of the global labour market are currently being reinforced by the social policies of governments of the Blair–Clinton tendency (and even in the more conservative welfare regimes of Europe, such as Finland). Public power is now deployed to shift people out of the moral economy of house-holds and mutual social support, and into paid work. But it is the nature of that paid work that should also be addressed in the debate about social justice. As in Finland, much of the new employment that will be created through this readjustment of incentives will be domestic labour in better-off households; hence the placard carried by lone parents protesting against the British cuts: 'We Won't Clean Harriet's Toilet'.

In these two examples, a broader issue becomes plain. The labour markets now operating in First World countries are themselves fulfilling two quite different functions. On the one hand, they reflect that part of the production for global markets that is located in the advanced capitalist countries. More precisely, they show how international capital is deployed in various kinds of organizations – mainly concerned with the financial sector of banking, insurance and share-dealing, and with business services in communications and information technology, and only residually in manufacturing itself. On the other hand, the main bulk of employment in these advanced economies is now in occupations concerned with social reproduction. The largest employers are health services, social care organizations, education and training establishments, and the small enterprises giving various kinds of personal services, from hairdressing to cleaning. Employment now takes place as much in retailing outlets and wholesale warehouses as in factories, and women are employed as much as men. And – in a strange twist of globalization – small ethnic-minority firms increasingly supply local First World markets with the goods they need for everyday consumption. Asian restaurants today employ more workers than the steel, shipbuilding and mining industries put together in the United Kingdom.[15]

The fact that most employment is now concerned with social reproduction is highly relevant to issues of social justice in the division of labour. In the 'golden age' of welfare states, when most employment was in agriculture, construction, mining and manufacturing, it could be credibly argued that the national labour market was an institution for structuring an efficient division of labour within the global system of production of goods and services for consumption. Even though most of the output of these industries was in fact consumed within the national economy, the nature of the global division of labour, and of the forms of protectionism practised in welfare states (Keynesian economic management, imperial preference, and other barriers to free trade) were such that the relevant notion of an 'efficient' division of labour could be claimed to be achieved by just these methods of sheltering national industrial firms and their workers. Now that these protections have been largely blown away, and labour markets restructured, the majority of industrial employment is located in developing countries, and increasingly in very large economies such as China and Indonesia, India and Brazil. Efficiency in the division of labour for production for global markets in finance, manufactured goods and information services is achieved by competitive forces, not by the management systems of nation states.

Conversely, however, national economies in First World countries have to the same extent become primarily concerned with social reproduction rather than the production of such goods. In so far as most employment is in these sectors, employment policy is disproportionately focused on issues of *equity* in the division of labour, rather than pure competitive efficiency. The national economy has become 'domesticated'; its division of labour is now akin to that of a domestic household, and the issues at stake are similar to those struggled over between men and women over the centuries. How can the division of labour over social reproduction reflect fairness in the allocation of roles and burdens, and what principles should apply to decisions about the tasks to be performed in the moral economy of shared unpaid activities, and which through 'free' exchange in formal labour markets?

## The main theses of the new orthodoxy

There are two quite different traditions in which these issues have previously been debated. Each has a characteristic view about human individuality and social relations. In the liberal tradition of the Anglo-Saxon countries, individuals are supposed to be competent actors who take critical responsibility for the success of their projects and commitments in a competitive economic environment. Their projects include all those clusters of actions that give a life its consistencies and overall trajectory, including the accumulation of property rights and the pursuit of wider economic interests. Their commitments include all their interactions and their interdependencies with others, which they incur through these processes. Simply by following their preferences and sympathies, they come to be bearers of all these rights, interests and obligations, but they remain autonomous decision makers in a world of free exchanges between such actors.[16]

In the continental (and especially the Christian Democratic) tradition, individuals are conceived as embedded in an environment of binding social obligations and a culture of enduring collective solidarities. Society is a hierarchy of unequally endowed but interdependent groupings, organically and functionally linked through occupational, civic and religious structures. Through the principle of subsidiarity, welfare provision devolves to the lowest possible level, and public power is minimized; hence members of the household, and specifically womenkind, are held responsible for providing the basic care and nurturance on which society ultimately depends. The embeddedness of the economy precludes a meaningful discussion of individual responsibility outside these structures of interdependence and solidarity, through which each member is included in a corporate unity.[17]

In the former tradition, labour markets are seen primarily as *markets*, with the emphasis on the freedom of the exchange relationship; in the latter, they are embedded in these other social relations, and government has responsibility for ordering their functions within the social system. Whereas labour markets are important means of incorporating citizens into the hierarchy of occupational status groups in Continental Europe, Anglo-Saxon liberalism requires citizens to take opportunities for economic self-development, and to achieve the status of free and equal members of the polity.[18]

The new orthodoxy claims that social justice is best promoted by well-functioning labour markets and an adaptable workforce, which is conscious of the need to update its skills, and of its obligations to contribute to prosperity and progress. In this view, the European institutional structures for employment now need to be updated and made more flexible, if they are not to fetter growth and cause high unemployment.

There are three main theses in the new orthodoxy on social justice and labour markets.

1  *National prosperity is crucially related to the skills of the workforce.* Despite globalization, the downward pressure on wages at the lower end of the labour market, and the phenomenon of the 'working poor' in the USA, social justice through equality of opportunity can be achieved by a well-educated workforce willing constantly to update its skills. The aim is to find a 'middle way' between the deregulatory US – where the lowest third of workers have been losing ground since the 1970s, and the bottom 10 per cent, the real value of whose wages has declined by one third in this period,[19] now earn roughly four and a half times less than the top 10 per cent – and over-regulated Germany, with its high unemployment, where the ratio is between two and three times between the bottom and top deciles.[20]

The combination that can provide both dynamic economic performance and social cohesion is flexible labour markets and an adaptable workforce, in this view. Employers need to have the power to dismiss employees whom they do not need at short notice, and to fire less productive workers who are underperforming. Workers' protection should not act as a barrier to this flexibility, nor should wages and fringe benefits be set too rigidly; they should be closely related to productivity. But, on the other hand, workers should be adaptable, and thus empowered by having access to improve their education and skills. This balances the power of employers, and allows workers to move quickly into new posts, or acquire new expertise. Instead of job security, the new aim is 'employability' and the test how quickly a redundant worker finds a new post.[21]

One policy implication of these principles is that the government should invest in education and training, and especially in the technological infrastructure of computers, modems, satellites and down-links. As technological innovation makes skills redundant twice as quickly as in the 1970s,[22] workers need a good basic education and constant opportunities to 'add value through lifelong learning'.[23] Another is that welfare systems should supplement low wages, in order to make the workforce more adaptable. Traditional social insurance and social assistance programmes encourage people to remain unemployed because they lose their benefits when they re-enter the labour market. Instead, income maintenance systems should function as an 'intelligent welfare state', to promote participation. As a model, earned income tax credits in the USA represent a means to top up family incomes, and this support can be withdrawn only gradually as earnings rise.[24] Indeed, the new Labour government is planning to integrate the tax-benefit systems to replace family credit with an American-style system of tax credits for the working poor.[25]

With these measures in place, it is then possible for governments to pursue expansionist monetary and fiscal policies, so as to provide the demand to achieve high levels of employment. A flexible labour market, adaptable labour power and a government willing to invest in a skilled workforce, all guarantee that the economy can safely be run at close to full capacity, and in this way every citizen will have the opportunity to achieve their full potential.

2  *A strong work ethic benefits the whole polity.* The new orthodoxy argues for an intensification of work as a contribution to the success of its project for social justice and the inclusion of marginal groups. According to this view, the puritan cultural norms of hard work and personal discipline are valuable public goods that benefit the whole economy, and hence the cohesion of society. Tony Blair has promised 'to put the work ethic at the centre of the welfare state'.[26]

It might be thought that a preference for leisure and refinement over sheer hard work was a mark of an advanced civilization and a mature culture. However, economists have recently reasserted the importance of the work ethic, and of maximizing contributions to the formal economy, even when this seems to impoverish the informal interactions that constitute civil society and the democratic political life. High rates of labour-market participation and long working hours allow the economy to expand, and the division of labour to be more refined. This enables productivity to be increased and the volume of exchanges to grow, hence improving rates of economic expansion and employment since – as has been clear since Adam Smith's work on the division of labour in 1776 – 'much more value can be generated in an economy where different persons, or groups of persons, produce different goods and then exchange these goods among themselves'.[27] Thus an increase in the supply of labour to markets means a bigger market, specialization developed further, and a faster growth in the productivity and output of the economy as a whole. Each person in society is therefore better off if others work more, because the amount that each can purchase for any unit of labour will be greater than if others worked fewer hours.[28] The work ethic is therefore a normative aspect of the social capital of a society, and a public good that contributes to the welfare of every citizen.

This analysis justifies the emphasis on the promotion of formal economic participation in the Blair–Clinton orthodoxy. Welfare-to-work programmes aim to shift people from the informal to the formal econ-omies, as well as moving them from dependency on public provision to the independence of earned income.[29] Part of the justification for this is the economist's argument that unpaid work is almost always too unspecialized, and hence too low in productivity, to be a more efficient use of time than paid work.[30]

But the main thrust of the welfare-to-work programme is to change *character*, not just behaviour. The idea of a 'dependency culture', developed by neo-conservatives in the USA, and taken up by Margaret Thatcher's ministers,[31] posited a set of attitudes and practices which discounted work, thrift and independence, and built the claiming of social assistance into expectations of everyday lifestyles, as a means of supporting the reproduction of the population (lone parenthood for women, long-term unemployment for men loosely attached to families). The academic debate about the underclass,[32] while challenging the notion of a distinctive group of people with such cultural characteristics, has not dispelled this idea; even the black American sociologist William Julius Wilson,[33] uses the term to denote a group of the black ghetto poor whose structural situation has been altered by the 'disappearance' of employment opportunities in their neighbourhoods, and the exit of better-educated members of their communities to the leafy suburbs.[34] The very notion of an underclass is therefore pounced upon by those who see a need to restore the work ethic by processes of social engineering – through blocking the option of long-term claiming, and insisting on labour-market participation as a means to resocialization (or even remoralization) of the poor. Among the foremost advocates of this approach was Frank Field,[35] formerly a British minister for welfare reform, with a brief to 'think the unthinkable', and a mission to reinculcate puritan values, and reinvent civil society through the rediscovery of working-class institutions for thrift and mutual protection.

3 *The principle of reciprocity applies to civic obligations.* One of the strongest moral themes in the new Blair–Clinton orthodoxy on social justice is the insistence that rights imply responsibilities, and benefits entail contributions.[36] It is widely asserted that the kind of social citizenship created by postwar welfare states was one-sided in its emphasis on rights. Even the conditions (work tests, cohabitation rules and requirements to demonstrate incapacity and not to retard recovery from illness) that were built into the Beveridgian national insurance benefits for unemployment, widowhood, disability and sickness are now seen as far too weak – hence the much stricter tests of availability for work, the emphasis on 'contract' in the new Jobseeker's Allowance, and the re-emergence of tests for working capacities. The Jobseeker's Agreement turns conditional social rights into individual obligations sanctioned by an individual contractual agreement.[37] In other words, collective protection is replaced by individualized compulsion. The 'integrity tests' for disability benefits turn entitlements for life into benefits that are open to discretionary administrative review.

These issues are even more fundamentally at stake in Continental Europe, where basic social rights were written into constitutions after the experiences of Nazism and Fascism. These are now seen, by market-minded critics in the USA and the UK, as at the root of the inflexibilities of their labour markets, and the exclusions experienced by their unemployed citizens.[38]

The redefinition of social justice in the new orthodoxy focuses on the need to create a 'something for something society' in which 'rights are matched by responsibilities'.[39] The principle of reciprocity states that those who enjoy the economic benefits of social cooperation have a corresponding obligation to make a productive contribution to that community.[40] This principle appeals to the theme of the British civic liberal tradition – in Hobhouse, Tawney and Beveridge, for example – that rights must never become detached from the performance of social functions.[41] It emphasizes the injustice of 'free-riding' on the efforts of others, and the requirement of institutional arrangements for social justice to forbid the exploitation of the hard-working by the idle that is allowed by unconditional benefits.[42]

The principle of reciprocity is derived from small-scale voluntary associations, in which labour services are exchanged by members. Clearly, it would be impossible to provide the mutual benefits of such an association if there were not a rule to require such contributions of members, and to exclude from membership those unable or unwilling to make them.[43] The problem of 'free-riding' relates to the interest that each individual has in minimizing his or her contributory efforts, and maximizing their returns – hence cooperation is only possible through the exclusion of non-contributors.[44] A variant of the same problem is the 'tragedy of the commons' – that all users of those resources that are shared, because it would be too costly to divide them physically into private portions, have an interest in over-exploiting them, with the result that they deteriorate, and are eventually made worthless.[45] Here too the remedy is exclusion and the contributory principle; commons are conserved where users are restricted by traditional rules, and where they reciprocally manage their shared and valued resource according to good principles of social and ecological sustainability.[46]

Hence the principle of reciprocity demands a willingness from all able to do so that they should offer productive contributions through the formal labour market. Welfare-to-work measures and the New Deal for Lone Parents are thus in line with both efficiency and justice. They increase national prosperity by widening the system of social cooperation; and they increase equality of opportunity as well as reducing exploitative free-riding and the depletion of the common stock of benefits.

The principle of reciprocity is taken to apply more widely than the formal economy – to the moral economy, of course, from which it is derived, and to the concept of community itself, which forms the basis of an ideal society of contributors in a 'giving age'.[47] However, the cornerstone of social justice remains the labour market, because it alone can enable the link to be made between the social rights of citizenship and the functional efficiency of the economy which generates these benefits.[48]

Thus there is a symmetry and coherence in the three new theses of social justice. The notion of equality of opportunity can only be implemented through a workforce that is empowered by its employability; the work ethic is the cultural capital that ensures that all benefit from the growth of productivity and output; and the reciprocity principle promotes the minimization of exploitation as well as the maximization of participation.

## The weaknesses of the three theses

These three theses have come to be very widely accepted, not merely by politicians of the Blair–Clinton tendency, but also in the academic social policy community, and in the public at large. Furthermore, this orthodoxy is increasingly adopted in Continental Europe also as a rationale for the future of the welfare state, with German analysts agreeing that more flexible labour markets and more employment-friendly income maintenance systems are required,[49] and that individuals must become more responsible for their own welfare, through a willingness to make private contributions and bear higher risks.[50]

In the rest of this chapter, I shall develop a detailed criticism of all these theses, and the links between them. The central point in my critique is that processes of globalization have altered the nature of interactions within the national polity, so as to undermine the force of these three arguments. In a world economy where international corporations are larger and stronger than nation states, where the division of labour over the production of most traded goods is global rather than national, and where First World countries are increasingly emerging as the centres for the *financing* of such production rather than the manufacture of these goods, a model derived from a national industrial economy does not make sense. The crucial change of the final quarter of the twentieth century is that – for purposes of the production of raw materials and manufactured commodities – it is the *world economy* that is the relevant unit of account, and not the national economy. This means that it is necessary to consider issues of efficiency *and equity* in a global context, not a national one. Many of the analyses that sustain the three theses conspicuously fail to do this; as a result, their conclusions can be revealed as unconvincing. Above all, the links between social justice and more extensive and intensive participation in the formal labour market are fatally weakened, and this brings down the whole edifice of the policy programme like a pack of cards. Intuitive doubts about the fairness of cutting benefit rates, and increasing conditionality and coercion, are seen to be well founded.

The new Labour government in Britain sets much store by its *values*.[51] It stands for justice in relations between British citizens, and in its dealings with other nations and their citizens. None of the criticisms developed below are intended to impugn these values, or the sincerity of those who proclaim them – politicians or academics. My analysis essentially supports the aims of the Blair government's policy programme, but questions its philosophical basis, and above all the measures by which it is implemented. Paradoxically, although New Labour proclaims a radical break with the past, its central weakness is to cling to ideas and policies which ceased to be appropriate with the passing of the industrial age; they are 'modern' in precisely the sense that the real economy of the new age has become 'post-modern'[52] and post-Fordist.[53] It is necessary to update the principles and the policies, in line with the shifts attendant on globalization, in order to achieve either efficiency or justice, and to make a more sustainable link between them.

*The division of labour in present-day society*

The idea that national prosperity is crucially related to an empowered workforce of citizens who constantly improve their employability is cast under serious doubt by patterns of employment since the 1970s. As manufacturing expands at an extraordinary rate in countries like China and Indonesia, Brazil and India, it correspondingly contracts in First World countries. The kind of employment that has grown most rapidly in those countries of the advanced industrialized world is uniformly low-productivity, labour-intensive work, concerned with social reproduction – social and child care, health and community services and miscellaneous private services, often again in the nature of personal or domestic care. The idea that a larger investment in education and training will make the population more employable ignores this reality. The real problem faced by the advanced industrial economies is the decline of most forms of skilled technical employment (traditionally taken by men) and the lack of incentives for many citizens to take low-paid, labour-intensive jobs in the work that is increasingly necessary for social reproduction.

The statistics to demonstrate this are readily accessible. On the one hand, at 150 million, the numbers employed in manufacturing in the new economic zones of China already far exceed the entire manufacturing workforce in Europe put together, or the United States.[54] There are some 1.2 billion peasants in China and Indonesia, earning less than US$3 per day, who are likely to enter the global economy as industrial workers, producing for world markets, during the first quarter of the twenty-first century.[55]

The economic crisis in South Korea and Japan in the final months of 1997 was closely related to a shift in the location of manufacturing expansion in South East Asia. Already the 'tiger' economies of the region have passed through the phase of exceptionally fast economic growth, based on the absorption of low-productivity rural labour power into new industrial employment. In the case of Korea, a combination of trade union bargaining power, high wages and artificially cheap capital (much of it from Japan) have now caused a collapse of profitability which threatens the whole 'miracle' of rapid development, and leaves the country as a supplicant before the International Monetary Fund. In the case of Hong Kong, of course, its re-annexation by China means that it can quite smoothly be accommodated as a centre for banking, insurance and financial services, while the sites for manufacturing production are developed on the mainland.

In the First World countries (now including Japan) the growth in employment has for 20 years been focused in the service sector. Of course there has been an expansion of jobs in the financial sector and in information technology, and many of these have been very well paid. However, numerically the largest growth has been in part-time work for women, mostly low-paid. Especially in the USA, the UK, France and Portugal, women's employment is rapidly catching up with rates of male participation in the labour market, which in turn has been declining.[56] In the UK, almost half of employed women work part-time, and there are actually fewer women in full-time employment than there were in 1973.[57] Part-time women workers earn only around 60 per cent of average male wage rates.[58] Conversely, only just over half of working-age males were full-time employed in 1993, compared with three-quarters in 1973[59] – a change resulting from longer education and earlier retirement, as well as the decline in industrial employment. In other words, in the UK economy (and all other advanced economies), men still earn more, because they are concentrated in managerial posts, and in the remaining skilled technical jobs; but women are more employable, because they are willing to take low-paid, part-time work in the services sector.

Furthermore, it is a complete fallacy to suppose a correlation between high standards in education and technical training and high levels of economic participation. Germany has what is by common consent one of the best education and training systems in the world. An extraordinarily high proportion of young people in Germany go on from school to universities, colleges or apprenticeships in skilled manual occupations. German students are twice as likely to reach the standard of two 'A' levels as British.[60] Yet Germany has one of the highest rates of unemployment in Europe today, and an increasing crisis over the employment prospects of young people. Furthermore, it has a rather low rate of overall economic participation, with only 48.2 per cent of women and 69.7 per cent of men over 15 in any formal

TABLE 2.2  *Economically active population (over 15): selected countries, 1995*

|             | Men (%) | Women (%) |
|-------------|---------|-----------|
| Denmark     | 83.4    | 70.7      |
| Finland     | 67.1    | 55.2      |
| France      | 62.6    | 47.6      |
| Germany     | 69.7    | 48.2      |
| Netherlands | 80.8    | 59.1      |

*Source*: International Labour Office, *International Labour Force Statistics*, 1996, Table 1A

labour market position, and only half of those men aged between 55 or 65 in employment.[61] France, whose educational standards at the point of leaving school are comparable to Germany's, has very similar figures on labour-market participation and unemployment (see Table 2.2).

The reasons for this lack of correlation between high educational and training standards and high employment levels are not difficult to understand. Since a very low proportion of the workforce in any First World country is now employed in skilled technical occupations, the capacity for such industries to absorb trained staff is very low. Of course it is true that there has been a rapid growth of jobs in information technology and communications, and that a well-educated workforce is in a far better position to attract investment from international companies in this field than one with illiterate and unskilled workers. It is also true that the UK has been very successful in the field of fashion, design, music and the arts, and leads the world in many creative occupations. Indeed, there are now more members of the actors' and musicians' union (Equity) than of the National Union of Mineworkers in the UK.[62] However, none of these sectors accounts for a large proportion of employment, nor could it ever do so in any conceivable scenario of the future.

This is partly because there will be fierce competition between First World countries for dominance in financial services, and in information technology and communications. Even the most successful centres for such activities will face constant attempts by rivals to displace them in such leadership roles; hence the opportunities for rapid expansion of employment will be strictly limited. Indeed, in the UK previously expanding sectors like banking are now experiencing redundancies, as British banks look for efficiency gains in order to compete in global financial markets.

As a result of all this, the demand and opportunities for highly educated and technically skilled employees is quite limited, as manufacturing becomes highly specialized and concentrated in high-tech, high value-added industries, with generous efficiency wages and fringe benefits for the small staff of technicians, as the payoff for high productivity, loyalty and willingness to undergo frequent retraining. Only in the UK has there been an increase in the kind of semi-skilled assembly work that characterized the Fordist era, and here mainly as a result of inward investment by Japanese and Korean firms. Even so, in a period of rapid overall growth, engineering employment declined by 3 per cent and output grew by 3 per cent between the end of 1993 and the end of 1995.[63] Meanwhile, in France and Germany there is increased evidence of graduates and skilled technicians among the long-term unemployed, indicating that 'employability' (if such a concept is meaningful at all) is not directly related to high levels of education and training. Indeed, the German system of retraining redundant skilled workers is open to strategic use by formerly high paid staff, who wish to avoid the inferior types of employment now available there.

On the other hand, the expansion of work for social reproduction is clearly related to the characteristics of First World populations. As medical science has advanced, and the benefits of better diet and hygiene and the more relaxed lifestyles associated with the era of welfare states have come through to present ageing generations, so the mortality rate has declined and the proportion of people living to their late eighties and beyond has grown rapidly. Between 1961 and 1995 the proportion of people over 75 years of age in the UK population increased from 4 to 7 per cent, with 16 per cent of the population now aged 65 and over.[64] In addition to this, better care and measures for social inclusion have greatly extended the life expectancy of people with handicaps and disabilities – but they of course need extra care to cope with everyday life. Hence the growth in public health and social services employment is a universal feature of First World patterns, along with a parallel increase in private services of all kinds.

These developments have not been uniform in all the advanced capitalist countries. In the United States, women have benefited from a rapid growth in private health and welfare employment – both in higher, better-paid managerial posts, and in lower-paid direct care work.[65] In Scandinavia, the expansion has taken place in the public sector, with women again the main beneficiaries, at decent rates of pay, but often in part-time roles. More than 80 per cent of the new jobs created there since the 1970s are in social services.[66] In the Continental European countries, the growth in employment in these services has been far slower. In Germany between 1961 and 1984, jobs in health, education and welfare grew by only half the rate of Sweden.[67]

The UK is somewhere between the American and Scandinavian patterns, with an expansion of women's employment in both the public and the private sectors of education, health and social care. In 1997 there were 4.2 million workers in education, health, social work and other community, social and personal activities (public and private) in Great Britain, out of a total of nearly 16.9 million employees – almost exactly 25 per cent of the total in employment.[68]

Productivity in these jobs has not risen, and cannot rise, except in so far as medical technology changes the possibilities of curative interventions. People do stay in hospital for less time after operations, but this is mainly because the tasks associated with recuperation are now carried out by district nurses, home helps and community care assistants, by residential and nursing home staff, or by family members. It takes the same amount of time to help a fragile elderly person to do their shopping, or look after their garden, or tend their feet, or have a midday meal, as it did 20 years ago. Most of the changes in the care of severely disabled people have been driven by pressure from these groups themselves for independent living, and not by considerations of efficiency. Even when changes in the organization of services do result in money being better spent – as in the transfer of resources from residential care to more flexible packages of care in the community – the result is not necessarily a diminution of costs in the longer term. In the Kent Community Care Project, which provided the basis for the reform of service for elderly and disabled people in the UK in the 1990s, those receiving community services lived longer still, and eventually needed *more* expensive hospital care.[69]

Much the same is true of all the work in miscellaneous private personal services, that has generated so many new jobs in the US and UK economies. The productivity of hairdressers, cleaners and caterers has not increased, nor has that of domestic servants, drivers, dogwalkers or housesitters. All that has happened is that – as incomes have become more unequal – better-off people have been able to afford to buy services that previously they performed for themselves and each other. There are important issues of justice around these developments, but those of efficiency are far less clear. By and large, the average productivity of the formal economy tends to be lowered rather than raised by the addition of more of this work to the overall pool of paid employment.

Important progress in upgrading the quality of this work, and improving standards, has been made through the National Vocational Qualifications (NVQ) system in the UK. From the point of view of dignifying the tasks of social care, and allowing a good quality of life for those who need it, this is very significant. But it is misleading to suppose that better training for these tasks actually increases efficiency. Indeed – as the experience of the health service and community care have illustrated since the reforms of the early 1990s – there is a constant tension between the value-for-money priorities of the purchaser–provider split and the market in care on the one hand, and the drive towards quality standards, better training and service-user choice on the other.[70] The logic of the contract culture favours private-sector care, where savings are often made by employing fewer trained staff, worse paid and on non-standard contracts; in the public sector, the logic of the NVQs, individual care plans, quality control and increased professional responsibility points to more expensive ways of providing better care.

Overall, then, the issues at stake over social justice in the division of labour in present-day societies are not clarified by insisting that better education and training will improve both efficiency and equity, as proponents of the new orthodoxy often do. There are difficult questions about how a declining proportion of the workforce, which will earn high wages and salaries for work connected with the global system of pro-duction and exchange, can best share these earnings with the growing proportion who are engaged in tasks of social reproduction, and whose productivity cannot be increased because of the nature of their work. The issues are rather like a macro-version of the household economy: how is social justice possible between one member (usually a man) who gains substantial resources in the wider public world of paid work and the organized pursuit of collective interests, and his 'dependants', who earn little from the formal economy, and who spend most of their energies and time on domestic activities of care or maintenance, and on servicing the public career of the 'head' of the household?

*The work ethic as a public good*

The idea that each individual member of a First World society is made better off if all others work harder and longer in formal employment is an equally unhelpful one in trying to clarify current issues of social justice. Empirical evidence immediately casts doubt on its validity. The countries with the highest participation rates for men and women in the 1970s and 1980s were the Soviet Union and the Eastern European countries, now branded as monuments to inefficiency and low produc-tivity. The great improvements in productivity achieved in the UK in the early 1980s were gained by reducing participation and creating high levels of unemployment.[71] The Netherlands had a very low rate of participation, and was a rather successful economy; much the same is true of Canada.[72] The most flourishing economies of these two decades, Japan and West Germany, had participation rates around the average[73] – similar to those of Austria, Australia and Hong Kong. In the rest of

the world, some of the richest countries had low participation rates
(Kuwait, Libya) and some of the poorest had high participation rates
(Vietnam, Thailand, Mali).[74]

Of course, these figures tell us nothing about the *quality* of the work
done by participants in these economies, or how well it was organized.
But this should alert us to the dangers of supposing that – simply by
driving or counselling people into the labour market through benefit
reductions or gentle persuasion – efficiency will automatically be
improved. Whether or not a strong work ethic is a public good, and
improves each individual's welfare, must depend as much on what
work is available and how it is organized. In Nazi Germany, a strong
work ethic contributed to efficiency in making armaments and
exterminating minority groups.

In the present situation, an even more important point concerns the
international division of labour. Using the economic methods discussed
in the first chapter (see pp. 3–6), Buchanan demonstrates the relevance
of a society's work ethic through a thought experiment. He invites his
reader to imagine him or herself on a space ship, with a choice of
whether to land and live on one planet with an average 40-hour
working week, or another with a similar population and natural
resources but a 20-hour working week. If economic advantage is the
criterion, the first is clearly preferable because (whatever one's preferences for work and leisure) the value of output purchasable per unit of
labour supplied to the market is higher – since specialization is more
developed because of the greater size of the economy, and technology is
better utilized.[75]

But this fable does not conclusively make the point Buchanan seeks
to prove. Because the two planets may be at quite different stages of
economic development, the relevant consideration is not how hard the
current population works, but how hard past generations did. It is quite
true that, in an industrial economy, a greater work effort will produce
the phenomena he mentions. But suppose that people on Planet A now
live on income derived from investments in manufacturing plants
located on Planet B. Under these circumstances (the situation, for
instance, likely to pertain in Hong Kong, as it becomes a financial centre
rather than a manufacturing one in relation to the Chinese mainland)
the welfare of each individual on Planet A will depend much more on
the work ethic of inhabitants of Planet B than on that of inhabitants of
that individual's own planet. People on Planet A will tend to be better
off because of the more advanced state of their economic development,
however hard they work, so long as those on Planet B continue to be
very industrious in their factories.

With globalization along the pathways discussed in Chapter 1 and in
the first section of this chapter, advanced capitalist countries of the First
World are increasingly in the situation of Planet A, while the former
communist countries of the Second World have regressed to a point

where re-industrialization on the model of Planet B is just taking off, and several large Third World countries are also at the point of takeoff in the industrialization process. For instance, although the German banking system was for several decades closely locked into industrial investment within the nation state, Germany is now the leading investor in Central Europe,[76] and hence facilitates the growth of productivity and output there, even when its own industrial production is stagnant or falling, and its own unemployment high. I shall use an example closer to real life to illustrate that the welfare of First World citizens is more influenced by the work ethic of societies like Poland, China and India than that of their fellow citizens.

Suppose that my neighbour, who works in a factory making plastic fittings, is made redundant because his boss has decided to move the whole production process to one of the new economic zones in China.[77] In terms of a public choice analysis of allocative decisions, this shift of resources clearly improves efficiency, if the fittings can be made at a lower cost there; and it improves equity too – in world terms – because the gain in welfare for a Chinese peasant previously earning £2.50 per week in a rural commune, and now receiving £50 per week as a factory worker, is far greater than the loss of welfare for my neighbour, given his stock of resources to fall back upon, and the protections offered by social insurance and social assistance in this country. Even if the Chinese government does not compensate my neighbour, the UK government can afford to do so. Furthermore, the shift improves my welfare, because the next time I want to buy plastic fittings, I shall benefit from the fall in price it allows.

The question is therefore whether my welfare is directly affected by my neighbour's decision about what to do next. In Buchanan's analysis, I should be concerned about the attitudes and practices of my neighbour, because these have an 'externality' – there is some inter-dependence between my welfare and his, through the public good of the puritan work ethic – and I stand to lose if the labour supply from other members of my society is limited by their reduced motivation to work. But, when I review the options open to my neighbour, it seems that this effect on my welfare is contingent on a number of circum-stances. My neighbour's choices seem to be:

1   to emigrate to another region or country where the skills my neighbour has are in demand;
2   to retrain for another factory job locally;
3   to retrain for another job in social care or private personal services;
4   to claim benefits and turn to self-provisioning activities, such as gardening, animal breeding or fishing.

None of these choices can be shown unequivocally to benefit me. Emigration reduces the size of the home labour market, and hence, on

Buchanan's account, the scope for specialization and productivity growth. The costs of retraining for factory work may outweigh the benefits to the economy, especially if the new employer quickly decides to tread the same pathway eastward as the previous one. Adding to the stock of social care and personal service workers may cost me more (in wage subsidies to exploitative private employers, or in local authority taxes to finance increased social services spending) than if my neighbour stayed on social assistance; if such labour power is being wastefully used, it may reduce efficiency without improving equity. Becoming a long-term claimant, but being active in the (legal) informal economy, could be the best outcome from any point of view. It might be the most or least efficient and equitable choice; this can only be determined when we know the actual costs associated with this and the other options, and the effects on output and productivity that they generate.

All this indicates that – since most of the material goods on which my comfort now depends are made in South East Asia – it is the work ethic and practices of Chinese workers that are likely to be more relevant for my welfare than those of my neighbour. Buchanan's argument that I should not be indifferent as to the work–leisure preferences of my neighbour because of the external benefits of the puritan ethic, and hence our interdependency within the system of cooperation constituted in our economy, turns out to be misleading. On the contrary (supposing that I am morally neutral about my neighbour's employer's decision to move to China), since the expansion of the labour market, the division of labour and productivity growth can all proceed faster there than here, it is clearly better for me if the Chinese work harder and more efficiently, even if this makes my neighbour redundant. As far as my neighbour is concerned, it will depend on many factors how his work–leisure preferences will affect me, because the main source of profits for my economy comes from investments in industries located in other societies, and because the most efficient and fair division of labour over social reproduction (especially that between paid and unpaid work) is a complex question that cannot be settled by using the analytic tools that Buchanan deploys in this essay.

Broadly speaking, taken in the global context, the puritan work ethic is only a public good in any society if it contributes positively to the quality of life shared by members of a community, through improving efficiency and equity. Under present-day conditions, it probably does so in China, but not in the UK. Applied uncritically to issues of public policy over welfare-to-work and lone parent benefits, it may well drive up the costs of public administration, and end up with more people in prisons and psychiatric hospitals, as well as making others neurotic, unhappy and mutually critical. Ultimately, if a puritan work ethic demands forced labour of a section of the population, it threatens the values of a liberal democracy, and even free markets themselves. Under these circumstances, the work ethic becomes a public hazard, rather than a public good.

### Civic obligations and the principle of reciprocity

The idea that the principle of reciprocity applies to civic obligation is strongly linked to the notion of the national economy as a system of cooperation.[78] But once the global economy is understood in the way suggested in the previous section, it becomes apparent that economic transactions can more usefully be represented as gainful exchanges, and national 'economies' as temporary clusters of such exchanges. If capital and some forms of skilled labour can move easily between countries – through the operation of international corporations – and if many commodities consumed in one country are produced in another, how can my civic obligations to a national polity be derived from my economic relations within markets?

The rules of social obligation are supposed to give reasons for favouring the claims of particular individuals over those of others. They are derived from the model of the small-scale voluntary association, in which benefits are restricted to those who offer labour services or other contributions to the exclusive 'club', and denied to others who have not qualified for membership. Hence these rules institutionalize the economics of such groups, by recognizing the interdependencies between members' welfare, and excluding the claims of outsiders who have not made the necessary contributions. But – as was shown in the previous section – now that there are stronger interdependencies between the welfare of individuals in one country and the actions and attitudes of workers in another far away, it is doubtful whether the obligations derived from economic relations can be a reliable guide to social obligations, still less to civic obligations in the national polity.

Although my own case is hardly typical, it does give some indications of the problem. In 1995–6, I earned most of my salary in Slovakia and Germany, and spent much of it in those and other European countries. The research fellows in those projects I directed were citizens of Brazil and Germany respectively, and I also employed a Slovak assistant. It is probable that most of my university pension fund was invested in overseas or international companies; the recession in the Far East will probably reduce the returns it can expect on these investments.[79] And when I fell ill, I received treatment in a German hospital, which was paid for out of a travel insurance policy I held in England. It is extremely difficult to see any of these transactions as contributing to a national 'system of cooperation'; but I was required to pay taxes in the United Kingdom on all my earnings, and hence to favour the claims of poor, unemployed, sick and retired UK citizens over those of far more indigent Slovaks, or my fellow patients in Germany.[80]

In one sense, this is the counterpart to the issue of capital's freedom to seek its highest return anywhere in the world. As shown in the previous section, it is advantageous for the welfare of citizens of this country that British capitalists should be free to relocate their factories in China. Hence the capitalist mentioned in the previous section was under no special obligation to his workers (other than those specified by their contractual conditions), or to the other citizens of that region of the UK. Conversely, where Japanese and Korean companies locate factories in depressed regions of the UK, they bring managers and designers with them, who participate in our productive processes, but remain citizens of (and under civic obligations to) their home countries.

Liberal political theory and institutional arrangements must somehow reconcile the freedom to pursue economic advantage by gainful exchanges across borders (i.e. globalization of all kinds) and the obligations of a political association that makes rules of justice through collective decisions for the common good. It is obvious that a totally unregulated global market would be impossible to achieve, however desirable it might seem in the eyes of neo-liberal Utopians. Such a system would require a ban on virtually all forms of collective action, since any cooperation of this kind between members of a group is – virtually by definition – a restraint on competition, and hence on 'free exchange'. The central problem of politics would then become how to *prevent* collective action, reversing the question of how individuals could ever come together in a polity or association to impose mutual restraints on competition when they could gain more immediate payoffs from rivalrous action, and asking instead how groups would be prevented from acting together to protect themselves by renouncing rivalry.

As Polanyi[81] showed, there has never been a human society in which groups did not take collective action to further or protect their interests; indeed the 'double movement' of society since the Industrial Revolution (and earlier in Britain) has been for the expansion of free markets to be offset by the organization of communities in defence of shared cultural practices. Cartels and trade unions (like corporations and guilds before them) used rules for restraint of competition to raise profits and wages, and every bourgeois voluntary body or working-class society was a way of sheltering a communal system of mutuality from the destructive force of markets. In this sense, the welfare state was the collectivization of these exclusive groups into a national system for economic and social protection, that redistributed resources at the same time as it restrained competition between organized capital and labour.

However, social justice in a globalized economic environment cannot rest on the same foundations as those of postwar welfare states. There are no 'social contracts' to be struck now between national capital and national labour; the former has dissolved into ethereal international exchanges, and the latter no longer represent the bulk of the population of working age. As welfare states have weakened, the pathways of the economy and society have diverged. The economy is based on individual exchanges and international forces – it is global and competitive, and knows few boundaries or barriers. Society is fragmented into exclusive groups – cooperation is more selective, narrower and more parochial. We seek gainful exchanges in a world of unrestrained and unembedded markets, and then look for protection among groups of citizens very much like ourselves.

The question is therefore whether societies, whose 'domestic' economy is now more unequivocally a system for the reproduction of a national culture and political life, can reach internal settlements on issues of social justice that embrace these plural, polarized and often conflictual groupings, and reconcile the global, competitive sector of the economy with the needs for social reproduction. These will be the topics for the remaining chapters of the book. But for the rest of this section, the task is to clarify the relevance of the principle of reciprocity for these questions.

This part of the argument is so important for the rest of the book that it will be developed in some detail.

*The intuitive appeal of the reciprocity principle*    The intuitive appeal of the reciprocity principle is that free-riding of all kinds is unjust, whether this takes place in a small-scale association, or takes the form of a defection from civic obligations by citizens. The same idea is often expressed in the notion that the social rights of citizenship (such as benefits to unemployed people and lone parents) imply reciprocal obligations.

Something in present-day political culture – especially in the Anglo-Saxon world – makes this notion specially persuasive. It first occurred to conservatives,[82] and now is enthusiastically endorsed by social democrats.[83] But I shall argue that it is a misleading basis for a theory of, or institutions for, social justice. There is at best a contingent connection between the elimination of free-riding and the principle of reciprocity, and neither on its own provides a convincing analysis of justice between members of a liberal polity.

Free-riding means failing to make an appropriate contribution for those collective goods which are shared because it is impossible or too costly to divide them up into items, each of which can be exclusively owned, and therefore bought and sold for a price.[84] Free-riding becomes possible when those who have not made a contribution benefit from a service like flood defence or firefighting. Hence the goods are under-supplied, unless contributions are made compulsory,[85] or they are limited to members of an association whose rules require contributions.

In a market economy, most public goods provided by the state (such as those mentioned in the previous paragraph) are paid for out of taxes. Others are supplied by restraints on actions that would cause negative externalities. Take the example of clean air: citizens are forbidden to burn noxious substances, or release harmful gases into the atmosphere. Neither taxpaying nor restraint of negative externalities is an instance of reciprocity. Contributions are simply the economic means of ensuring an efficient supply of public goods; how these are levied raises issues of social justice about the distribution of burdens, but not of reciprocity. Sanctions against polluters are also relevant for justice, since it is now recognized that people should pay in some ratio to the harms they cause to others – but this again is a principle of proportionality, rather than reciprocity.

Far from belonging in the public sphere of social obligation, the principle of reciprocity has, since the Middle Ages, been characteristic of the moral economy of households, voluntary groups and communities, not the formal economy or the polity. In particular, it applies to transactions in which payments in money or in kind are inappropriate. Anthropologists[86] distinguish between *balanced* reciprocity (for instance, if I borrow my neighbour's lawnmower, I should be willing to lend her my power drill later this week), and *generalized* reciprocity (when I shelter a homeless cousin I have only a vague expectation that he will help me out in some distant future emergency, or that I am possibly returning a longstanding moral debt by my branch of the family to his mother, my aunt).

Wherever direct barter or cash payment are possible, the notion of mutually gainful exchange substitutes for reciprocity, and markets arise. In this sense, the morality of reciprocity ceases where markets begin. Reciprocity is an appropriate way of dealing in long-term relationships of interdependency, where multi-faceted interactions occur between the parties, where issues of human value, dignity and stigma are at stake, and where flexibility and adaptability are required. Hence reciprocity is the obvious interactional code for the household and the wider family, where sensitivity to such issues is vital, and ambiguous situations have to be constantly negotiated.[87] In sexual relations, the most delicate and intimate of such transactions, ideas of choice and reciprocity are linked in complex ways – the crude notion of a *quid pro quo* would be as inappropriate as that of *compulsory* reciprocity for partners. It is the idea of spontaneous mutual giving, without rules, that sustains sexual intimacy – reciprocity under cover of dual unilateral selflessness.

In the moral sphere, the notion of free-riding is certainly linked to that of reciprocity. For example, a lazy husband might be said to free-ride on the efforts of his industrious wife, if he provided only half of the family income from employment, did little of the unpaid work about the house, and consumed a large proportion of the domestic budget.

Reciprocity would demand that he 'did his share', both in the formal economy and in the domestic division of labour.

This example clarifies some of the differences between the interactional codes of the formal and the informal spheres. In the household, fairness in the division of labour takes precedence over efficiency. Even if the woman is a much more efficient worker in the labour market *and* in the domestic arena, the man is expected to do his 'fair share' of work in both. Second, this fairness in the division of labour is supposed to function through the *sense* of obligation, and only if this fails through persuasion or negotiation, as reciprocity is meant to stem from mutual love and concern, or mutual commitment to a common project, and not the outcome of a bargaining process or a power struggle.

The other important difference is that reciprocity in the moral sphere of voluntary associations often takes the form of *labour contributions* to the production of goods that are collectively consumed. In the formal economy and in the public life of the polity this is hardly ever the case, for reasons that will be clarified below.

Consider an amateur hockey club, that owns its ground and club-house. The rules of the club define the dues payable by playing and non-playing members (financial contributions); the privileges of membership (e.g., over Cup tickets); and the various prohibitions on rivalry, disloyalty and disorder among members (playing for other teams, fighting in the clubhouse, etc.). Finally, and most importantly, they prescribe the duties of members, such as training sessions, work to maintain and mark the pitch, and the rota for teas and the bar. Hence – for the sake of the collective consumption of intrinsically rewarding shared goods (hockey matches) – members are required not only to mobilize themselves for organized competition with other clubs, and to restrain from damaging conflicts with fellow members, but also to give labour contributions to the cause. Here again, reciprocity is 'doing one's fair share'.

This example might be contrasted with the interaction code of a trade union, as a typical collective actor in a market environment. Here the paramount rules are those forbidding members to break strikes, to offer their labour for less than the union rate, or to do work that is not prescribed as appropriate for union members. Indeed (apart from making financial contributions) most of what such members agree to when they join the union is in the nature of *restraint* of labour contributions – promising *not* to work, except under prescribed conditions. Far from reciprocal labour being required to avoid free-riding, what is promised is *not* to work too hard, *not* to do others' tasks, *not* to work during strikes, *not* to work with non-union labour, and so on. This is because the collective benefit that accrues to trade unions comes mainly from restricting the supply of labour in their trade, forbidding actions that might weaken collective bargains, and limiting the sphere of labour appropriate for their members. A scab is not a free-rider but an egoistic opportunist.

So we can see that there is a complex and contingent relationship between free-riding and reciprocity in all human associations. Free-riding comes to be associated with failures in reciprocity in those groups and organizations where labour contributions are relevant for the production of collective goods. The idea that everyone should 'do their share' of the work of a cooperative unit is intuitively powerful but, as we have already seen in this section, it is by no means a universal feature of interactional codes. On the contrary, it applies to particular forms of informal associations. In formal organizations, the dominant code is one of *financial contribution* and *restraint of rivalry* among members. As we shall see, there are strong reasons for favouring these latter principles, rather than the principle of reciprocity, in issues of social justice and civic obligation in a liberal polity.

*The new orthodoxy, obligation and reciprocity*   In this section I shall argue that the intuitive appeal of the principle of reciprocity, captured in the new Blair–Clinton orthodoxy on welfare, stems from a number of muddles in current political thought. These muddles are specific to the age of global economics and domestic insecurity in First World societies.

The first part of the muddle is to confuse the interactional code of reciprocity with the rules for fair exchange. These are essentially *alternative* modes of interaction. Reciprocity relies on precisely those bonds of personal obligation that are absent in market (including labour market) transactions. Markets are efficient and convenient ways of making decisions about the allocation of resources, because they eliminate such moral considerations. Reciprocity would (as Adam Smith pointed out) require us to consider the sensibilities of the butcher, the brewer and the baker every time we went shopping. It would make us ask ourselves what duties of loyalty and fealty we owed our employers, rather than lead us to consult our contracts. Reciprocity requires us to strive to please others, by behaving in ways that are visibly caring, fair and cooperative (as in friendship groups and social gatherings). Reciprocity is for mutuality among members of an informal group, not customers or employees. Markets free us from such obligations. They allow us to pursue our interests as bargain hunters in an impersonal environment, where we offer only our money and our skills for exchanges conducted in a spirit of civil indifference.

Why then should these obvious distinctions be fudged in present-day thinking? The muddle seems to stem from growing concern that this same impersonal rational egoism that is appropriate for markets cannot provide the cement for society.[88] In the era following the market-minded reforms of Margaret Thatcher and Ronald Reagan, and the conscious denial of the mass solidarities of the postwar era ('there is no such thing as society . . .'), political theorists and politicians themselves have become increasingly desperate to discover a reliable source for the sense of obligation. Globalization increases transactions across *all* borders, and these include the artificial ones that are created by mutual associations of all kinds, from families to nation states. Unregulated markets tend to destroy all forms of community, and the institutions that protect human values. Hence it is not surprising that in the 1990s theories of citizenship should turn to the duties and virtues of members of the polity,[89] and attempt to show that these are reciprocal with the rights of citizens. This idea, often repeated by politicians like Tony Blair, is as obscure and meaningless to most people – especially the young[90] – as a Taoist mantra. Their lives are mainly made up of exchange in markets, most of which have some transnational elements. The duties of citizenship are largely unknown territory.

The second part of the muddle is to extrapolate from intimate associations (and especially from the family) to large-scale impersonal ones (society, the polity). Reciprocity is, as we have seen, the very stuff of family and friendship interactions, where life becomes unbearable if members do not pull their weight or take their turn. The sense of personal obligation is essential, because there is no other way to reconcile freedom with cooperation. Individuals have to experience the *desire* to do certain things for certain people, a desire that stems from affection, gratitude, loyalty, concern and interdependence. By definition, such feelings are absent in cosmopolitan societies, especially urban ones. Today we see a huge growth of people living alone in cities – the essence of a non-reciprocal lifestyle.[91] In 1961, 4 per cent of households under pensionable age consisted of one person, in 1995–6, 13 per cent.

Extrapolation from the family to the polity is a recipe for tyranny, as Locke[92] pointed out in his critique of Filmer's *Patriarcha*.[93] The Divine Right of Kings was a claim to moral authority as the head of the political household, and demanded absolute obedience. In more recent times Big Brother[94] – the fictional dictator of Orwell's communist totalitarianism – was strong on reciprocity, and had ways of making citizens do their bit. It seems extraordinary that, at the end of a century in which fascism and communism put obligation to the state above individual liberty, we should be forgetting the distinction made by Hume in the eighteenth, between associations based on sentiment and those based on utility.[95] There are many reasons why individual rights must be prior to political obligations in any form of liberal constitution (these will be discussed in the next chapter); without these, the dangers of authoritarianism are overwhelming.

If the family has become the only viable form of human association in a globalized economy (as the rest of Margaret Thatcher's famous aphorism implied), then it is little wonder that reciprocity should be claimed to be the primary element in all associations, and a necessary condition for a stable society. The threat of tyranny may seem a lesser evil to our rulers than the threat of anarchy.

The third part of the muddle is about the welfare state. It insists that reciprocity has always been a central idea of large-scale, state-sponsored schemes for replacing the incomes of people who are excluded from the labour market, or who have lost the support of a working partner. On this analysis, the *social insurance* principle contains strong rules against free-riding, and about reciprocal duties to work and earn (see pp. 42–3). However, this is quite misleading. Like other impersonal systems of insurance, it is simply a system that relates benefits to contributions, and excludes non-contributors, as well as forbidding actions that threaten to deplete collective funds. The fact that contributions are deducted from earnings is an administrative matter; it is the contributions that are compulsory, not the work.

This muddle is connected with the conditions for unemployment benefit, which insist that claimants must be available for and willing to take suitable work. But this rule simply defines the contingency in which benefits are paid (involuntary unemployment) in such a way as to protect the funds from excessive claims. All insurance funds and comparable mutualities (such as sickness clubs and friendly societies) have similar rules against depletion; they exist to restrict eligibility, not to demand reciprocal labour. A funeral club (i.e. a mutual-benefit burial club) excludes claims from members who are not dead, but this is fund management, not reciprocity.

The muddle arises because of confusion between the institutional rules of social insurance schemes and labour markets. Social insurance systems pool risks among large groups; they also control potential competition from 'outsiders', which would undercut the living standards of 'insiders' with protected jobs and wages. In Germany, for example, generous early retirement and 'disability' pensions keep older workers out of the labour market to defend the living standards of remaining workers.[96] In the labour market, he or she who does not work is not paid – this is the principle of exchange, where nothing is for nothing. In social insurance, the principle of past contributions guarantees a livelihood to those excluded from the labour market, in part to allow those in it to continue to prosper.

Another subsidiary reason for this particular confusion lies in the differences between social insurance and *social assistance* (income support in the UK, 'welfare' in the US). This is a system, derived from the late medieval Poor Law, which pays benefits to certain people whose incomes fall below a defined level (the 'poverty line'). Social assistance – which used to be administered at the local level of 'parishes', under varying discretionary regimes – was supposed to be abolished, or relegated to a small subsidiary role, by postwar welfare states. In fact it has expanded in scope, especially in Britain, where means-tested benefits (family credit, housing and council tax benefits, as well as income support) have come to make up over a third of income maintenance spending,[97] now loosely referred to as 'social security', or even – by Tony Blair himself – as 'the welfare state'.[98] Because social assistance is funded out of taxes, those who pay income tax in particular are not usually beneficiaries, so it is socially divisive – the rich pay, the poor receive – unlike social insurance, which redistributes over the life cycle, mainly from working age to old age.

The social assistance system is far older than liberalism and democracy. Its traditions were openly coercive, and included loss of liberty (the workhouse) and forced labour (the Speenhamland and roundsman systems).[99] It is to this tradition that politicians appeal when they say, for instance, that claimants should be 'made to jump off the welfare wagon and push it'.[100] Systems of compulsory 'workfare' and welfare-to-work, that require claimants to demonstrate their worthiness of assistance by taking low-paid employment on basic training, are systems of forced labour, not of reciprocity. These rules define free-riding in terms of being poor, and give taxpayers the right to impose work duties on anyone who is forced through poverty to claim against collective funds. So-called 'reciprocity' in these circumstances is simply the imposition of the labour-contribution principle in the form of forced labour, by the state.

The fourth part of the muddle over obligation and reciprocity is the idea that labour contributions are the usual ways in which free-riding is eliminated in large-scale, formal, impersonal membership organizations. In fact, as we have seen above (pp. 55–58), this is not the case; the main institutional features of such organizations are rules requiring financial contributions and those that outlaw forms of rivalrous behaviour between members. There are very good reasons, of efficiency and equity, why labour contributions are seldom the means of eliminating free-riding in such organizations.

In larger scale, more formal interactions, reciprocity is not an effective interactional code for preventing free-riding because the conditions conducive to the efficient use of moral sanctions – face-to-face contacts – are absent. Reciprocity works well where the voluntary efforts of a small group are ruled by mutual obligations, usually policed by persuasion, negotiation and ultimately by shaming. Such methods are efficient in the improvised order of the household[101] or the social club, but not in interactions between large groups of anonymous actors.

Large-scale systems for compulsory labour service are notoriously inefficient. Feudalism and slavery ultimately gave way to labour markets not because they were immoral but because those who practised them could not, except under very special conditions, compete successfully with systems based on 'free' exchanges of money for labour power. The largest-scale modern system of forced labour, state socialism, was ultimately revealed to be inefficient, because it could not raise the productivity of unwilling workers. The famous slogan 'we pretend to work, you pretend to pay' summed up the reluctance with which citizens made their labour contribution under state socialism, while the buoyancy of the secondary, 'shadow' economy revealed how well a (then illegal) labour market could work by comparison.

Reflection on our own society reveals that compulsory labour contributions are an improbable solution to problems of free-riding. If the issue over public goods is a way of ensuring that all make the contribution necessary for their optimal supply, why do we not have conscription into the police and the fire services? The obvious reason is that they would not be as efficient as ones financed out of compulsory financial contributions (taxes). A lifeboat crewed by ten pressed landlubbers would save few of those in peril on the seas; paid rescuers and volunteer professional fisherfolk are far more reliable. And if reciprocity were the guiding principle for contributions to public goods, the criterion for rescue service would have to be the experience of having been saved from mortal danger in some earlier incident. A lifeboat crewed by (reciprocity-driven) former rescuees would be a danger to shipping, not a contribution to social justice.

Furthermore, the objections to the notion of forced labour from equity are even stronger than those from efficiency. It violates the principle of self-ownership, which is one of the most basic tenets of liberalism. Self-ownership implies that each individual has an inalienable right to liberty in certain decisions, including the choice of what work to do in order to earn a living; it was a principle that was incorporated into liberal political philosophy specifically to rule out serfdom and slavery. This liberty overrides considerations of efficiency. There is inevitably some loss of productivity because brilliant scientists have the right to retire early, or to turn in whimsical middle age to painting or pottery. But liberal societies make this sacrifice of efficiency for the sake of a fundamental rule forbidding the alienation of the human body and spirit.

The new orthodoxy sometimes argues as if individuals forfeit this right when they throw themselves on the mercies of the public power as welfare dependants. This is a variant of Locke's justification of slavery,[102] when he suggested that those defeated in battle owed their lives to the mercy of their conquerors, and hence had no rights to liberty. In the nineteenth century, similar arguments were used to show why paupers should lose their civil and political rights on claiming assistance, and could validly be forced to enter the workhouse, and to submit to its disciplines of labour and segregation.[103] In postwar welfare states, Marshall argued, social rights completed the concept of liberal citizenship, by giving claimants the right to assistance without the shame and mortification of this loss of self-ownership.[104]

In the present-day world, many of the most obvious examples of abuses of human rights take the form of forced labour or slavery. There is still slavery in parts of sub-Saharan Africa, and variants of it in parts of India. Women from Eastern Europe are being imported into the Netherlands and Belgium and forced to work as prostitutes after their passports have been confiscated by racketeers. In South East Asia, children are sold to the sex trade for tourists. But we should not forget, either, that in recent history totalitarianism used extreme forms of forced labour as its basic instruments. In the 1920s and early 1930s, camps for unemployed men, required to do public work in exchange for benefit, were the norm all over Europe; indeed, in a report before the First World War, Beveridge recommended them for Britain.[105] Labour camps were used for land reclamation in Germany, and for the construction of the dykes in Holland. It was only during the Second World War that these camps came to be adapted for the purposes of the Holocaust in Poland, and later in Germany, and finally into the system of gulags in the Soviet Union. The exponents of the Blair–Clinton orthodoxy would do well to remember that the slogan 'Arbeit macht frei' at the entrance to Auschwitz was not a piece of random hypocrisy, but the fundamental principle of social policy of the Nazi regime, as well as in the Soviet state.

The fifth and final muddle in present-day political thought over the relationship between civic obligation and the principle of reciprocity is about exploitation. The new orthodoxy defines exploitation in terms of free-riding on the efforts of others, and especially claiming against the earnings and property of others. The image of the 'welfare cart' being pulled by exploited taxpayers, with idle, feckless claimants taking a leisurely ride, has been promoted first by Republican populists like Newt Gingrich in the USA,[106] and more recently by Democrat politicians there, and New Labour ones in the UK.

However, to focus exclusively on this aspect of exploitation is very misleading. A proper analysis of social justice requires us to look at various kinds of exploitation that can arise within relationships of interdependency between members of an association that cooperates, makes collective decisions and shares certain resources. To concentrate on welfare claims as the defining form of exploitation is like looking at women's roles in the patriarchal household in terms of unjust dependence, and not addressing issues of power and access to autonomy and public participation. Exploitation stems from the inability of individuals to achieve autonomy, to exit from situations of subordination, to have a voice in collective decisions, and to participate as full members in the activities of the wider association. Unless all these aspects of exploitation are considered, the analysis of injustice will be very distorted. For further discussion of this issue, see Chapter 5, pp. 166–79.

*Reciprocity and the conditions for social justice*     In the remaining chapters of this book, I shall consider all these aspects of interdependency in the present-day economies of First World states. To conclude this chapter, it is only necessary to point out that nation states, as systems for the reproduction of particular national cultures and practices, are interdependencies of this kind, and that the rules governing membership must be analysed as systems for social justice, and not taken in isolation from each other. The lone-parent protesters who carried the banner proclaiming 'We Won't Clean Harriet's Toilet' had a far clearer understanding of exploitation than the Secretary of State for Social Security (Harriet Harman), who was proposing the cut in their benefits. They saw that this measure, in combination with the New Deal, was aimed at making it more difficult for them to resist pressures to take low-paid, menial work, including domestic service. The power relations implicit in the employment of lone parents to do such work in the households of better-off couples are just as relevant to exploitation as are claims from taxpayers' contributions.

During the present era of globalization, nation states' capacities to sustain obligations in the form of compulsory contributions to collective goods have been eroded. At the same time, a proportion of the population have become more reliant on these collective resources. Some factors of production have become more mobile, and more resistant to making the contributions necessary to sustain those that are less mobile. Denied access to decently paid, secure jobs, the latter resist declining living standards by resorting to strategic use of welfare provision.

Injustice is endemic in this situation. If we imagine the labour market as an archaic daily gathering in the town square, these issues can be made concrete. How would a just division of labour be organized in this counterfactual situation? On the one hand, the requirement of efficiency is that all should be deployed so that the marginal utility to the economy of an extra job equals the marginal cost of creating it, and none could shift his or her labour supply without reducing overall productivity (output per person). And the optimum income maintenance system is one that best supports such a deployment, given that the demand for labour may change over time, and hence those temporarily outside the labour force should be kept as healthy and capable a reserve force as possible.

But from the point of view of equity, the demands of liberal justice include an opportunity for everyone to gain some economic advantage by exchanging their labour power for money, and that all should in turn contribute financially to the common fund. To comply with these requirements, the rules for labour market participation and income maintenance must allow even the least productive to do *some* paid work, and compel even these to make *some* contribution to revenues – even if this actually lowers overall productivity, and these contributions do not match their subsistence costs.

Thus in our imaginary daily labour auction, every adult man and woman should have a (formally) equal chance of being hired for the day (equality of opportunity); but no employer should have an incentive to pay less for labour power than the price that would lead him or her to use it most productively, given the (worldwide) technological possibilities. Behind this labour auction must lie a system of income maintenance such that each potential worker must know that if he or she is not hired for that price, there is an adequate level of support available; but that he or she is free to *offer* to work for less, if they wish to do so. On the other hand, all must know that, in order to benefit from such a scheme of income maintenance, they are required to contribute an amount of tax, such that the total sum of contributions, however levied, is sufficient to sustain the fund.

It is clear that the present situation in the USA and the UK does not anywhere near meet these criteria, and that that in Continental Europe does not either, for slightly different reasons. The former's labour auctions might be schematically represented as involving five categories of applicants for work, each with very different prospects at the start of the day:

1   *'Insiders'*, who are already guaranteed secure employment, decent rates of pay and working conditions, fringe benefits and insurance against a variety of contingencies, including redundancy.
2   *'Outsiders'* who are unprotected by any such collective agreements, or by any satisfactory income maintenance provision, and who are therefore motivated to work for wages which allow employers to use their labour power inefficiently, thus lowering the potential overall productivity of the economy, and exploiting them unfairly.
3   *'Claimants'* with established rights to various kinds of benefits, which allow them to protect themselves against some of the exploitation suffered by 'outsiders', but whose terms also deny them opportunities legally to participate in labour markets, even on a part-time basis.
4   *'Forced labourers'*, who are required to participate in state schemes for special employment or training, who are not paid wages at the level required by efficiency or justice, and who are denied the income protection given to claimants – and are therefore exploited by virtue of being used for purposes not required by optimization, and under coercive conditions constituting a denial of basic freedom.
5   *'Opportunists'* and *'Fiddlers'*, those employers who offer cash work to claimants, and thus avoid making the appropriate contributions to the funds, and those claimants who do such cash work 'on the side', without declaring it to the benefits authorities.

In summary, therefore, inefficiency and injustice are endemic to our labour markets, and the proposed measures of the Blair–Clinton orthodoxy will increase rather than diminish them. In the Continental European variant, claimants have better income protection, outsiders are shielded by various regulations governing pay and conditions, and workfare schemes are less coercive – but opportunities to contribute through formal labour markets are even more limited to those in 'insider' roles. All this indicates that free-riding is only one part of the problem of social justice to be addressed in labour markets. Indeed, attempts to tackle free-riding in isolation from these other sources of injustice compound the problems, because they ignore other central issues.

## Conclusions

The image of the town-square labour auction at the end of the last section captures the main argument of this chapter. The new Blair–Clinton orthodoxy on welfare policy claims that social justice is best achieved if all the citizens attend the auction, if all are skilled and motivated, and if all are moved by motives of responsibility to the prosperity of the polity. Its policy programme is to shift resources out of expensive income maintenance payments, and into the education and training of the workforce, to get them back to work – if necessary by cutting or withdrawing their benefits. In this sense, labour markets are seen as the keys to social justice.

My critique has shown that issues of justice lurk behind the auction, and are obscured rather than clarified by the new orthodoxy's arguments. In the wider context of a global division of labour, resources should be free to flow to those parts of the world where they can be most productively allocated. Local labour markets have to equilibrate demand for workers to produce for global markets, and to keep the local economy functioning. Over time, this polarization has become institutionalized in the different conditions and pay enjoyed by 'insiders' with secure, well-paid jobs and fringe benefits, and those endured by 'outsiders' with low pay, little protection and 'non-standard' contracts.

On the supply side, households have adapted to this polarization by a strategy in which one member (usually a man) tries to occupy an 'insider' role, while others (women and young people) do 'outsiders'' work.[107] But those families that could not sustain this strategy have been pushed beyond the labour market, and into claimant roles. For instance, in the UK in addition to the 1½ million long-term unemployed and one million lone parents, there are now nearly 2½ million claimants of incapacity benefits in the UK, compared with only 300,000 in 1979.[108]

The Blair–Clinton orthodoxy rightly draws attention to the way that welfare benefits expenditure has grown inexorably over the past 20 years, yet poverty and social exclusion have increased rather than diminished. It rightly insists that the income maintenance system must function so that labour markets work more smoothly, rather than acting as a barrier to claimants' participation. But it is wrong to suppose that the best way to achieve this goal is to make benefits more restrictive and conditional. Paradoxically this can have exactly the opposite effect to that intended,[109] as I shall argue in Chapters 4 and 5. Although in the USA the number of welfare claimants has been reduced by over 10 per cent each year since 1995, spending per head has risen. Wisconsin, which has had a large fall in welfare rolls, now spends 62 per cent more per claimant on those remaining; and only half of those who have left welfare move into jobs.[110]

My critique in this chapter has been focused on the three main theses of the Blair–Clinton orthodoxy. 'Education, education and education' as the priorities of policies to empower an adaptable, employable work-force have been shown to be only a part of the solution, since an increasing proportion of work must necessarily take the form of low-productivity tasks for social reproduction. This is essential and poten-tially intrinsically rewarding work, that determines the quality of citizenship of those who perform it as well as those who receive services. But it is not susceptible to technological change or enhanced efficiency.

'Putting the work ethic at the centre of the welfare state' has been demonstrated to be an inappropriate slogan. The work ethic – in the sense of motivation to work long hours in physically or mentally demanding toil, as an investment for future wealth – is certainly still relevant for the expansion of the world economy, and the improvement of the welfare of the great majority of its inhabitants. But in those post-industrial economies that rely primarily on capital- and information-intensive production and on the financial sector for their share of global markets, the puritan ethic of hard work can be counterproductive, if it leads to a blaming attitude towards those for whom there are no longer roles in traditional industries, or to costly social divisions, punitive policies and a breakdown of the trust and cooperation that are necessary conditions for prosperity and good democratic governance.

Finally, the 'something-for-something society' is an excellent prin-ciple, so long as this is not taken simplistically to reflect the kind of reciprocity – based on labour contributions to a system of cooperation – that characterize small informal groups of family and friends. I have shown that, in large-scale anonymous societies organized through market economic relations, the attempt to extrapolate from the moral codes of such groups to the civic obligations of social citizenship is totally inappropriate for a liberal democratic polity. Instead of ushering in the 'Giving Age', it reverts to pre-modern forms of serfdom, or the barbarity of the workhouse. Human rights, in whose name state socialism was laid low in almost every corner of the world, would be given no respect in such an ironic replication of the most totalitarian features of those dead regimes.

It is not the goals of the new orthodoxy that are wrong, but its programme of measures to try to implement social justice. It is as if the council of the town in which the labour auction is taking place attends solely to the conditions of the auction itself (how many citizens are present, how many are hired) and not at all to the conditions under which they arrive at the market place. If some drive up in luxury coaches from their already-guaranteed workplaces, while others limp in cold and bedraggled from sleeping in doorways or ditches, while others still turn up in chain gangs, escorted by officials, this is not a free and fair auction. It cannot possibly provide the institutional basis for social justice.

In the next chapter, I shall turn to an analysis of principles of social justice in a liberal democratic state. It is only by returning to these underlying issues that we can unravel the background to the problems of the labour market.

## Notes and references

1 G. Esping-Andersen, *The Three Worlds of Welfare Capitalism*, Cambridge: Polity, 1990, p. 12 and ch. 2.
2 Ibid, p. 21.
3 Department for Education and Employment, *Labour Market Trends, December 1997*, London: Stationery Office, 1997.
4 M. Walzer, *Spheres of Justice*, Oxford: Blackwell, 1983.
5 K. Polanyi, *The Great Transformation: The Political and Economic Origins of Our Time*, Boston, MA: Beacon Press, 1944.
6 D. Thompson, 'Fetishizing the Family: The Construction of the Informal Carer', in H. Jones and J. Millar (Eds), *The Politics of the Family*, Aldershot: Avebury, 1996; H. Dean (Ed.), *Parents' Duties, Children's Debts: The Limits of Policy Intervention*, Aldershot: Ashgate, 1995.
7 J. Keane and J. Owens, *After Full Employment*, London: Hutchinson, 1986.
8 A. Revenko, 'Povety in Ukraine', paper given at the Third International Conference on the Social History of Poverty in Central Europe, Lodz, Poland, 3–6 December, 1997.
9 C. Handy, *The Age of Unreason*, London: Hutchinson, 1989.
10 R. Solow, *The Labour Market as a Social Institution*, Oxford: Blackwell, 1990.
11 Revenko, 'Poor Strata of Population in Ukraine'.
12 P. Van Parijs, *Real Freedom for All: What (If Anything) Is Wrong with Capitalism?*, Oxford: Oxford University Press, 1995.
13 B. Jordan, M. Redley and S. James, *Putting the Family First: Identities, Decisions, Citizenship*, London: UCL Press, 1994.
14 BBC Radio 4, *Eurofile*, 22 November 1997.
15 B. Archer, 'Marques out of 10', *Guardian*, 6 October 1997.
16 A. Weale, *Political Theory and Social Policy*, London: Macmillan, 1983, pp. 42–6; B. Jordan, *The State: Authority and Autonomy*, Oxford: Blackwell, 1985, ch. 1.

17  M. Dean, *Towards a Theory of Liberal Governance*, London: Routledge, 1991.
18  R. Plant, 'Citizenship, Employability and the Labour Market', *Citizen's Income Bulletin*, 24, July 1997, pp. 2–3.
19  E. Balls, 'Danger: Men Not at Work', in E. Balls and P. Gregg, *Work and Welfare*, London: IPPR, 1993.
20  R. Reich, 'New Deal and Fair Deal', *Guardian*, 14 July 1997, p. 16.
21  Commission on Social Justice, *Social Justice: Strategies for National Renewal*, London: Vintage, 1994, p. 154.
22  US Department of Labor, *Labor Market Problems of Older Workers*, Washington, DC: Department of Labor, 1989.
23  Commission on Social Justice, *Social Justice*, ch. 4.
24  Reich, 'New Deal'.
25  G. Brown, 'Why Labour is Still Loyal to the Poor', *Guardian*, 2 August 1997.
26  T. Blair, speech at Durham, 22 December 1997.
27  J.M. Buchanan, *Ethics and Economic Progress*, Norman, OK: University of Oklahoma Press, 1994, p. 13.
28  Ibid, p. 16.
29  Commission on Social Justice, *Social Justice*, ch. 5; Brown, 'Loyal to the Poor'.
30  Buchanan, *Ethics*, pp. 13–15.
31  H. Dean and P. Taylor-Gooby, *Dependency Culture: The Explosion of a Myth*, Hemel Hempstead: Harvester Wheatsheaf, 1992.
32  K. Mann, *The Making of an English Underclass*, Oxford: Oxford University Press, 1991; L. Morris, *Dangerous Classes: The Underclass and Social Citizenship*, London: Routledge, 1994.
33  W.J. Wilson, *The Truly Disadvantaged: The Underclass, the Ghetto and Public Policy*, Chicago, IL: Chicago University Press, 1989.
34  W.J. Wilson, *When Work Disappears: The World of the New Urban Poor*, London: Vintage, 1997.
35  F. Field, speech to Conference on the Future of the Welfare State: British and German Perspectives, Humboldt University, Berlin, 18 November 1997.
36  T. Blair, speech to Labour Party Conference, *Guardian*, 22 October 1997.
37  H. Dean, *Welfare, Law and Citizenship*, London: Routledge, 1994.
38  N. Barry, 'Markets, Citizenship and the Welfare State: Some Critical Reflections', in R. Plant and N. Barry, *Citizenship and Rights in Thatcher's Britain: Two Views*, London: Institute of Economic Affairs, 1990.
39  Commission on Social Justice, *Social Justice*, p. 362.
40  S. White, 'Rethinking the Strategy of Equality: An Assessment of the Report of the Commission on Social Justice', *Political Quarterly*, 1995, pp. 205–10, at p. 208.
41  R.H. Tawney, *The Acquisitive Society*, London: Allen and Unwin, 1921.
42  S. White, 'Reciprocity in the Defence of Basic Income', paper given at Basic Income European Network Conference, Vienna, 12–14 September 1996.
43  B. Jordan, *A Theory of Poverty and Social Exclusion*, Cambridge: Polity, 1996, ch. 2.
44  M. Olson, *The Logic of Collective Action: Public Goods and the Theory of Groups*, Cambridge, MA: Havard University Press, 1965.
45  R. Hardin, 'The Tragedy of the Commons', *Science*, 162, 1968, pp. 1243–8.
46  E. Ostrom, *Governing the Commons: The Evolution of Institutions for Collective Action*, Cambridge: Cambridge University Press, 1990.
47  Blair, speech to Labour Party Conference.

48 White, 'Strategy of Equality', pp. 207–8.
49 G. Schmid and J. O'Reilly, 'Future Patterns of Work and Employment', paper presented at the Conference on the Future of the Welfare State: British and German Perspectives, Humboldt University, Berlin, 17–18 November 1997.
50 S. Bergmann-Pohl, 'Keynote Address' to the Conference on the Future of the Welfare State; K. Hinrichs, 'Demography and Pensions', paper given at the Conference on the Future of the Welfare State.
51 Blair, speech to Labour Party Conference; Brown, 'Loyal to the Poor'.
52 Z. Bauman, *Intimations of Post-modernity*, London: Routledge, 1992; B. Smart, *Modern Conditions, Post-modern Controversies*, London: Routledge, 1991; N. Parton, *Social Work, Social Theory and Social Change*, London: Routledge, 1996.
53 B. Jessop, 'The Transition to Post-Fordism and the Schumpeterian Workfare State', in R. Burrows and B. Loader (Eds), *Towards a Post-Fordist Welfare State?*, London: Routledge, 1994, pp. 13–37.
54 S. Hoggart, 'Is China Trading Places? Why are our plastic bags produced in China and not Telford?', *Guardian*, 28 September 1996.
55 P. Kennedy, 'Globalisation and Its Discontents' (Dimbleby Lecture), BBC Radio 4, 30 May 1996.
56 European Commission, *Employment in Europe*, Luxembourg: Office of the Commission of the European Communities, 1993.
57 Department for Education and Employment, *Labour Market Trends, November 1997*, Table 1.1, p. 57.
58 C. Nichol, 'Patterns of Pay: Results from the 1997 New Earnings Survey', in *Labour Market Trends, December 1997*, Table 1, p. 470.
59 Office for National Statistics, *Social Trends, 1997*, London: Stationery Office, 1997, Table 4.2, p. 73.
60 A. Green and H. Steedman, *Educational Provision, Educational Attainment and the Needs of Industry: A Review of Research for Germany, France, Japan, the USA and Britain*, National Institute for Economic and Social Research, Report Services No. 5, 1993.
61 International Labour Office, *International Labour Force Statistics, 1996*, Geneva: ILO, 1996, Table 1.1.
62 D. Donnison, *Politics for a Just Society*, Basingstoke: Macmillan, 1998, p. 62.
63 Department of Employment, *Labour Market Trends, June 1996*, Tables 1.2 and 1.8.
64 *Social Trends, 1997*, Table 1.5, p. 29.
65 Esping-Andersen, *The Three Worlds*, Table 8.1, p. 199.
66 Commission on Social Justice, *Social Justice*, p. 168.
67 Esping-Andersen, *The Three Worlds*, p. 78.
68 *Labour Market Trends, June 1996*, Tables 1.2 and 1.8.
69 D. Challis and B. Davies, 'Long-Term Care of the Elderly: The Community Care Scheme', Discussion Paper 386, Canterbury: Personal Social Services Research Unit, University of Kent, 1985.
70 R. Hadley and R. Clough, *Care in Chaos: Frustration and Challenge in Community Care*, London: Cassell, 1996.
71 International Labour Office, *Yearbook of Labour Statistics, 1989–90*, Geneva: ILO, 1990, pp. 27 and 42.
72 Ibid., pp. 21 and 39.
73 Ibid., pp. 31 and 37.
74 Ibid.

75 Buchanan, *Ethics*, p. 17.
76 *Central Europe Productivity Reporter*, 4th edition, March 1997, p. 3.
77 Hoggart, 'Is China Trading Places?'.
78 White, 'Strategy of Equality', and 'Reciprocity'; Brown, 'Loyal to the Poor'.
79 M. Woollacott, 'Watch That Pension', *Guardian*, 15 January 1998.
80 B. Jordan, 'Justice and Reciprocity', *Critical Review of International Social and Political Philosophy*, 1 (1), 1998, pp. 63–85.
81 Polanyi, *The Great Transformation*.
82 C. Murray, *Losing Ground: American Social Policy, 1950–80*, New York, Basic Books, 1985; L.M. Mead, *Beyond Entitlement: The Social Obligations of Citizenship*, New York: Free Press, 1989.
83 Blair, Speech to Labour Party Conference, October 1997; Brown, 'Loyal to the Poor'.
84 J.M. Buchanan, *The Demand and Supply of Public Goods*, New York: Rand MacNally, 1968.
85 Olson, *Collective Action*, ch. 1.
86 M. Sahlins, *Stone Age Economics*, London: Tavistock, 1974, ch. 5.
87 Jordan et al., *Putting the Family First*, ch. 4.
88 J. Elster, *The Cement of Society: A Study of Social Order*, Cambridge: Cambridge University Press, 1989.
89 W. Kymlicka and W. Norman, 'Return of the Citizen: A Survey of Recent Work on Citizenship Theory', *Ethics*, 104 (2), 1994, pp. 352–81.
90 Alan France, '"Why Should We Care?": Young People, Citizenship and Questions of Social Responsibility', *Journal of Youth Studies*, 1 (1), 1998, pp. 97–111.
91 *Social Trends, 1997*, Table 2.2.
92 J. Locke, *Two Treatises of Government* (1698), Ed. P. Laslett, Cambridge: Cambridge University Press, 1967.
93 Sir Thomas Filmer, *Patriarcha*, in P. Laslett (Ed.), *Filmer's Patriarch and Other Political Writings*, Oxford: Oxford University Press, 1949.
94 G. Orwell, *Nineteen Eighty-Four*, London: Secker and Warburg, 1949.
95 D. Hume, *A Treatise of Human Nature* (1739), Ed. L.A.S. Bigge, Oxford: Clarendon Press, 1928; *Essays Moral, Political and Literary* (1742), Oxford: Oxford University Press, 1985, pp. 42, 175, 309–10.
96 G. Esping-Andersen, 'Welfare States Without Work: The Impasse of Labour Shedding and Familialisation in Continental European Social Policy', in G. Esping-Andersen (Ed.), *Welfare States in Transition: National Adaptations in Global Economies*, London: Sage, 1996, pp. 66–87.
97 Department of Social Security, *Social Security Statistics, 1997*, London: Stationery Office, 1997.
98 Blair, speech at Durham.
99 S. and B. Webb, *English Poor Law History*, London: Allen and Unwin, 1929.
100 N. Gingrich, speech during mid-term elections, *Guardian*, 20 October 1994.
101 Jordan et al., *Putting the Family First*, ch. 5.
102 Locke, *First Treatise of Government*, sections 42 and 43.
103 S.G. and E.O.A. Checkland (Eds), *The Poor Law Report of 1834*, Harmondsworth: Penguin, 1974.
104 T.H. Marshall, *Citizenship and Social Class*, Cambridge: Cambridge University Press, 1950.

105 Sir William Beveridge, *Unemployment: A Problem of Industry*, London: Longman Green, 1909.
106 Gingrich, speech during mid-term elections.
107 Jordan et al., *Putting the Family First*.
108 *Social Security Statistics, 1997*, Fig. D104a.
109 H. Dean, 'Undermining Social Citizenship: The Counterproductive Effects of Behavioural Controls in Social Security Administration', paper given to ISSA Second International Research Conference on Social Security, Jerusalem, 25–28 January 1998.
110 V. Keegan, 'A New Deal – But a Great Gamble', *Guardian*, 1 January 1998.

# 3

# Social Justice: Rights, Equality, Need

In a sense, there is only one principle of justice – that every individual should get his or her due. But what is due to each is made up of a complex mixture of elements (entitlements that arise from equal membership, from particular merits, and from acknowledged needs), and derived from a number of different 'spheres of justice', each with its own criteria for distributing its goods.[1] Any new perspective on social justice is required to juggle these elements – reordering them and rearticulating the connections between them – and to reprioritize these spheres, giving a revised account of what is due to each individual through a fresh analysis.

The Blair–Clinton orthodoxy is an explicit example of this process. On the one hand, it emphasizes those claims that arise from contributions, and especially economic contributions to the common good. It reasserts that those who work hard are entitled to more, because they merit (or deserve) it. On the other, it refocuses equality on opportunities for all, rather than on redistribution to produce equality of outcome. This kind of equality is far easier to reconcile with claims from merit (or desert), and hence more suited to the new design. Finally, it demotes claims from need, and insists that any such must be shown to be genuine. The needy must therefore demonstrate (or even parade) their neediness, and mark themselves out from those whose claims rest on contributions, merits or deserts.

At the same time, the new orthodoxy prioritizes various forms of procedural justice over the substantive elements of redistributive systems. Justice is defined in terms of fair exchanges and fair contracts in markets, as well as decisions arrived at by due process and according to law. Criminal justice is given a higher priority, with retribution and deterrence as recognizable features of these processes. Conversely, social justice in the form of claims against the incomes and property of fellow citizens through collective schemes for redistribution are relegated in priority, and made more restrictive and conditional in form.

Finally, the sphere of formal economic activity is elevated in importance over other spheres of justice. 'It's the economy, stupid', as Bill Clinton told himself during his first election campaign, is now the watchword of the new orthodoxy. The moral economy of households, associations and communities is dignified by rhetorical praise, but relegated to a less important role. But the economy is remoralized, by the importation from the ethical sphere of concepts like responsibility, reciprocity and obligation.[2] Yet despite this process of extrapolation from the moral sphere, informal activity is deliberately given lower priority than formal labour supply; the work ethic implies high participation rates and hard work, even when this means that duties of care to children, friends and neighbours must be neglected as a result.

The overarching institutional forms in which liberal conceptions of justice have been framed – those of constitutional democracy – are strongly asserted in the new orthodoxy. This is most clearly the case in Tony Blair's version, with its strong appeal to more explicit constitutional principles over civil rights, justifiable claims, open government and the devolution of powers to new assemblies in Scotland, Wales and Northern Ireland. Justice is located in a framework of impartial law, which aims to create conditions for harmonious co-existence of citizens committed to various beliefs and causes, and a plurality of cultural practices. Impartial justice aims to reconcile these potentially conflictual forces,[3] and create a community of interest through a unified economic purpose; punishment underpins this code (see Figure 3.1).

But – as I have already argued in the previous chapter – there are obvious and already visible tensions between the liberal democratic framework of the new orthodoxy's version of social justice, and the substantive content of its policies. These were well captured in the first public outcry about the proposed cuts in British disability benefits, announced in December 1997. Jane Campbell, a disabled woman who had been nominated as a member of the new government's working party on civil rights and citizenship, asked how she was supposed to take part in this if her mobility allowance was cut.[4] The quality of membership of a political association is determined – for other disadvantaged people as well as those with disabilities – by their capacity

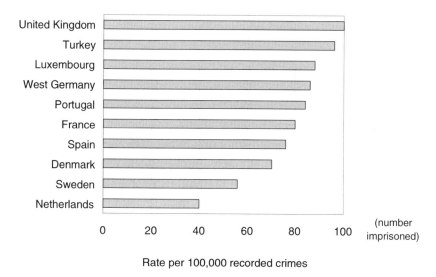

FIGURE 3.1   *Prison populations: an international comparison (Barclay, 1991, p. 61)*

to implement their social rights, and attain a minimum necessary for participation, debate and deliberation.

In the USA, the issues are raised more starkly by the trends in criminal justice policy. With almost all states now practising capital punishment, and no political party opposing its extension, the execution of mentally handicapped people is already happening, and that of juveniles is being debated. The numbers of prisoners in federal and state prisons there rose from 196,000 in 1974 to 1,100,000 in 1995 – more than a fivefold increase; if local jails are counted, then the number is over one and a half million. In the city of Baltimore, the majority of young men are black, and the majority of these are now in prison, on probation or on parole. Yet between 1970 and 1994, the city's homicide rate had increased by 75 per cent.[5] Civil rights in this context are defined not by the procedures of the courts, but by the political climate in which politicians campaign for election, and win votes by promises to restrict the liberty and enforce the control of groups defined as deviant and threatening for the mainstream.

These issues are now most urgently at stake over the rights of unemployed and disabled people and lone parents, in questions about whether they should be compelled into economic participation for the common good. These issues force us back into the theoretical debate about justice, in a search for reliable principles to regulate a society in which work roles are contested at the same time as income shares are being allocated through more competitive processes.

Procedural and constitutional rules for justice cannot settle disputes of this kind. We must also deal in substantive issues about the distribution of responsibilities for society's work efforts, and the division of its income. These will be the subjects of the chapter.

## Rights and obligations

A central feature of the new orthodoxy is the idea that rights must be balanced by obligations. In the UK, for example, the former Labour Minister for Welfare Reform, Frank Field, argued that rights without corresponding duties are not sustainable, so obligations should be regarded as prior to rights.[6] All small-scale associations (such as those of the voluntary sector) are obligation-based; their rules define the contributions required of members. Hence political life should be governed by explicit obligations also, especially in matters concerning claims against the public purse.

In the USA, this principle has been much more fully developed. Under Bill Clinton's presidency, the word 'responsibility' has appeared with increasing frequency in welfare reform legislation. He adopted the slogan of a 'New Covenant' at the 1992 election; in his speech commencing his candidacy he used the world 'responsibility' 12 times, calling for justice, but appealing to the middle class (13 mentions).[7] His policy emphasizes deservingness and independence, and the need to reduce the numbers of families on social assistance (see Table 3.1). His proposed Work and Responsibility Act of 1994 would have limited time on Aid to Families with Dependent Children to two years, required lone mothers to name the father of their children, and established a set of teenage pregnancy prevention programmes. The eventual Personal Responsibility Act of 1996 (introduced by the new Republican majority) substituted Temporary Assistance for Needy Families for the AFDC programme, gave states more discretion to modify eligibility criteria, and required adult claimants to work within two years of receiving benefits, only parents with a child under one year of age being exempted. Teenage mothers could be denied benefits until they reached their eighteenth birthdays. The disability criteria for children's benefits were tightened; legal immigrants would not be entitled to benefits until five years after their arrival, and legal and illegal aliens were denied most federal benefits.[8]

This aspect of the new orthodoxy reflects recent developments in political thought. The communitarian turn of the 1980s refocused attention on duties and virtues, and the necessary conditions for a responsible political body. In their critique of liberalism, communitarians represented it as an abstract and empty universal code, that could not mobilize members in pursuit of higher values,[9] or articulate their aspirations for a shared improvement in the quality of their collective culture.[10]

TABLE 3.1  *Average monthly numbers (thousands) of AFDC families and recipients, 1980-1993*

|  | **1980** | **1985** | **1988** | **1990** | **1991** | **1992** | **1993** |
|---|---|---|---|---|---|---|---|
| Families | 3,574 | 3,692 | 3,748 | 3,974 | 4,375 | 4,769 | 4,981 |
| Recipients | 10,597 | 10,813 | 10,920 | 11,460 | 12,595 | 13,625 | 14,144 |

*Source*: Committee on Ways and Means, US House of Representatives, 1994 Green Book, p. 325

This has led to renewed interest in the institutions of civil society, and how associational networks make democratic politics possible.[11] The family and the voluntary association as the formative experiences that inculcate responsible and virtuous activity are claimed to be the necessary conditions for a self-governing, free and prosperous society.[12]

Interest in association, community and active membership has been carried over into theory about citizenship, which has been a feature of political thought in the 1990s. On the left, notions of participatory democracy are recognized as requiring a greater sense of responsibility as well as involvement among citizens.[13] Civic republican theory has been revived, with its emphasis on the necessity for active participation in the political life of the community for the full flourishing of human potentials;[14] this in turn requires a sense of mutual obligation among members. Liberals too have developed an interest in political virtue, and in citizens' responsibilities at least to engage in debate and discussion about important issues,[15] and to exercise 'public reasonableness' in coming to collective decisions.[16]

All these ideas converge around the notion of the citizen as a competent and responsible actor, who deliberates, decides, takes part in the economic and political life of the public sphere, and contributes to collective choices. It also echoes the New Right's critique of the welfare state in the 1980s, when public provision was blamed for passivity and dependence,[17] and the decay of civic obligation and economic energy was attributed to an overgenerous[18] or excessively unconditional[19] welfare system. Ultimately, the fault was traced to the postwar settlement, and the creation of social rights – to complement civil and political rights – at the time when citizenship was being redefined to include all members of a democratic system.

It should be pointed out that T.H. Marshall's famous analysis[20] of this historical moment is an Anglocentric one (see p. 7). Social rights came far earlier in Germany and Scandinavia especially, and were introduced as alternatives to democratic political rights, as part of monarchical, paternalistic attempts to pre-empt liberalism and socialism. In order to give social provision the status of a right of citizenship, liberal polities had to overcome the objection, first articulated by Malthus in 1798,[21] that public assistance allowed the poor to transfer the costs of childrearing on to the rest of the community, and discouraged work and thrift. They did so only when liberal collectivists like Beveridge were able to argue that social insurance could eradicate poverty without destroying individual initiative or the duty to provide for one's dependants,[22] and hence was consistent with the fundamental conditions for a free society.[23]

Social rights were necessary because the lack of material resources could prevent an individual from becoming an autonomous economic agent or a competent political actor; they were feasible through a system of mutual insurance against measurable contingencies and risks. The first argument had justified universal public-funded primary education in the United States long before it was implemented in Britain; the second allowed the New Deal there in the 1930s, and the early development of unemployment insurance in New Zealand.

In Marshall's analysis, the historical emergence of civil rights (individual freedoms of speech and belief, and protections against arbitrary coercion) in the eighteenth century were followed by the gradual emergence of full democratic political rights in the nineteenth and early twentieth. These were largely negative rights, consisting of prohibitions on state interference and compulsion, and powers to replace unpopular governments and control collective decisions through the ballot box and popular mobilization. Social rights were different, in that they contained substantive elements of redistribution, and claims against the generality of others in the political community. But they were granted because they gave a kind of basic equality of status, appropriate for a postwar social democracy, rather than an actual equality of material resources. Marshall considered social insurance to be the equivalent for workers of legal aid for citizens, which gave them access to the civil rights that would otherwise be denied them by their poverty.[24]

In this way, Marshall was able to maintain that social rights were part of a new postwar version of that bundle of liberties that surrounded the individual citizen of a liberal polity, and allowed him or her to develop projects and commitments as an autonomous actor. Social rights complemented civil and political rights, rather as property rights complemented personal rights in the bourgeois conceptions of the nineteenth century.[25] They were necessary to give substance to the human potential that was protected by the rights to freedom and choice, which could not otherwise be operationalized. In other words, they democratized John Stuart Mill's famous defence of liberties as a capsule surrounding individuals, and allowing them to flourish as innovators, critics, originals, creators or resisters against conformity, and hence permitting them to develop a plurality of forms of human flourishing and prosperity.[26] Social rights – provided through the proper institutions – could extend these freedoms to the working class which hitherto lacked property and security; and also to those minorities which liberal rights sought to protect against the possible tyranny of the majority under democratic political institutions.

This view of social rights as a new kind of democratized property rights, appropriate for the postwar world of inclusive citizenship, was strongly challenged by those who revived Malthusian and Benthamite doubts about the sustainability of claims against the resources of productive members of the economy. The neo-liberalism of the 1980s appealed specifically to the fear that the poor would be feckless, idle, improvident and fecund if not subjected to the 'natural' law of the labour market, in which those who did not work could not eat, find shelter, rest or breed.[27] The notion of an underclass culture of dependence and predation, fed on welfare generosity, was later modified by Mead's argument that it was the unconditional nature of welfare provision that undermined morals and responsibility. Like the authors of the Poor Law Report of 1834, Mead maintained that he had discovered a way of separating out those with valid claims for relief from public funds, and those with no such case. If welfare provision were made more conditional, by stricter tests of willingness to work, the obligations of social citizenship could be made more visible and enforceable, and the underclass remoralized and fitted for the labour market.[28]

The new orthodoxy takes up Mead's arguments by insisting on a necessary and close connection between rights and obligations. This is put forward as a general argument about social interactions of all kinds, rather than a specific requirement for collective provision. The point is particularly strongly made in the writings of Frank Field,[29] but it is also a central feature of Tony Blair's speeches, and the justifications given by New Labour for its reforms of the British welfare state at the start of its term of office.

## Liberal obligation

This view of the relationship between rights and obligations flies in the face of several centuries of liberal thought and its institutional out-workings. Contrary to the new orthodoxy's central thrust, it could be more plausibly argued that liberalism's project has been to disconnect all economic activity from the notion of obligation, and to substitute that of mutually advantageous voluntary exchange. The Great Transformation of the nineteenth century was based on just these institutional shifts.[30] Rights were the conceptual tools for accomplishing this disconnection; they allowed individuals' actions and choices over goods and services to be uncoupled from their moral duties to each other, through the spread of markets in a growing sector of their interactions.

Take the example of property rights. Locke can be regarded as the first liberal theorist precisely because he provided arguments for the economic sphere to become detached from the moral domain of the household, and political authority from the power relations of the family. Locke's *Two Treatises of Government* was first and foremost a new theory of property.[31] He justified the enclosure of the common lands that belonged jointly to all human beings by natural right, on the grounds that this enabled them to be 'improved', and hence become more productive.[32] This greater productivity of land could in turn be translated into higher productivity of labour also; thus even unskilled day labourers could earn much more by selling their labour power than the value of the fruits and berries that a native savage could gather from the common land in 'the wild woods of America'.[33] Money, whose invention enabled wealth to be accumulated and stored, was the means by which the higher productivity of land and labour was translated into exchanges of goods and services, which in turn freed people from the bonds of obligation that drove interactions under feudalism. Instead of landowners being tied by duties of paternal responsibility to tenants, who in turn owed them labour services, both could be free to pursue their interests, and to interact through the anonymous processes of the market. Property rights were henceforth to be unencumbered by moral obligations – a freedom which still allows capitalists to locate their factories according to global economic opportunities, rather than be tied by their duties to the working classes of their homelands.

It is to Locke too that we can trace the idea that political authority can be legitimately resisted, because the rights of individuals include an entitlement to freedom from unjust coercion and arbitrary compulsion. The legitimacy of governments was not the same as the moral authority of fathers over sons and daughters, of husbands over wives, or masters over household servants.[34] The natural rights of human beings (what we would today call human rights) included the inalienable liberty to manage one's own economic decisions in conditions of freedom. As the American colonists insisted in their War of Independence (citing Locke), political obligations could not override these economic liberties; the monarch could not claim paternal power over free citizens, as Locke had asserted against Filmer's arguments for the Divine Right of Kings.

In other words, Locke was the founder of a liberal tradition in which public obligations of all kinds became conditional, because rights were absolute and unconditional. The obligation to obey the government was conditional upon it ruling justly, and avoiding coercive infringements of the natural rights of subjects – this was indeed the basis of the rule of law. The obligations of the moral sphere did not spill over into the economy, because individuals must be free to contract with each other according to purely instrumental criteria of material advantage, for the sake of justice as well as for efficiency.

This was the first step along the road of freeing all public sphere relationships from the archaic bonds of moral obligation. Liberalism does indeed specify civic duties, but wherever possible these take the form of financial contributions, making them as anonymous and impersonal as possible, and leaving the freedom of the individual intact. The obligation to pay taxes is the only one which is enforced by law in most liberal polities. Other duties – such as that to vote during elections – are merely indicative and permissive. The law, as a framework guaranteeing the rights of individuals against undue interference by the state or their fellow citizens, and protecting them against theft, force or fraud, or any other infringement of their property or persons, became the source of a new rational authority, with a new (neutral, impartial) obligatory force to replace the personal, blood or religious ties of the medieval era.

Of course, this 'ideal' form of liberalism never found expression in an actual political regime. For instance, the British form of liberalism in the nineteenth century can be seen as a compromise between classical liberal thought and the utilitarianism of Jeremy Bentham and his followers. The latter allowed a large number of social engineering projects by the state, for bringing individuals into line with public interests (see pp. 79–89 and 162). The utilitarian tradition interacted with and influenced British Fabianism, which in turn modified Continental socialism in the twentieth century. But throughout these processes, liberal thought provided a set of principles to evaluate institutions and policies, from the standpoint of equal liberty and economic efficiency – just as Hayek[35] and others did in their critique of welfare states that proved so influential in the 1980s (see p. 85). The new orthodoxy on welfare borrows much from this tradition, but neglects its central thought on liberty.

Crucially, the new orthodoxy's claim that civic duties correspond to rights, or are attached to them, is quite misleading. The liberal theory of citizenship insists that fundamental rights are only to be suspended for the most serious offences, and then only after careful judicial considera- tion. But any instances of suspending citizens' rights – loss of liberty, of civil or political rights, or rights to basic protection – are seldom directly linked to the obligations that accompany them in their manner of enforcement. For instance, citizens who are imprisoned or detained in mental hospitals may lose their votes; but citizens who fail to vote are not disenfranchised. Citizens who evade taxes may be fined or even sent to prison, but not put on special punitive tax codes. Indeed, it was the crude linkage between highly conditional citizenship rights and the performance of duties demonstrating loyalty to the state that formed the substance of Western criticisms of the Soviet Bloc regimes during the Cold War. The fact that those who did not accept state employment were put in forced labour camps, and that those who did not subscribe to state ideology were put in psychiatric hospitals to have their values changed, were taken as the strongest evidence that these regimes had no rights worth the name. Rights that are trumps[36] in contests over the limits of authority do not have such obligations corresponding to them; still less are defections from the duties loosely associated with them enforced by methods that extinguish them without due process.

There is just one exception to this general rule. The duty to do compulsory military service (especially in wartime) is an obligation involving labour service, and is usually strongly enforced, even in liberal countries. This is because the successful defence of the polity against foreign invasion is taken as a necessary condition for all personal freedoms and property rights. Without military protection from external attack, liberty itself would be unsustainable; hence the state can compel military service. But even in this instance, a conscript who refuses to be enlisted is imprisoned, not sent to the front line.

It is therefore very surprising that the new orthodoxy should maintain that there are civic obligations that correspond to rights, and that the public power can therefore compel claimants of social entitlements to work or train for the public good. The first principle of liberalism – strong unconditional rights, weak and conditional duties – is clearly breached if rights are hedged about with restrictive obligations, and if public power can be used to enforce these through administrative processes. But of course social rights are not accessible for all citizens, and not all are therefore affected by these obligations. It is only those experiencing the contingencies associated with insurance benefits – unemployment, sickness, accident, injury, disability – who are required to fulfil these conditions, along with those so poor as to require social assistance through means-tested benefits. Those with enough property or income to live without recourse to benefits are not obliged to work at all – and many of them choose not to do so.

The paradox of the new orthodoxy's line on obligations is that it seems to fly in the face of the logic of globalization. On the one hand, it is often maintained that governments can no longer enforce obligations on their citizens, because the opportunities to move themselves and their assets abroad are now so much greater. But the new orthodoxy's response to this situation is to maintain that obligations must be made more explicit, be strengthened and then far better enforced, as the new basis for social citizenship. This paradox is more an apparent than a real one. Claims for social benefits are made by just those immobile members of the population who cannot shift themselves or their resources to other countries. It is these immobile factors of production whose fortunes have waned with globalization, and who now rely on state support. Governments have lost the power to compel mobile factors; but they can now compensate themselves by coercing immobile ones, with a double dose of their authority.

The result is a strange and contradictory situation. Under the new orthodoxy, governments constantly proclaim that they cannot increase taxes, because of the requirements of international competitiveness, and the threat that capital will move abroad. In other words, the main obligation of citizens – to pay taxes – is less enforced, because less enforceable, than in the postwar era. On the other hand, the importance of obligation to the public good is emphasized in the case of claimants, and this takes the form of work placements; they are required to take 'employment' which cannot attract them through the wages and conditions that it offers. Yet at the same time, there are many thousands of foreigners – citizens of poorer countries – only too willing to do this work, if they were allowed to enter the country to take it. Indeed many do enter the country – disguised as tourists or students[37] – and undertake this work as part of the shadow economy. Governments spend a good deal of their revenue from taxes forcing claimants to do these tasks, and trying to stop undocumented immigrants from doing them.

The new orthodoxy claims that it derives its principles from small voluntary associations. Its view of civic rights and obligations is based on the idea of a club, whose members collaborate and give reciprocal service for the benefit of all. But it is a strange kind of club in which the committee spends part of the funds on bullying some of the members to do unpleasant tasks like scrubbing the floors, when it could far less expensively get these same things done by non-members, simply through paying them a basic wage.

The new orthodoxy's main muddle over rights and obligations is to confuse the idea of civic duty with that of the cement for society. The obligation to contribute for the provision of public goods in liberal constitutions is very carefully defined so as to eliminate the notions of moral duty and reciprocal labour service. It is not for the state to provide society's morality, or the interactional codes which are to regulate the many different forms of association that thrive outside the formal economy and the public life of democratic political institutions. The cement of society is supposed to be made up out of all the norms and practices of every such social unit, from families to religious movements, sports clubs and cultural groups. The sense of obligation, and of society itself, is either derived from these interactions, or it is deficient, and needs to be replenished by a rejuvenation of civil society's vigour. But – as many recent commentators have argued[38] – societies whose social capital in terms of trust, cooperation and voluntary association becomes depleted run into difficulties in their economies, and in the functioning of governance. These cannot be remedied through the substitution of political authority for societal norms. Indeed, the attempt to impose obligations through third-party enforcement creates conditions in which trust and cooperation between citizens cannot readily be spontaneously replenished.[39]

Of course there are real issues about how a state can ensure that its economy functions efficiently, and how all citizens can be motivated to contribute to national prosperity, and to supply their labour to the market. There are also real questions about how to minimize free-riding over social benefits. But these questions should be sharply distinguished from ones about morality and social cohesion on the one hand, and about political obligation on the other. Governments should indeed enable a social system in which citizens trust and cooperate with each other in reciprocal interactions; and they should ensure that laws and regulations are respected. But the issues of economic motivation and the minimization of free-riding are not questions of this kind. In a liberal polity, they are matters to be addressed through policies on wages, job security and other labour market conditions, and the rules that protect the funds available for social benefits and services.

Social justice under liberal arrangements is served by systems of rights that grant equal liberties to all citizens, under rules that try to harmonize interests and minimize conflicts. Within this framework, which seeks the least coercive regulatory regime possible, individuals should be free to interact without external interference, both in order to make voluntary exchanges for mutual benefit, and to organize themselves into associations to pursue common ends. Obligations are supposed to be the least prominent features of such systems, that rely on impartiality, the rule of law and a strong protection for liberty in the form of rights protecting personal freedom and private property. The difficulty – as we shall see in the next section – is how social justice can reconcile the liberty granted under these arrangements with any substantive measures for equality.

## Equality and freedom

Liberal justice demands equality for citizens in the distribution of several fundamental rights and duties of the political association. Equality before the law is a basic principle for a regulatory regime that promises impartiality to all individuals and neutrality between different conceptions of the good life. Equal voting rights for all citizens is a requirement of a democratic system of accountability that allows all the same degree of influence on collective decisions. Equal responsibility for jury service demands something like a lottery to apportion duties. And equal contribution to defence demands a system of conscription that falls on each able-bodied person (usually each man in fact) who is capable of taking up arms for the defence of the nation. Procedural justice generally guarantees equality (in the sense of due process for all, and the like treatment of like cases). Justice stipulates that all should receive equal consideration in decisions over benefits and burdens, irrespective of their sex, skin colour or religious affiliation.

But issues of substantive equality are far more contentious in the liberal tradition. It is generally held that freedom and equality come into conflict over questions about the possible redistribution of wealth and income, because the freedom to use one's personal skills and material resources is fundamental for free exchange in markets, for getting the best returns on one's long-term investments, and for the transfer of accumulated assets from one generation to the next. According to this view, the entitlements of liberal justice forbid the compulsory confiscation of property, or the compulsion of any individual for the good of others.[40] In this view, it is freedom itself that should be maximized and shared equally among citizens; substantive equality through authoritative redistribution always infringes liberty, as the Soviet system illustrated.

One of the main exponents of such arguments has been F.A. Hayek, whose criticisms of 'patterned distributions' of all kinds have been associated with an attack on the whole concept of *social* justice. For Hayek, justice is necessarily procedural, and deals in the ways in which resources are allocated, rather than the outcomes of these processes.[41] Institutions that are neutral over who gets what, that allow individuals to exchange for mutual advantage, and that give rise to no particular patterns or regularities, are preferable to those that try to impose a certain disposition on the myriad transactions that make up the 'catallaxy' of the economy of society.[42]

But resistance to attempts at substantive equality is a far longer and broader part of the liberal tradition than the work of Hayek, which was so influential in the Thatcher–Reagan period. The new Blair–Clinton orthodoxy appeals to the tradition of Rawls, and further back to J.S. Mill and Locke. Inequalities should only be addressed if they can be shown to harm the interests of the poorest and most vulnerable – a difficult demonstration to accomplish.

Rawls' theory of justice is based on liberal assumptions about people's preferences for security and freedom. It sets out to show that individuals who were ignorant of their own endowments might contract together to draw up impartial rules that applied to all, and were in the interest of each to keep. This involves a just distribution of 'primary goods' (rights and freedoms, opportunities and powers, income and wealth[43]), such that

1   each person is to have an equal right to the most extensive basic liberty compatible with a similar liberty for others; and
2   social and economic inequalities are to be arranged so that they are both: (a) reasonably expected to be to everyone's advantage, and (b) attached to positions and offices open to all.[44]

What is to everyone's advantage is defined in terms of the 'difference principle', that a gain for anyone in society must contribute to the expectations of the worst-off person in society (and hence presumably also to every person in an intermediate position between the two). This is supposed to justify redistributions from the richest to the poorest, but in fact it can be used to legitimate a stratified society, because the well-off can always claim that what is to their advantage will also benefit the poor. Rawls' principles can certainly be adopted by the Blair–Clinton orthodoxy without threatening the considerable degree of inequality that exists in the USA and the UK.

This is possible because the assumptions built into Rawls' theory (and into the new orthodoxy itself) are a typically liberal compromise between liberty and equality, providing a trade-off between them.[45] If the individuals in Rawls' thought experiment of the 'original position' were assumed to have a greater tolerance for risk (or even a liking for a gamble) they would be much more likely to favour the priority of freedom over equality, such that the fortunate would profit more fully from their endowments or their luck. If they were assumed to have a greater preference for security, or to be more likely to envy the success of others, then a much more egalitarian principle of distribution would be more appropriate. After all, socialists can claim that justice is best served if need is the first priority in the distribution of all basic goods, and in the allocation of opportunities for using talents. Equality would be the second criterion, in those spheres where need is not the paramount consideration, and merit then used to distribute whatever surplus of goods is then left over – for instance, through an incentive scheme for workers who exceed the basic earnings for an adequate living.[46]

The Blair–Clinton orthodoxy relies on the typically liberal solution of equality of opportunity when it is pressed by socialists (or other egalitarians) about why it allows the rich to get so much richer, and why its policies are actively seeking to take money from the poor. Once some basic equality has been established through free primary and secondary education for all, and affordable health care (for most but not all in the US), then merit is supposed to get its just reward through regulated competition for positional goods (like well-paid jobs), and between interest groups, representing various productive factors and occupational organizations, for shares of national income.

The clearest exposition of this position was provided by Gordon Brown, the UK Chancellor of the Exchequer, in his reply to the criticisms of the former Labour Party deputy leader, Roy Hattersley.[47] First, the new orthodoxy has an ethical commitment to the equal worth of every human being – all have a claim to equal social consideration by virtue of being human. Everyone should have the chance to bridge the gap between what they are and what they have it in themselves to become. The government has a duty to get the best out of all its citizens, for the sake of efficiency as well as justice. Hence it must focus on their employability.

The policies which correspond to this commitment are investment in education and training (see pp. 39–40). Equal rights to increased potential contribution through the labour market imply equal opportunities through lifelong learning for all. But Brown insists that equality of outcome, through the increases in redistributive benefits that Hattersley has demanded, is not desirable or feasible.

Predetermined results, imposed (as they would have to be) by a central authority and decided irrespective of work, effort or contribution to the community, is not a socialist dream but other people's nightmare of socialism.[48]

He maintains that what makes citizens resentful is lack of opportunities to work, not the inequalities that stem from the achievements of those who have worked hard. It is unemployment that is wasteful and unfair – benefits increases would only trap more of the unemployed in inactivity, and exclude them from society. Hence it is welfare-to-work measures and reforms in the tax-benefit system to improve incentives that can combat exclusion and allow a sustainable, employment-friendly welfare state to be established.

One part of Brown's retort is difficult to dispute. It is true that the Labour Party has never favoured the welfare state, and especially not the social security system: the implementation of the Beveridge Report was delayed by Labour,[49] benefits upratings were lower under Labour in the Wilson years than under Heath's Conservative government,[50] and more generally, socialist governments prefer to uphold workers' rights than those of people outside the labour market. As for Marxism–Leninism, it used public spending mainly for massive industrial investment, and not for redistribution to the non-working groups within the population. So it is true that socialism has not, in reality, promoted redistribution through social security or other benefits systems.

However, the rest is, as we have already seen (pp. 36 and 46–9) much more questionable. If the new orthodoxy acknowledges that people need a good basic education, health care and some degree of physical security to allow them to get to the starting line for participating in the economy on equal terms, why should it draw the line at providing financial support for the same purpose? For instance, benefits paid to lone parents with respect to the costs of bringing up their children only trap them in excluded roles if they are withdrawn when they take work. If they are tax-free and non-means-tested then they make it easier for lone parents to work, because they cover some of the costs of child care. But the new Labour government cut these benefits. Similarly, benefits paid to disabled people in relation to their extra costs for everyday living do not act as any kind of disincentive to work, and actually promote inclusion of every kind. Making them means-tested, as the new Labour government has proposed at the time of writing, and restricting them by abolishing rights of appeal against refusal, or imposing new tests of incapacities, as it has already done, only act as barriers to participation in the labour market, since these benefits alone allow many disabled people to be able to afford the costs associated with employment.

A system of social justice based on equality of opportunity assumes that:

1   the national labour market is a set of comparable opportunities for employment (like the daily auction described at the end of the previous chapter on pp. 64–6), and ordered according to a hierarchy of pay, related to merit or contribution to the common good;

2   the division of labour within a national state reflects a single system of cooperation between the citizenry, and hence an internally coherent set of relationships among people committed to a common purpose (national prosperity and a shared way of life);

3   the global division of labour is such that any advanced national economy which realizes the full potential of its citizens can effectively and legitimately capture a set of employment opportunities such that its workforce can perform technologically sophisticated tasks as its contribution to the global economy (a high-technology, high-value-added national economy, with a highly educated and skilled workforce);

4   the international division of labour is beyond the scope of any national system for achieving social justice. The establishment of a fairer distribution of resources worldwide is addressed, if at all, through foreign aid and foreign policy. Social justice is exclusively concerned with the domestic (i.e., national) division of labour.

All these assumptions have already been questioned in Chapter 2. For the purposes of the following discussion, it will be useful to summarize briefly here a number of the problems not addressed by this perspective.

1   Labour markets are not open competitions between equals. 'Insiders', 'outsiders' and 'claimants' have different statuses, which are related to organizational power. Access to 'insider' status depends on gender, race and age.

2   Because of the high proportion of goods and services now traded in global markets, national labour markets cannot be regarded as systems of cooperation between citizens.

3   Because of international competition, no one country can appropriate the highly rewarded work of the financial sector or the most technologically advanced sector of industrial production.

4   Because of extensive emigration and immigration, social justice must be analysed in a global context. Policies to encourage trade but discourage settlement from abroad are in considerable tension with each other.

In the following section I shall suggest that the proposed compromise between equality and freedom postulated by the principle of equality of opportunity does not address any of these issues, and suggest that there are inescapable questions about substantive, material equalization that must enter any credible analysis of social justice.


## Equality and markets


The first argument that can be advanced against the new orthodoxy over equality of opportunity is the one which is derived from radical free-market principles. This is that justice is best served by strict adherence to the 'invisible hand' in issues of distribution, because individuals pursuing their own interests are able to come to the optimum outcomes in such an environment. It is important to distinguish between this view, which claims that the poorest will gain most in global interactions for which all organizational barriers to free exchanges have been eliminated, and the Blair–Clinton principle of equality of opportunity. The former insists that free market distributions have nothing to do with merit or contributions to the common good, but only with mutual advantage; justice is a procedural feature of the rules regulating exchange, or at best is an accidental by-product of free trade. The latter claims that institutional arrangements must ensure, first that those able to contribute most to the welfare of their fellow citizens receive the highest offices and the highest rewards, and second that all make their contribution to national productivity, if necessary by making them enter the labour market.

The idea that equalization of incomes and life chances is best promoted by free trade can be traced to Adam Smith. He argued that it would allow the spread of trade and industry, which would benefit all those who entered the global market place, by maximizing the international division of labour. In the long run, this included the most undeveloped regions of the world. He also maintained that it would tend towards an international balance of power between nations, because 'nothing seems more likely to establish this equality of force more than that mutual communication of knowledge and of all sorts of improvements which an extensive commerce from all countries to all countries naturally, or rather necessarily, carries along with it.'[51]

The mechanism by which this was to be accomplished was first identified by Joseph Tucker in 1756, when he claimed that 'the universal mover in human nature, self-love, may receive such a direction in this case (as in all others) as to promote the public interest by those efforts it shall make towards pursuing its own'.[52] Adam Smith more memorably argued that the rich

> are led by an invisible hand to make nearly the same distribution of the
> necessaries of life, which would have been made, had the earth been

divided into equal portions among all its inhabitants, and thus without intending it, without knowing it, advance the interests of society, and afford the means to the multiplication of the species . . . In ease of body and peace of mind, all the different ranks of life are nearly upon a level, and the beggar, who suns himself by the side of the highway, possesses that security which kings are fighting for.[53]

The complete version of this famous passage is specially striking for its contrast with the new Blair–Clinton orthodoxy. The invisible hand, working through the self-interest of the rich, gives an almost equal share to the poor, not because of any work effort of the latter, or any good intention of the former. It is as hard to imagine that Tony Blair would have chosen an idle beggar to illustrate the justice of free market institutions or the equality of the advantages to be gained from them as it is to suppose that Bill Clinton would praise the American labour market for the advantages it bestows on black mothers who claim welfare.

In case this should be thought to be a case of special pleading by an apologist for free markets, we should also remember that Marx and Engels were fulsome in their praise for capitalism's achievement in freeing workers from the bonds of feudalism and the 'idiocy of rural life'.[54] And their follower, Liebknecht, commented on the Great Exhibition of 1851 that 'egotism has, albeit unintentionally, done more for humanity than the most humane and self-sacrificing idealism'.[55]

The important difference between free market advocates and adherents of the new orthodoxy is that the former claim that formal equality before the law and the absence of barriers to mutually gainful exchange by self-interested actors are necessary and sufficient conditions for the greatest sustainable improvements in the incomes of the poor, not just nationally but globally. For instance, Von Mises attributed unemployment to the combined effects of trade unions keeping wages at levels where only a proportion of the labour force could be employed, and governments providing unemployment benefits.[56] More recently, Olson has argued that investment would flow to those regions of the national and the world economy which are least developed, and hence benefit those most vulnerable to unemployment and poverty, if the barriers created by trade union collective action and government benefits systems, as well as tariff and exchange controls, did not tie them to less productive allocations, and hence distort the economy to the disadvantage of the poorest and least well organized.[57]

It may seem strange to draw attention to these arguments at this stage of the discussion, especially as members of the twentieth-century Austrian school (such as Von Mises and Hayek) were adamantly opposed to government measures for equality and social justice. Indeed, Hayek claimed that social justice was a 'mirage', since the distribution of incomes, benefits and burdens brought about through markets is the consequence of billions of separate decisions and exchanges, and reflects a 'spontaneous', evolutionary order, rather than anything that anyone has intended or planned.[58] Hence the outcomes are accidental, and as such cannot be either just or unjust. Incomes are not distributed according to merits or contributions to society, but simply for the goods and services that others value. 'It is not good intentions or needs but doing what in fact most benefits others, irrespective of motive, which will secure the best reward'.[59] The idea that differences in earnings are in some way 'deserved' is misleading; they are simply signals about how labour power can most profitably be employed.[60]

So the point is that these arguments undermine the claim that income differentials are related to merits, and indeed that labour market participation is in itself meritorious in any sense. Like Adam Smith's image of the beggar sunning himself on the bank, they substitute a notion of accidental, unintended consequences for the idea that higher earnings are a reward for greater contributions. But they do also maintain that competition and free trade break down organizational and organized power, that protects privilege and the restrictions it places upon free exchanges. Both monopolies of capitalist interests and those of organized labour are distortions of efficient allocations, and the poor and disorganized have most to gain from the systematic dismantling of the barriers that they have created through collective action.

The idea that the equalization of incomes through the globalization process is a contribution to social justice is an obvious conclusion from these arguments. Less developed countries that have industrialized during the postwar period can be cited as examples of the process of 'catching up' with First World economies. Those who doubt the reality of globalization would do well to imagine themselves in the shoes of a South Korean factory worker who has seen his wages increase by up to 10 per cent per year for the last 25 years, to the point where they have overtaken those of his counterpart in the UK, but who now faces the prospect of a fall in earnings, as Chinese peasants, at present many times poorer than himself, begin the process of catching up and overtaking him, now the Chinese economy has launched into a new phase of capitalist industrialization.

From the point of view of justice, such changes – though they stem entirely from the self-interest of international businesses in their global pursuit of profits – result in greater proportional gains in the welfare of newly recruited industrial workers in less developed countries than the corresponding losses of welfare to workers in more developed ones. Hence they can certainly be justified, if the whole world is taken into account as the relevant unit for the analysis of distributive justice.

Exactly the same considerations should apply to the possibility of improving the welfare of the poorest 'outsiders' in a national labour market, at the expense of the advantages enjoyed by 'insiders'. If the protections enjoyed by those with well-paid secure jobs and fringe benefits rest on collective agreements that prevent capital from being invested in its potentially most profitable allocation (i.e., giving job 'rents'), then they are unjust collusions against the interests of the poor. The latter do not need better education, or training, still less workfare. What they need is the opportunity to compete fairly in labour markets that give them an equal chance of decently paid employment. This can only be achieved by further restrictions on the power of trade unions and professional associations, and by weakening the existing legal protections for 'insiders', as well as acting against the oligopolistic practices of cartels.

Are there any circumstances in which it might be fair for 'insiders' to retain their advantages over 'outsiders'? The only ones that come to mind are when a sudden opening up of competition could so drastically erode the earnings and security of existing asset holders that incomes could suddenly fall, causing 'outsiders' themselves to suffer. Even so, it would still be in the long-run interests of 'outsiders' to have the opportunity to compete on equal terms, so to leave things exactly as they stand would be a greater injustice than to change them. The solution might therefore be for 'insiders' to pay 'outsiders' compensation in return for being allowed to retain their job assets for a transitional period, to avoid damaging and disruptive sudden change. This compensation might take the form of an income transfer, such that all those whose earnings fell below a certain level became net beneficiaries of the tax-benefit system. In this way, those with high earnings would automatically be net contributors to the transfer system, and compensate those whose earnings were much lower.

This implies that compensation is offered in return for restraint of rivalry over job assets. Restrained competition is, as we have seen (pp. 56–7), the essence of cooperation for the common good. By compensating fellow citizens who refrain from competing away their advantage, 'insiders' could favour their claims over those of foreigners, without damaging the efficient and just allocation of resources through global free trade – a process that would, of its own accord, tend to erode their advantages over a longer period. At the same time, they could find institutions for doing this in such a way as to allow the tasks of social reproduction in the domestic economy to be allocated and rewarded as fairly as possible.

This kind of problem arose in the UK after the Second World War. The wartime economy had been efficiently run mainly by women, who took roles in factories and agricultural production previously occupied by men. But the return of men from the armed forces to the civilian economy was seen as requiring women to leave these jobs, and go back into unpaid work within the household. Women were excluded from the labour market to avoid the competitive pressures that had led to unemployment and falling wages after the First World War. This was achieved through much political rhetoric about women's 'place' in the home, their contribution to the maintenance of 'British stock' and 'British civilization',[61] and their status as equal 'partners', with an equally important role with that of men. It was reinforced by inducement in the tax system, and allowances for them as 'dependants' in new benefits for unemployment and sickness, and in retirement pensions. In effect, women were compensated for restraining their labour-market activities, and persuaded to return to domestic roles, or to subordinate positions in mainly service occupations.

A rhetoric of equality of this kind would clearly be inadequate in the present age. Women's consciousness of their situation in a patriarchal order, and their gradual return to the labour market in the years since the 1950s, have meant that the equality offered under any present day compensatory deal would have to be more substantial and material than this. Women remain the majority of 'outsiders', but not content to occupy these roles purely by virtue of being women, and certainly not by virtue of unpaid household roles. The minimum acceptable conditions for continued restraint in competition would be likely to include:

1   the acknowledgement of equal citizenship, and equal and independent status in the tax and benefit system;
2   equal status in the household, with tax and benefit inducements for men to share unpaid domestic responsibilities and tasks;
3   equal tax rates when women do enter the labour market, and equal rates of pay for part-time as well as full-time workers;
4   some form of income, corresponding with existing unpaid duties, but allowing these to be shared (or some child care and domestic assistance to be purchased); and which ensures that women have a real choice over whether and how much of these to do for themselves, *and* that poor women should not have to do them for rich others;
5   equal access to training and retraining.[62]

In other words, what would be at stake in such a settlement would be a form of compensation that did not confine women in their homes, but recognized unpaid work as an essential element in the reproduction of the national social system, and that offered some income to men and women willing to forgo labour-market opportunities in order to do it. This income would not jeopardize their present or future rights to more extensive or intensive labour-market activity. This would serve both to protect 'insiders'' job assets, and to compensate 'outsiders' for their restrained competition for these posts. And it would protect unskilled men and women (but particularly women) from being exploited by a return to Victorian-style domestic roles as low-paid nannies and servants.

It is difficult to see what form this compensatory payment might take, other than an unconditional basic income, paid to individual men and women, irrespective of household status.[63] This would allow them to form households, cooperate and share unpaid duties in ways consistent with the equality demanded by the above principles. It would also mean that, whoever did hold job assets, or increase their labour supply, would automatically contribute to the fund out of which the basic income was paid to those who remained as 'outsiders' (or worked less), because they would become net contributors to the system through taxation.[64]

In this way, the equalizing effects of market forces, which are indeed highly destructive of protective institutions of all kinds within a national or local economy, might be mitigated by redistributive systems between citizens of a nation state. The principle of equality would be observed in the terms on which income was distributed (equal basic incomes for all citizens), but the effect would be to reduce rivalry over certain positional goods, where the effect of this might in the short run be to harm efficiency and damage the welfare of all. The policy programme associated with a basic income approach to distributive justice will be discussed in Chapter 5.

## Exploitation

The supposed trade-off between freedom and equality in the new orthodoxy's account of social justice conceals another issue. Equality of opportunity cannot give rise to social justice if some people are exploited by others, even if there is fair competition between them for the positions of exploiter and exploited. There must be some safeguards in the system against exploitation of the 'Cleaning Harriet's Toilet' kind – demeaning, badly paid work by those who have been unsuccessful in the competition for highly paid posts for those who hold them.

Towards the end of Chapter 2 (pp. 64–6), we considered the issue of exploitation through the thought experiment of a daily labour auction. Justice demands that there should not be opportunities and incentives for those employing the workers offering their services to use their labour power in ways that are inconsistent with the most efficient possible allocation of their energies and skills. It is efficient to provide more employment up to the point where the marginal utility of an extra job equals the marginal cost. The price of labour power used, in classical economic theory, to be related to the costs associated with its reproduction. A 'living wage' was one which allowed the working class to be maintained in reasonable health and fitness. Hence the value of the additional output produced by one extra worker was supposed to be equal to the cost of hiring him or her (wages plus taxes and contributions paid by the employer).

In today's economy, several factors complicate this equation. The first is the very high costs now associated with employment. In Continental Europe, social insurance contributions by employers now constitute a formidable part of the costs of hiring workers.[65] In the USA, it is the costs of health insurance that are most deterrent. Taking these costs into account, it becomes too expensive to take on full-time, permanent staff. In the UK, the costs of possible redundancy pay and other benefits (like holiday pay) make employers reluctant to offer long-term security to workers where the need for their services varies because output fluctuates in response to changes in demand. They prefer to employ them temporarily through an agency, which gets a higher hourly amount for their work than the employer pays to its regular staff, but gives them considerably less than this amount after it has taken its commission. Such workers are exploited, in relation to those receiving as much as a third more for doing the same work, as well as enjoying long-term security and various fringe benefits.

Governments that want to boost employment can offer selective concessions to employers by giving them rebates of these on-wage costs, or suspending them altogether for various kinds of work, or categories of employees (such as long-term claimants or disabled people). An example of this was given on p. 36, where better-off Finnish households are excused all social insurance contributions if they employ domestic servants. In Germany, 5.6 million people were employed in 1997 under a concession to employers who take on workers for one year, paying them only DM 610 (around £210) per month.[66] Here again, workers used in these ways are exploited in relation to those on standard contracts, because employers have incentives to use them in ways that would be grossly inefficient if they were paying the full costs associated with hiring full-time permanent staff.

The second complication is that people come to the imaginary labour auction in various relationships of interdependence with each other, as household partners, offspring and parents, house-sharers, friends and kin. These relationships allow them to share some of the costs of their lifestyles through informal transactions and the unpaid work they do for each other. Adult male wages used to be based on the idea that working-age men were either supporting a wife and children, or saving up to do so; the 'family wage' was one of the traditional demands of organized labour. Nowadays, with almost as many women in employment in the UK, the USA and the Scandinavian countries as men, this idea is an anachronism – even though it is still a popular one in Germany and France. On the other hand, the numbers of lone-parent households and single-person households are growing in all societies. These have higher costs per person, especially in relation to housing, than the traditional family.

The labour-supply strategy adopted by most couples in the UK (and increasingly also in Continental Europe) is for the man to seek an 'insider' post with job security, an efficiency wage, training and promotion prospects, incremental rises, an occupational pension and perks, while the woman and young people of the household take 'outsider' employment at considerably lower rates of pay, often on a part-time basis, or on some other form of non-standard contract.[67] This strategy was particularly successful in the 1980s, when the incomes of such households rose considerably in the UK. On the other hand, where no member can gain an 'insider' post, or the main jobholder loses one, the strategy breaks down, because it is extremely difficult to coordinate the decisions of two or several people doing the kind of irregular, short-term or part-time work that makes up the 'outsider' sector.[68] As a result, in Britain there are 3.4 million households with no member in formal employment; the available work does not offer them sufficient incentives to draw them into the fragmented labour market of low and unreliable earnings (see pp. 144–5 below).

The disparity between the wages and conditions of 'insiders' and 'outsiders' constitutes a form of exploitation of the latter, since employers have an incentive to use part-time and short-term workers in a very different way from their deployment of full-time staff. Research suggests that women part-time workers are often more trained and skilled than men full-time ones, yet paid as much as one-third less.[69] Part of this disparity results from the division of labour in the household; despite the labour-market changes of the past 25 years, women still do the bulk of unpaid child care and domestic work, and even those with high educational and professional qualifications define themselves as 'supportive' of their husband's careers, rather than developing careers of their own.[70]

Although women form the largest group of 'outsiders' in the labour market, there is also exploitation of women by women. One version of emancipatory justice and anti-sexism sees access to better-paid jobs and powerful positions as the only route to equal status for women. Yet this point of view often involves selective blindness to the inequalities and injustices built into the relationships between themselves and those they employ for domestic service and child care. By recreating nineteenth-century social relations of household paid employment, they exploit the labour power of those women who are constrained to work, either by the low earnings of the other members of their households, or by pressures from the benefits authorities. This selective blindness was illustrated in the following quotation from an interview with a young woman with an 11-month-old child, who was asked whether she ever had difficulty in getting her childminder to provide extra cover when she was working more than the 17½ hours of her contract.

> *Mrs Ash*: No, I think she's fairly short of money, which is handy [. . .]. So, if I need to, thankfully, 'cause my job demands that . . .[71]

The new Blair–Clinton orthodoxy is able to win support from this wing of the feminist movement precisely because it prioritizes the needs of upper and middle class women over poor ones.[72] We should be suspicious of arguments for social justice that create social relations that are identical to those of colonial Africa and India – wealthy women pursuing lives in the public sphere, or simply enjoying leisure and social activities, by virtue of employing black or Asian servants. Hillary Clinton, Cherie Blair, Harriet Harman and Patricia Hewitt[73] might all reflect more critically upon this situation.

In the new Blair–Clinton orthodoxy, the problems of social justice that arise from these developments in the labour market are addressed through the promotion of higher rates of participation, but not by trying to equalize the terms on which workers are hired. Selective incentives for employers to take on long-term unemployed claimants or lone parents will not increase fairness if they are wastefully used during such a contract, if they receive little or no training, and if they are then discarded and return to unemployment and claiming. These unfairnesses will be compounded if employers lay off workers on permanent staff contracts in order to take advantage of these government incentives, and if workers are forced to take this employment unwillingly under threat of losing benefits entitlements.

How might the injustices of exploitation be countered by an employment-friendly state welfare system? The long-term solution favoured by the new orthodoxy is one of subsidization of labour-intensive jobs through the tax system – tax credits for the working poor, on the US model.[74] Low earners would be able to submit their payslips for the previous six months or year, and qualify for a credit that would automatically then be used to supplement their weekly earnings. The assessment would be based on the income of the whole household unit.

But this system offers a different kind of selective incentive to those employers using workers inefficiently. Working Family Tax Credits will go to those households where there are the lowest-paid individuals, and where part-time and irregular employment is most prevalent. Those who receive tax credits will therefore be subsidized for employers to use their labour power less efficiently than that of workers who receive no credit; it is an incentive to discriminate in the terms on which they employ parts of the workforce.

In the UK, this tendency will be partly offset by a new national minimum wage, that will apply to almost all employment. This does address the issue of equalizing the terms on which potential workers present themselves at the imaginary auction, because it sets a baseline below which their hourly rate must not be allowed to fall, and therefore makes it uneconomic to use them in very wasteful ways. However, it seems certain that employers will be able to get around this by insisting that many of those they hire to do peripheral tasks, where demand for labour fluctuates, are technically 'self-employed', and hence not covered

TABLE 3.2   *Self-employment in the UK, 1982–1996 (thousands)*

| 1982 | 1985 | 1988 | 1990 | 1992 | 1996 |
|------|------|------|------|------|------|
| 2,183 | 2,588 | 2,954 | 3,345 | 3,216 | 3,279 |

Source: Department for the Education and Employment, *Labour Market Trends*, December 1997

by the minimum wage legislation (see Table 3.2). This device was increasingly used in the 1980s to evade other employment costs, or pass them on to employees. In the UK there are now over 3 million such workers.[75]

In the imaginary daily auction, every adult man and woman should have a (formally) equal chance of being hired for the day, for the sake of equality of opportunity; but in order to prevent exploitation, behind the labour auction must lie a welfare state that gives each worker the security of knowing that if he or she is not hired at the wage appropriate for optimum efficiency, there is adequate support available for their needs until the following morning. Of course all must pay taxes on their earnings to contribute to the fund, such that the total revenue is sufficient to sustain the necessary subsistence.

Suppose that there were in place a basic income (or citizen's income) of the kind described in the previous section (pp. 93–4). It would be equal for all the would-be workers presenting themselves at the daily auction, so no one of them would be more subsidized than any other – formal equality of opportunity would be observed. On the other hand, all pay for employment would be taxable, at a rate sufficient to sustain the fund, and to pay benefits at a level that would give them no incentives to work in ways that exploited them by using their skills and energies inefficiently.

The aim of such a system would be to eliminate exploitation of the kind discussed in this section, without creating new forms of injustice in its place. But this measure would raise the seemingly knock-down objection that it would greatly increase the possibility of exploitation of the kind discussed in the earlier section on reciprocity (pp. 42–3), by making it possible to free-ride on the efforts and contributions of others.[76] Why should anyone work if their subsistence needs were guaranteed? And if some choose to do so, why should they pay taxes to support those who choose not to?

But these arguments are the converse of ones about exploitation through the inefficient (wasteful or hazardous) use of labour power. Too low a basic income would certainly increase the latter type of exploitation, because more people would be motivated to accept such badly paid and dangerous work than they are at present, assuming that basic incomes would replace existing benefits for partial disabilities, lone parent status and unemployment. Too high a basic income would lead too many to choose leisure over work, and hence mean that the economy was undersupplied with workers willing to take the kind of jobs needed to keep society functioning at maximum efficiency.

But between these two must in principle lie a rate of basic income just enough to protect the potential workforce from exploitation, but not so much as to encourage free-riding of the kind discussed in the earlier section. Of course there will still be questions about which individuals prefer income from earnings, and which a life of (relatively less affluent) leisure, because preferences in these matters vary. Issues of reciprocity and justice over the burdens of society's work cannot be so easily and neatly dealt with. These will be more fully discussed in the next two chapters. But, for the purposes of this one, the possibility of an overall equilibration between demand for and supply of labour power, that reconciles freedom with the requirements of efficiency, is an important indication of an alternative to the new orthodoxy's notion of equal opportunity.

## Need

Need has always been one of the main principles governing redistribution according to social justice. But it has been given lower priority by the new Blair–Clinton orthodoxy, because it implies passivity, incompetence and dependence. Advocates of the new orthodoxy constantly emphasize that those who receive welfare benefits and services would rather work and be independent, and that it is very important not to provide these in a way that excludes them from active, participatory and contributory roles. Hence need has tended to be demoted below merit and equality of opportunity in the justification of social provision.

Of course it is quite true that any claimant seeking to give a morally adequate account[77] of his or her citizenship would emphasize that they would prefer to be active and to participate in economic life. It is also right to argue that some welfare benefits – especially those provided under means tests – discourage labour supply and trap claimants in unemployment and poverty. But these are very general and abstract arguments. People who are sick would rather be healthy and working, but this does not make them fit for work, or guarantee that there are jobs suitable for them to go to. Benefits that pay more than the employment available in the labour market do discourage claimants from working, but this is only partly because of the level of benefits provided. It is also because the work available is too low paid, too insecure and unreliable, or too unpleasant in its conditions, to attract people off benefits and into employment. To reduce benefits rates, or make eligibility more conditional, or disqualify those who refuse the work that is currently on offer, does not address the latter causes of exclusion and injustice.

The new orthodoxy is equally adamant that its policies are designed to provide for 'genuine need',[78] and to focus benefits and services on those who really should receive them, and cannot do without them. It seeks to deflect criticism, for instance about reductions in provision for lone parents and disabled claimants in the UK, by insisting that its only intention is to help such individuals more, by restricting payments to those who are not really in need. This 'targeting' of benefits and services is accomplished by various kinds of tests – interviews, assessments, lengthy questionnaires and surveillance – designed to discriminate between the genuinely needy and others.

One consequence of this is that claimants are required to parade their disadvantages, to prove their disabilities, to demonstrate their incompetences and substantiate their illnesses. For example, the new Disability Integrity Procedure in the UK makes people who had been granted benefits for life complete a 33-page questionnaire, or give answers to an administrative interviewer, to re-examine eligibility for assistance. The implication of all this is that need is an exceptional and special feature of the human condition, and the only 'genuine' versions of it are those that can be recognized by bureaucrats or experts, giving close scrutiny to its manifestations. The 'needy' are a category of unfortunates who qualify for selective assistance by jumping (or more accurately failing to jump) through the hoops designed to test their inabilities.

This approach to need is the opposite of the one originally pursued in the postwar welfare state, where universal benefits and services were supposed to meet the basic needs that were common to all the members of the political community. The pooling of risks, to protect everyone from shared vulnerability to the contingencies of industrial society, and to establish common standards in the provision for universal needs, were supposed to substitute for the selectivism and stigma of the earlier era. This was the basis for the health and education services, and for social insurance, which was intended to relegate public assistance to a very small service for exceptional and emergency needs. It has been the gradual expansion of public assistance (income support and means-tested benefit for the working poor) that has led the UK government to concentrate its programme of welfare reform on the notion of 'better targeting', as if the selection of the most needy were the main function of the welfare state. Indeed, its plans to apply means tests to child benefit and various schemes for giving extra income to disabled people take a further step towards transforming income maintenance systems back into the forms they took before the Beveridge revolution.

Some theorists have tried to reassert the claims of universal needs, shared by all human beings, and to make a case for services that recognize these in the way that they provide for citizens. Doyal and Gough[79] have argued that universal and objective needs exist, and that no political programme can plausibly argue that it seeks to promote welfare which does not recognize:

1    that humans can be seriously harmed by alterable social circumstances, which can give rise to profound suffering;
2    that social justice exists in inverse proportion to serious harm and suffering;
3    that when social change designed to minimize serious harm is accomplished in a sustained way then social progress can be said to have occurred; and
4    that when the minimization of serious harm is not achieved then the resulting social circumstances are in conflict with the objective interests of those harmed.[80]

Doyal and Gough go on to criticize the subjectivist and relativist basis of most recent analysis of welfare issues. Economists insist that all choices must be treated as stemming from preferences rather than needs, since any individual may prioritize a particular desire over what may conventionally be treated as a basic need. Hence only individuals can judge their interests, and markets (except for a limited number of cases of indivisible or non-rivalrously consumed goods) are the best ways of coordinating demand to satisfy their requirement.[81] Justification of state provision derived from notions of need is used to argue for authoritarian systems and compulsory redistributive measures.[82] Since needs are also relative to their cultural context,[83] and also socially constructed within discursive communities,[84] market-minded political theorists and postmodern sociologists converge around their criticisms of universal, objective human needs. But Doyal and Gough insist that needs are preconditions for human action and interaction, and physical health and autonomy (in the sense of being able to make informed choices about what should be done and how to get it done) are necessary conditions for participation in any form of life to achieve any other valued goals.[85] Hence they claim that these are basic, universal needs.

They go on to conclude – from a careful review of statistical evidence from the whole world, much of it relating to the early and mid-1980s – that the best strategy for satisfying universal needs is a combination of markets and central planning, in which state intervention and active democracy balance a vigorous private sector. 'The case for positive social rights provides the justification for state responsibility for health, education, income maintenance and a host of other public services . . . Our theory of human need propels us towards a radical extension, plus a codification, of the citizenship-based welfare entitlements presently found in Western welfare states'.[86] These include a minimum income for all, which could either be provided by means of the basic income approach discussed above (pp. 93–4) or by guaranteeing the right to work.[87]

The problem with this whole approach is that it is difficult to specify the institutions to be derived from these principles, except in the most general terms. Doyal and Gough compare regimes across a whole range of constitutional, political, health and income-distributional features, and draw some highly generalized conclusions about the satisfaction of need under different institutional arrangements. The USA comes out badly from these comparisons on most measures, except the educational and housing ones, because of the prevalence of poverty there, and the lack of access to health care of a substantial proportion of the population. However, it is more difficult to distinguish between the performances of Germany, with its insurance-based income maintenance and health system, and Australia, where almost all redistribution systems are income-tested; or to know how much the apparent superiority of Sweden to either the United States or the UK on almost all their measures is due to its relatively egalitarian distribution of earnings and benefits, or its (now shaky) full employment policies; or to tell how important the proportion of government expenditure is for equalizing life chances, when the low-spending Japanese regime produces rather egalitarian outcomes.

Developments since Doyal and Gough's book was published have also complicated the picture. The relative stagnation of the Continental European economies, and the rise in unemployment in that region, are widely attributed to their excessive reliance on state redistributive systems and over-generous health care provision. The USA and the UK now claim the leadership roles in economic growth, and maintain that this is due to flexible labour markets and the enforcement of social obligations. The real argument in all these countries is now between two quite different approaches to distributive issues – the one insisting on enforcement of work obligations, and the priority of measures to combat social exclusion through education and training, and the other emphasizing the importance of retaining the protections afforded by unconditional rights, and enabling rather than enforcing economic participation.

There is no contradiction in recognizing that certain needs are universal, yet insisting that they should be satisfied by a combination of hard work and saving against equally universal risks and contingencies. In the past 15 years, the pendulum has swung in favour of those political groupings which have favoured just this combination. In the name of 'tough love', the Blair–Clinton orthodoxy embraces many of the values of the Thatcher–Reagan era, but grafts them onto a more universalist conception of human needs and vulnerabilities. In one sense, they turn the participation requirements of the advocates of need and inclusion into aspects of this universalist programme, by emphasizing the need for work and contribution to the common good and seeking ways of operationalizing this through social programmes.

Even the selectivist rhetoric of 'genuine' need can be reconciled with these policies. The Blair–Clinton orthodoxy can claim that it is looking for mechanisms to identify exceptional needs that constitute exemptions from the universal need to work. Those it forces to parade their impediments are not being shamed or humiliated on this account, because they can demonstrate that they would have wanted to participate, if only they had not been so handicapped.

This approach links universal needs with a universal desire to satisfy them by individual efforts. Far from justifying extensive state provision, as Doyal and Gough seek to argue, it justifies the widening of the scope for individual action and private provision; hence the further commercialization of welfare, and the privatization of state services. The scope for private initiatives and commercial provision will be analysed in the next chapter.

The arguments in this chapter and the previous one are designed to question whether the particular policy programmes chosen by the Blair and Clinton governments are consistent with their principles. It should be possible to promote equal access to employment and training without such a heavy price in loss of liberty, and the selective enforcement of obligations. It should be feasible to increase social cohesion without intensifying inequalities and exploitation. And a government ought to be able to deliver social justice without a massive transfer of resources from welfare benefits to subsidies for low-paying employers, and for criminal corrections. At this stage of the analysis, the basic (or citizen's) income principle has been offered as a tentative alternative proposal for a social justice programme; this will be developed in the next two chapters.


## Conclusions


In this chapter I have shown how the new Blair–Clinton orthodoxy re-articulates the central features of a liberal theory of social justice, and hence new connections between freedom, equality and need. By emphasizing the obligations that accompany rights, and linking these to work contributions, it justifies a kind of equality of opportunity that is formal rather than substantive. It also insists that most needs of the working-age population must be met from earnings in the labour market, and that private provision should replace some of the collective benefits and services that were given as social rights in welfare states.

In all this it is innovative only in so far as it gives a different emphasis and priority to the three elements in liberal justice, and forges new links between them. There is no unambiguous status for social rights in liberal theory, and little protection for the freedoms of those who cannot look after themselves in market competition. Furthermore, the ambiguities in liberalism can always be used to turn it inside out, and use aspects of its curriculum for extremely authoritarian ends.

This was well demonstrated in an insufficiently famous book, *The Irony of Liberal Reason*, by Thomas Spragens, junior.[88] The Enlightenment hope that rational beings could perceive the coincidence of long-run self-interest and the common good was supposed to confine coercion to a last resort in the social order, to be used only for those who deviate from the rational norm. But 'a doctrine that started as a method of emancipating the middle class changed, after 1789, into a method of disciplining the working class'.[89] 'American liberalism, especially, seems to oscillate between legalistic and pacifistic protestations, on the one hand, and binges of largely unrestrained force on the other'.[90] 'State power, the classic enemy of early liberalism, became the only recourse against this new threat [monopoly capitalism] to basic liberal goals'.[91] Spragens argued that the separation of moral principles (which were not susceptible to reason) from political practice (which was founded on the interplay of interests, derived from preferences), left power as the only basis for the essential order necessary for such a system of contending and conflicting interests; and power could easily become the (irrational) *raison d'être* of political movements. Thus liberalism could quickly slip into totalitarianism, because the equal value of all human life could soon make all individuals equally worthless.[92]

In the light of this twentieth-century history, it is doubly ironic that it is those states that best resisted totalitarianism – the UK and the USA – that now lead the field in a return to authoritarian programmes, and punitive measures towards social deviants. In Germany particularly, where the liberal tradition was weakest and most fragile, the social institutions established by Christian Democrat governments in the postwar era (under the tutelage of the occupying powers) have proved more durable, and have been tenaciously protected by the majority of the electorate. This is both an achievement and a problem for these countries. The facts that most citizens have a stake in the preservation of collective systems for redistributing income over the life cycle, in protecting the wages and working conditions of the minority engaged in full-time work, and in providing high standards of rather expensive health care, all constitute important bulwarks for a version of social justice that is fast becoming outdated in the USA and the UK. But there are political groupings who now blame these institutions for the poor performance of most Continental European economies, and would like to see elements in the Blair–Clinton orthodoxy introduced into the politics of welfare in these corporatist regimes.

It is difficult to see quite how this might come about. The success of Bill Clinton and Tony Blair in mobilizing majority electoral support has stemmed from skilful manipulation of constituencies largely created by the Thatcher–Reagan era of deregulation, privatization, the weakening of trade union power and the polarization of society into comfortable majority and excluded minority factions. The new politics of welfare mobilizes those on the borderline between these segments of society, by appealing to traditional nineteenth-century liberal values of hard work, thrift, family mutuality and retributive criminal justice (as Thatcher and Reagan did), along with working-class ideals of self-help, community and moral duty. It is rather easy to persuade those with the most to fear from global economic forces – those whose semi-skilled jobs are most vulnerable to technological change or a slight movement in exchange rates – that they have suffered unfairly from the processes of economic change, while those outside the labour market have been adequately protected. Because taxes (especially consumption taxes) do fall disproportionately on relatively low-paid individuals and households, and because means-tested benefits exclude large groups living only just above the poverty line, it is no wonder that they can be mobilized in favour of radical reforms of welfare benefits and services, and have little sympathy with those who look like free-riders, cheats or opportunists, and far less deserving than themselves.

However, this political strategy faces a dilemma. On the one hand, it is difficult to contain the populist emotions released by such appeals to the moral sentiments of the deserving poor. For instance, why should the new politics of welfare stop at cuts at the margin of benefits to lone parents – why not take them away altogether, and make them the main targets for workfare measures, as has been done in many states in the USA? And why allow such unpopular groups as paedophiles or violent offenders to have any civil rights at all? Why not restore the death penalty, as most states in the USA have done? Once populist moral authoritarianism is released as a political force, it is very difficult to contain.

On the other hand, there is a risk that, instead of producing a new reconciliation between efficiency and justice, in practice it will achieve neither. By driving the least productive citizens into the labour market, and forcing them to work at unchosen tasks, it will actually damage the hard-won productivity gains of the Thatcher years. By depriving the poor of benefits, it will provoke resistance, increased deviance and conflict. In the end it will have to spend more on enforcement, especially on anti-fraud surveillance in the benefits system and criminal justice corrections. In the end, taxation will have to be increased to provide for these expenditures, and the resentment of the better-off will grow. The new Labour government in the UK runs the risk that all this will happen just as its term of office expires.

In this chapter I have argued that a good deal of this dilemma stems from having appealed to moral principles from the private sphere in drawing up a policy programme for the public welfare system. The politics of welfare in the Blair–Clinton orthodoxy invites voters in the upper working and lower middle classes to make moral judgements about the actions of a whole range of individuals on the margins of society, and to support policies which aim to penalize them, or deny them options open to them under previous welfare regulations. But the moral principles are applied selectively, and only to those who claim benefits and services from the state. If political institutions are supposed to encourage moral choices for the common good, then they should be applied across the board. For instance, which (if any) of the following individuals can be judged to have behaved in a blameworthy way, according to principles of social justice?

1   A top woman executive has turned a company around, creating new jobs for 350 people, as well as high returns for shareholders, and increased her own salary by 200 per cent in 5 years. She decides to leave the firm, to spend more time with her children.
2   A young black man has been raised and educated on a deprived outer-city council estate, and employed by the tenants' association as a community worker, both before university and during the vacations while he is studying economics and social science. On graduating, he moves to an up-market area, and takes a job in a bank.
3.   A top scientist, aged 41, holds a key position in a team investigating a possible genetic factor in stomach cancer. He decides to leave to become a painter.
4   A doctor, educated and trained in the NHS, has recently been appointed consultant in a Scottish hospital. She decides to leave for a better-paid post in the USA.
5   A widely respected social worker, who has received a great deal of recent in-service training in child sexual abuse, decides to take early retirement.
6   An unemployed man, whose recent employment history has been a series of low-paid, unskilled jobs on short-term contracts, turns down a job as security guard at a local factory (£2.50 per hour) because the benefit rate for himself and his family (partner and 3 children) is higher than his wage (with overtime).
7   A top sportsman, earning over £200,000 per week in international tournaments, moves to a tax haven 'for the sake of his family'.
8   A single-parent mother with two young children takes an evening job as a barmaid, leaves her children in the care of her aunt, and does not declare her earnings to the benefits authorities.
9   The owner of a local mill decides to close it, sell up and reinvest his resources in a new factory in Indonesia; 250 workers are made redundant.

From a moral standpoint, all of these might be open to criticism for their failure to take full account of the interests of their fellow citizens (or fellow members of their particular communities) in their decisions. But from the standpoint of the Blair–Clinton orthodoxy, only numbers 6 and 8 are failing in their civic obligations, and should lose their social rights (and possibly be prosecuted). Morality is a matter of private conscience for the other seven citizens; it is only for the claimants that it becomes a question of public duty.

The Blair–Clinton orthodoxy would argue that this is because only these two are living at the expense of the taxpayer; their actions therefore become the object of public scrutiny and accountability, because the electorate should not subsidize behaviour that is damaging to the common good. But of course the great majority of public spending goes on benefits and services to the mainstream population – pensions and health services for the elderly, law and order to protect the property and persons of the middle classes, and education (especially higher education) for the better paid. Spending on subsidies to employment, and to sustain the business infrastructure, is the second highest category of public expenditure after social security,[93] if account is taken of contributions to the European Union's funds. The point about all these examples is that they represent possibly socially damaging choices, that take little or no account of the obligations to use the opportunities bestowed through the public goods available in a welfare state for the benefit of one's fellow citizens.

Instead, these obligations are more strongly enforced upon minorities, with little political clout, or capacity to resist through democratic processes. The Blair government chose lone parents and disabled people as the first targets for its welfare reform programme. It is difficult not to suppose that this was because they were in a bad position to oppose these cuts. By the same token, young people from minority ethnic groups are particularly likely to be required to participate in welfare-to-work programmes.

Liberal rights, including social rights, are supposed to protect minorities against the possible tyranny of the majority in a democratic political system. The new orthodoxy seems to ignore this danger, possibly because it is more alarmed by the evidence of a weakening in the cement of society, and the decay in integrative institutions and norms. It is more fearful of the threat of disorder than that of authoritarianism – an instance of the contradiction of liberalism in relation to state power, and how it can be turned into something close to its opposite.

There is, of course, an issue about order and political obligation in modern complex, plural and unequal societies. The new orthodoxy is right to seek to include outsiders, create the sense of mutual responsibility and involve all in cooperation for the common good. But there are other ways of doing this, as I shall suggest in Chapter 5.

# Notes and references

1 M. Walzer, *Spheres of Justice*, Oxford: Blackwell, 1983.
2 M. Kettle, 'White House Wise Guys', *Guardian*, 19 January 1998.
3 B. Barry, *Justice as Impartiality*, Oxford: Clarendon Press, 1995.
4 BBC Radio 4, *World at One*, 22 December 1997.
5 E. Currie, *Is America Really Winning the War on Crime, and Should Britain Follow its Example?*, London: National Association for the Care and Resettlement of Offenders, 1996.
6 F. Field, *The Reform of Welfare*, London: Social Market Foundation, 1997; see also G. Mulgan, 'Citizens and Responsibilities', in G. Andrews (Ed.), *Citizenship*, London: Lawrence and Wishart, 1991, pp. 37–49.
7 R. Cook, 'Arkansan Travels Well Nationally as Campaign Heads for Test', *Congressional Quarterly Weekly Report*, 11 January 1992, pp. 58–65.
8 A. Waddan, *The Politics of Social Welfare: The Collapse of the Centre and the Rise of the Right*, Cheltenham: Edward Elgar, 1997, pp. 158–63.
9 A. MacIntyre, *After Virtue: An Essay in Moral Theory*, London: Duckworth, 1981.
10 C. Taylor, 'The Liberal-Communitarian Debate', in N. Rosenblum (Ed.), *Liberalism and the Moral Life*, Cambridge, MA: Harvard University Press, 1989.
11 M. Walzer, 'The Civil Society Argument', in C. Mouffe (Ed.), *Dimensions of Radical Democracy: Pluralism, Citizenship and Community*, London: Routledge, 1992; D. Ivison, 'Excavating the Liberal Public Sphere', paper given at the Oxford Political Thought Conference, St Catherine's College, 9 January 1998.
12 M.A. Glendon, *Rights Talk: The Impoverishment of Political Discourse*, New York: Free Press, 1991.
13 Mulgan, 'Citizens and Responsibilities'.
14 B. Barber, *Strong Democracy: Participatory Politics for a New Age*, Berkeley, CA: University of California Press, 1984; J. Mansbridge, 'Does Participation Make Better Citizens?', *The Good Society*, 5 (2), 1995, pp. 1–7.
15 W. Galston, *Liberal Purposes: Goods, Virtues and Duties in the Liberal State*, Cambridge: Cambridge University Press, 1991.
16 S. Macedo, *Liberal Virtues: Citizenship, Virtue and Community*, Oxford: Oxford University Press, 1990.
17 N. Barry, 'Markets, Citizenship and the Welfare State: Some Critical Reflections', in R. Plant and N. Barry, *Citizenship and Rights in Thatcher's Britain: Two Views*, London: Institute of Economic Affairs, Health and Welfare Unit, 1990.
18 C. Murray, *Losing Ground: American Social Policy, 1950–1980*, New York: Basic Books, 1985.
19 L.M. Mead, *Beyond Entitlement: The Social Obligations of Citizenship*, New York: Free Press, 1989.
20 T.H. Marshall, *Citizenship and Social Class*, Cambridge: Cambridge University Press, 1950.

21  T. Malthus, *An Essay on the Principle of Population as it Affects the Future Improvement of Society*, London: J. Johnson, 1798.

22  W. Beveridge, *Social Insurance and Allied Services*, Cmd 6404, London: HMSO, 1942.

23  W. Beveridge, *Full Employment in a Free Society*, London: Allen and Unwin, 1944.

24  Marshall, *Citizenship*.

25  C. Reich, 'The New Property', *Yale Law Journal*, 73 (5), 1964, pp. 473–98.

26  J.S. Mill, 'On Liberty' (1889), in *Utilitarianism, Liberty and Representative Government*, London: Dent, 1912.

27  C. Murray, 'The Underclass', *Sunday Times Magazine*, 26 November 1989, pp. 26–45.

28  Mead, *Beyond Entitlement*.

29  Field, *The Reform of Welfare*.

30  K. Polanyi, *The Great Transformation: The Political and Economic Origins of Our Time*, Boston, MA: Beacon Press, 1944.

31  J. Locke, *Two Treatises of Government* (1698), Ed. P. Laslett, Cambridge: Cambridge University Press, 1967; see also J. Tully, *A Discourse on Property: John Locke and his Adversaries*, Cambridge: Cambridge University Press, 1980, especially p. 167.

32  Locke, *Second Treatise of Government*, sections 33 and 37.

33  Ibid., sections 37 and 42.

34  Locke, *First Treatise of Government*, sections 1–6, 42 and 43; *Second Treatise of Government*, ch. VIII.

35  F.A. Hayek, *The Constitution of Liberty*, Chicago: Chicago University Press, 1960.

36  R. Dworkin, 'Rights as Trumps', in *A Matter of Principle*, Cambridge, MA: Harvard University Press, 1985.

37  B. Jordan and D. Vogel, 'Which Policies Influence Migration Decisions? A Comparative Analysis of Qualitative Interviews with Undocumented Brazilian Immigrants in London and Berlin as a Contribution to Economic Reasoning', *Zes Arbeitspapier* 14/97, Centrum für Sozialpolitik, University of Bremen, 1997.

38  F. Fukuyama, *Trust: The Social Virtues and the Creation of Prosperity*, London: Hamish Hamilton, 1995; D. Gambetta, *Trust: The Making and Breaking of Co-operative Relations*, Oxford: Blackwell, 1988.

39  R.D. Putnam, *Making Democracy Work: Civic Traditions in Modern Italy*, Princeton, NJ: Princeton University Press, 1993.

40  R. Nozick, *Anarchy, State and Utopia*, Oxford: Blackwell, 1974.

41  F.A. Hayek, *The Mirage of Social Justice*, London: Routledge and Kegan Paul, 1976.

42  F.A. Hayek, *Individualism and the Economic Order*, Chicago: University of Chicago Press, 1980, ch. 1.

43  J. Rawls, *A Theory of Justice*, Oxford: Oxford University Press, 1970, p. 92.

44  Ibid., p. 66.

45  B. Goodwin, *Using Political Ideas*, 4th edn, Chichester: Wiley, 1997, ch. 16.

46  Ibid., p. 384.

47  G. Brown, 'Why Labour Is Still Loyal to the Poor', *Guardian*, 2 August 1997.

48  G. Watson, 'Labour's Welfare Lie', *Guardian*, 24 December 1997; see also P. Hollis, *Jennie Lee, A Life*, Oxford: Oxford University Press, 1997, pp. 104–6.

49 B. Jordan, *Automatic Poverty*, London: Routledge and Kegan Paul, 1981.
50 R. Solow, *The Labour Market as a Social Institution*, Oxford: Blackwell, 1990; B. Jordan, M. Redley and S. James, *Putting the Family First: Identities, Decisions, Citizenship*, London: UCL Press, 1994, ch. 9.
51 A. Smith, *An Inquiry into The Nature and Causes of the Wealth of Nations* (1776), Ed. R.H. Campbell and A.S. Skinner, Oxford: Clarendon Press, 1976, Part IV, sec. vii, ch. 80.
52 Quoted in Hayek, *Individualism and the Economic Order*, p. 7.
53 A. Smith, *The Theory of Moral Sentiments*, in H.W. Schneider (Ed.), *Adam Smith's Moral and Political Philosophy*, New York: Harper, 1948, Part IV, ch. i.
54 K. Marx and F. Engels, *The Manifesto of the Communist Party* (1848), in *Collected Works*, London: Lawrence and Wishart, 1976, vol. 5, p. 488.
55 W. Liebknecht, quoted in R. Ashton, 'Marx's Friends and Comrades', *Encounter*, February 1986.
56 L. Von Mises, *Socialism*, Indianapolis: Liberty Fund, 1981, pp. 439–40.
57 M. Olson, *The Rise and Decline of Nations*, New Haven, CT: Yale University Press, 1982.
58 Hayek, *Mirage of Social Justice*.
59 F.A. Hayek, *Law, Legislation, Liberty*, London: Routledge and Kegan Paul, 1982, vol. 2, p. 72.
60 Ibid., p. 80.
61 Beveridge, *Social Insurance*.
62 B. Jordan, 'Justice and Reciprocity', *Critical Review of International Social and Political Theory*, 1 (1), 1998, pp. 63–85.
63 H. Parker, *Instead of the Dole: An Enquiry into the Integration of the Tax and Benefits Systems*, London: Routledge, 1989; T. Walter, *Basic Income: Freedom from Poverty, Freedom to Work*, London: Marion Boyars, 1988.
64 B. Jordan, *The Common Good: Citizenship, Morality and Self-Interest*, Oxford: Blackwell, 1989, ch. 7.
65 G. Esping-Andersen, 'Welfare States Without Work', in G. Esping-Andersen (Ed.), *Welfare Status in Transition: National Adaptations in Global Economies*, London: Sage, 1996, ch. 3.
66 S. Bergmann-Pohl, 'Keynote Address' to the Conference on the Future of the Welfare State: British and German Perspectives, Humboldt University, Berlin, 17–18 November 1997.
67 Jordan et al., *Putting the Family First*, chs 1 and 6.
68 B. Jordan, S. James, H. Kay and M. Redley, *Trapped in Poverty? Labour-Market Decisions in Low-Income Households*, London: Routledge, 1992, ch. 6.
69 R.E. Pahl, *Divisions of Labour*, Oxford: Blackwell, 1984.
70 Jordan et al., *Putting the Family First*, ch. 2.
71 Ibid., p. 47.
72 Andrea Dworkin, 'Dear Bill and Hillary', *Guardian*, 29 January 1998; Barbara Eichenreich, 'How Bill Screwed Us All', *Guardian*, 24 January 1998.
73 P. Hewitt, T.H. Marshall, Memorial Lecture, in M. Bulmer and A. Rees (Eds), *Citizenship Today*, London: UCL Press, 1996, pp. 254–65.
74 Brown, 'Loyal to the Poor'.
75 Department for Education and Employment, *Labour Market Trends, December 1997*, London: Stationery Office, 1997.
76 J. Elster, 'Comment on Van der Veen and Van Parijs' *Theory & Society*, 15, 1986, pp. 709–22.

77 D. Silverman, *Qualitative Methodology and Sociology*, Aldershot: Gower, 1985.

78 T. Blair, interview on *Breakfast with Frost*, ITV, 11 January 1998.

79 L. Doyal and I. Gough, *A Theory of Human Need*, Basingstoke: Macmillan, 1991.

80 Ibid., p. 2.

81 Ibid., pp. 5–19.

82 D. Green, *The New Right*, Brighton: Wheatsheaf, 1987.

83 J. Gray, 'Classical Liberalism, Positional Goods and the Politicisation of Poverty', in A. Ellis and K. Kumar (Eds), *Dilemmas of Liberal Democracies*, London: Tavistock, 1983.

84 R. Rorty, 'Pragmatism, Relativism and Irrationalism', *Proceedings and Addresses of the American Philosophical Association*, 53, 1980, pp. 379–91.

85 Doyal and Gough, *Human Need*, pp. 49–54.

86 Ibid., pp. 298–301.

87 Ibid., p. 303.

88 T. Spragens, Jr, *The Irony of Liberal Reason*, Chicago: Chicago University Press, 1981.

89 H. Laski, *The Rise of Liberalism*, London: Harper, 1936, p. 236.

90 Spragens, *Irony of Liberal Reason*, p. 7.

91 Ibid., p. 8.

92 Ibid., pp. 285–7.

93 Office for National Statistics, *Social Trends, 1997*, London: Stationery Office, 1997.

# 4

# The Scope for Self-Responsibility and Private Provision

The existence of a world market gives important advantages to mobile individuals who can shift their resources quickly. It penalizes those who are tied to particular locations and relationships. In this chapter I shall show that the greater choices offered to individuals through globalization have consequences which are not adequately addressed in the new politics of welfare.

The new Blair–Clinton orthodoxy on social justice gives a higher priority to self-responsibility than was granted to it under postwar settlements. The mass solidarities of the welfare state were created by restraining class and individual rivalries, and giving citizens rights to claim – through their pooled risks and employment-based compulsory contributions – from mutual insurance funds. As the costs associated with these systems have grown (with an ageing population, and increasing numbers of claims from citizens of working age), the goal of policy has been to get individuals to carry a larger share of the burdens associated with these risks. In the name of fairness, the new orthodoxy argues that citizens should accumulate their own rights and claims, through saving against the various contingencies of the life cycle.

In this chapter, I shall look at this broadening of the scope for self-responsibility and private provision in the wider context of risk-pooling and the provision of public goods in present-day societies. Issues like pensions reform and health care insurance are particular examples of more general questions about the roles of individual and collective action in the supply of welfare goods. These issues seemed to have been settled with the advent of the various kinds of mass national solidarities created in welfare states. That they arise again is partly a result of the global economic changes identified in the first three chapters, and partly an outcome of the strategies pursued by individual, self-interested actors in existing institutional systems.

The analysis of these questions will inevitably be a bit more difficult than anything that has been undertaken in the previous chapters. It involves an understanding of the interactions between the (often unintended) collective consequences of individual actions; the emergence of new kinds of risks, and new methods of managing them; changing technologies in the creation of exclusive 'clubs' for sharing risks and collective benefits; and the role of nation states as providers of public goods in a global economic environment.

The new orthodoxy treats all these issues as being about the relative shares of responsibility of the state on the one hand, and individuals (through market institutions) on the other. It argues as if individuals and families, by accepting more of the costs of covering themselves against contingencies, can reduce collective burdens, and their resultant tax and contribution rates, to manageable proportions. Other issues of social justice, arising from the collective actions of smaller or larger groups and communities, are largely ignored.

But – as I shall show – this is a great oversimplification of the problems of the relevant unit for distributional issues of justice. The difficulty stems partly from the greater scope for narrower mutualities that has been created by the erosion of welfare states, and partly from the increased interdependency of people from different countries under global economic developments. All this casts doubt on the role of nation states, and whether they are most suitable institutions for the provision of public goods. In order to demonstrate the interconnection between these issues, it is necessary to go back to an examination of the problem of collective goods, and how it influences issues of social justice and the politics of welfare.

## Collective goods in a global context

In the theory of groups[1] and the supply of public goods[2] it has generally been assumed that individuals must be compelled to contribute (for example, through taxes) or the necessary infrastructural services for an orderly prosperous and just society will be undersupplied. This is the main justification for the nation state's monopoly of coercive power, and the fact that it supplies or licenses public services. But this need not necessarily be so, as the following example shows.

Let us imagine for a moment that a rich property developer decides to set up a new community for convenient, convivial and comfortable living, starting from a greenfield site. She chooses the Ukrainian coast of the Black Sea for this development, and acquires a sizeable tract of (previously agricultural and forest) land for her purpose. She sets about constructing a town and several satellite villages, complete with infrastructure of roads, power supplies, drains, sewers, parks, schools, hospitals, libraries and sports facilities – though of course none of these is yet operational. She then starts to sell the houses (or building plots) to would-be inhabitants of the new community, setting prices that reflect the costs of constructing the infrastructural services as part of her development profits, and also demanding a monthly charge for maintaining these services in good order.

What sort of people will buy these houses and plots? Presumably members of the new business elites and the mafia from Russia and the other former Soviet states, and from Central and Eastern Europe, along with other wealthy people from Greece, Turkey and the more distant Western World, and perhaps some from Asia also. Their perception of the desirability of these properties will be influenced as much by the quality of the infrastructural services provided as the natural environmental amenities, like the coast and climate. They will choose them only if they see that the rather artificial global community thus created will supply sufficiently secure and congenial surroundings for their chosen lifestyles, for whatever parts of the year they plan to spend in this location. In principle, it is in the landowner-developer's interests to provide collective goods of these kinds up to the point where marginal cost equals marginal revenue;[3] this level is the technically efficient amount of such goods which maximizes her profits. 'As a result, a landowner-controlled community will provide an efficient level of public services'.[4]

Having all bought their properties, and agreed to pay a monthly service charge, the new residents will then have a strong interest in forming an association to negotiate in order to protect themselves from her opportunistically charging more.[5] Whatever the practical difficulties of this might be (and it is amusing to imagine the chaotic meetings of this residents' group), they can be assumed to form a system of governance for their new community, which in turn sets rates of contributions for the provision of the services they choose to supply for themselves (the staff they will employ in various services, and the quality of provision for their various needs). Again in principle, this would be a wholly consensual form of governance, since residents would have voted with their feet to move there,[6] have paid for the particular bundle of collective goods on offer, and now have voting rights over the contribution rate and quality of services to be supplied.[7] In other words, the residents governing themselves in these ways would be fully sovereign individuals, with full control over the collective goods provided in this territory, and hence voluntarily consenting to the taxes imposed to supply these goods, rather than being forced to pay them.[8] Of course, residents must have the right to exit by selling their properties at any time, and members of the association the right to exclude them if they do not pay their dues.

In this way, economists and public-choice theorists have postulated a self-governing, consensual, territorial community, with fully sovereign individuals (modelled on a Lockean theory of moral autonomy, property, political authority and governance[9]), which supplies itself with collective goods in an efficient and equitable way. A number of landowner-developers in nearby districts of the Black Sea coastline could set up competing territorial communities of this kind. Since the potential residents would be rich enough to make the assumption of perfect mobility quite realistic, communities would compete over the provision of welfare goods and their average costs. Each community would have the characteristics of an exclusive 'club', with self-selecting members, up to the point where an extra one would cause congestion, or the additional cost exceed the contribution rate.

Suppose, however, that three such new communities are threatened by flooding from a river whose estuary passes through all three of them. The question then arises whether such competing territorial 'clubs' can cooperate over defence against an external threat, by sharing the costs of building a dam higher up the river. Here again there is – in theory – a solution that does not involve a third party in the form of a sovereign state. The three community associations can negotiate to meet the expenditures involved in building the dam, so long as these costs are less than those of insuring against the damage done by floods. The point about this voluntary solution is that the costs are likely to be lower than the ones generated by a state-provided dam, paid for out of taxes. In public-choice theory, special interest groups will lobby to provide a larger dam than is necessary, and residents will end up paying more than under the voluntary agreement.[10] In this sense, governments tend to undermine the cooperative systems under which groups and communities could efficiently manage shared resources and problems.[11]

This whole example is given some credibility by the choice of the Ukraine as a location for the new developments – a nation state so bankrupt, and so devoid of revenues to provide any of these collective services and goods, that it seems plausible that it might allow something like this chain of events to happen. But in fact there are 'private' communities with many of these features, especially in the USA,[12] and (more importantly) much of this dynamic now affects the development of new residential districts in all states, and mobility between existing communities. People are attracted to districts which offer the bundle of collective goods (local amenities, including schools, health clinics, residential homes and other public services) that they prefer, and they are willing to pay the prices associated with these facilities.

The difference is that these goods are mostly supplied by local and central governments, and that the latter impose uniform contribution rates (taxes) on citizens, remain monopoly providers of most public goods and services, and restrict entry by foreigners, even those willing to contribute the full amount required for these. So the imaginary example raises two kinds of questions about the scope for self-responsibility and private provision. First, how appropriate are nation states for the supply of collective goods under present economic conditions? And second, how do these spontaneous movements by individuals (voting-with-the-feet), through which they join self-selective residential communities, each with its own bundle of collective goods, influence attempts to achieve social justice by the redistribution of resources within nation states?

Our present international system of nation states did not evolve from the empires of the late middle ages at a particular moment in history. Sovereign national governments emerged alongside several other ways of organizing political authority, which were alternatives and rivals to nation states. In particular, city leagues and city states were quite successful for several centuries, in competition with nation states, and it was only in the seventeenth century that the latter began to gain clear advantages, and eventually to create a system of international relations from which the other types of government were excluded.[13]

Nation states adopted a concept of exclusive territorial sovereignty, which was a fundamental change from the feudal order. Under the feudal system a variety of authorities could claim the right to govern and exercise jurisdiction over the same territory. From the point of view of the individual under feudalism, 'one's specific obligations or rights depended on one's place in the matrix of personal ties, not on one's location in a particular area'.[14] Sovereign states, by contrast, claimed final authority over the inhabitants of their territory, but confined their jurisdiction to within their borders. City leagues were confederations of self-governing, independent cities, with no territorial integration or hierarchy of authority. City states were territorially unified, but their sovereignty was fragmented between constituent units.[15] In the ensuing centuries, sovereign territorial states were better able to create unified economies, with reduced transaction costs, to assert authority over their subjects and commit them to collective action, and to empower each other through international treaties.

The first question raised by the imaginary example of competing territorial 'clubs' is whether this way of organizing political authority is any longer advantageous under global economic conditions. According to the perspective adopted in the example, sovereignty is both unacceptably coercive and allocatively inefficient. Sovereign governments have authority over the persons and resources involved in all activities taking place within their territories. All legal rights, both of persons and of properties, are determined by the sovereign government, and citizens are, in the ultimate sense (for instance, in issues of the defence of the state) the property of the sovereign. The alternative radical notion of the sovereignty of individuals, which appeals back to Locke's concept of liberty as a natural right, can be used against this principle of unified sovereignty; the model of authority this alternative implies is a contractual relationship between members all of whom have equal rights to alter the constitution of the association, to quit it individually, or to secede as a group and form a new unit of their own. Hence from this perspective nation states are seen as monopoly cartels, exercising invalid, non-contractual authority.[16]

Individuals cannot easily break the sovereign power of states, but they can erode it by their strategic action within a global economy, and also through the collective action of international enterprises. Here the emergence of transnational institutions like the European Union is of crucial significance. The EU is an ambiguous entity, which is widely seen as a potential superstate, in which the sovereignty of member states is pooled, creating a new unified (and less democratically accountable) collective authority. But alternatively it can be seen as a new international regulatory regime, which sets the rules under which individuals from a variety of constituent states interact together in a shared economic environment.[17] Up to the present, it has certainly been more concerned with dismantling barriers to free trade and the mobility of productive factors than with building institutions for a federal political authority. Furthermore, its various treaties create a cross-cutting set of jurisdictions at the national and supranational levels, and the European Court has made decisions against the practices of member governments.

This development offers opportunities for individual and collective actors to pursue strategies that further weaken the sovereign authority of nation states. For example, if the costs of collective goods supplied by national governments are too high, it becomes far easier to shift resources within the EU at reduced transaction costs. In effect, nation states are no longer monopoly suppliers of such goods, because of this mobility, and because individuals and firms have rights to seek redress against compulsion or against barriers to free trade at the European level. The availability of multiple jurisdictions within the territory of the EU allows greater scope for such initiatives, and will over time further erode the monopoly power of national governments. Spontaneously, and without a political decision at any level, the new institutions of the EU will contribute to the processes by which individuals are increasingly able to join territorial 'clubs' of their own choice, and select which bundles of collective goods they prefer. Eventually nation states might become no more than super-landowners, responsible for a limited range of collective goods by contract to constituent communities.

The second question is therefore how such developments affect issues of social justice. As we have already seen (pp. 5–6), market-minded theorists point to the welfare gains that are achieved through the global increase in transactions driven by self-interested decisions of private actors. In this view, it matters little if nation states are reduced to the role of bystanders in these processes, since it is market forces which improve efficiency and also equity. The only risks to these improvements are that transnational diswelfares – like pollution and international criminal syndicates – will also increase, and that (as new international regulatory regimes are established to try to control these) nation states with strong economies will impose 'agreements' on weak ones, which are to their disadvantage.[18]

But general optimism about the benevolent effects of global market forces takes little account of the way that collective goods are produced and distributed among groups and between communities, or how the decreased autonomy of nation states affects distributive justice. For instance, a landowner who is descended from ancestors who improved agricultural land, and hence accumulated great wealth, is far better able to develop this in the ways described than one who inherited marginal virgin territory; and well-appointed communities will attract only rich residents, including successful racketeers and criminals. How will collective goods be supplied to the most vulnerable individuals?

The new orthodoxy argues that there should be more scope for self-responsibility and private provision, but it does not address the implications of the greater sovereignty of self-interested actors or the 'clubs' they form to pool risks and cooperate to their mutual advantage. In this respect, its analysis of social justice is not so much confused – as in its main theses that were criticized in the previous two chapters – as incomplete. It does not have an adequate or comprehensive theory of collective goods and their optimal provision, or show how social policy can tackle the phenomena discussed so far in this chapter.

This is particularly serious because, whereas rich individuals can choose to form communities with their prefered bundle of collective goods almost anywhere in the world, middle-income households in the First World are mainly confined to the pursuit of strategies within national institutional systems, including welfare states. The greater scope for self-responsibility and private provision that is given them by globalization's erosion of national governments' powers is mostly exercised in seeking advantage through the very institutions that were previously designed to limit rivalry and organize them into mass solidarities, based on large-scale risk pools and standardized contributions.[19]

In this chapter I shall argue that these individual and household strategies over collective goods must form part of what is to be analysed in a coherent account of social justice. This is partly because such strategies have collective consequences – they influence outcomes for others, because of interdependencies within these systems. But it is also because individuals and households start with different and unequal resources and risks, and hence how they choose to group themselves and pool these resources and risks will affect the costs they pay for collective goods, and the quality of such goods that they are able to enjoy. It is only by some process of equalization that these interactions can be shown to result in social justice.

## Collective goods, insurance, income transfers

The discussion in the previous section, and especially the example of the imaginary, 'private community', should alert us to certain important distinctions between kinds of collective goods which are very relevant to the analysis which follows. In the classical differentiation between private and public goods, the former can be divided up, exclusively owned and hence given a price; the latter are too costly to divide between exclusive owners, and thus impossible to provide through markets. But several other features of 'public' goods are variable and require more refined distinctions. Some – like the wind – are non-depletable, and hence non-rivalrous in consumption (any number of windmills could be constructed without increasing the costs of using each of them). Others – like stocks of fish in the oceans – can be depleted, and so are rivalrously consumed beyond the sustainable limits of catching, and require some form of regulation if they are to be conserved, even if no one can 'own' them. Others still are 'congestible', such as a stretch of sea shore; even though it is not depleted by use, its amenity value is reduced by too many users, which means there is a marginal cost for allowing additional people to enter it beyond a certain number. Finally, some are 'capacious',[20] like a political party, because extra members can be added without raising marginal costs. These characteristics may combine in several ways, as Table 4.1 shows.

For political authorities, issues of congestibility are important, because they involve rules about who can use a certain territory. Sovereign territorial governments are especially sensitive to such issues, since the collective goods which they supply to their citizens might be deteriorated through congestion, either through excessive concentrations of population around specific facilities, or through uncontrolled immigration. Social policy issues are often used to justify restricted entry and exclusive citizenship rules.[21] However, those goods which are both excludable and congestible (so called 'clubhouse' goods[22]) are often seen as the concern of civil society organizations rather than governments. I shall argue that they are relevant for issues of social justice.

TABLE 4.1   *Characterization of public goods*

|                | Congestible    | Capacious        |
| -------------- | -------------- | ---------------- |
| Excludable     | Swimming pool  | Pay-tv broadcasts |
| Depletable     | Common land    | Oxygen           |
| Non-depletable | Sea shore      | Sunshine         |

Another set of distinctions concerns the manner in which goods are consumed. Those goods which make up the infrastructure for daily living (parks, footpaths, roads, railways, museums, concert halls, cinemas, theatres) involve various forms of collective consumption, even if they are privately owned. Utilities, like gas, electricity, water and drainage, are mostly collectively supplied, but consumed individually, and charged-for according to consumption. All these goods may, as we have seen in the previous section, be supplied by private developers or landowners through markets. The technological options for providing them on a large scale yet measuring individual consumption, allow various possibilities. For instance, in two cities where I have lived (Aalborg, Denmark, and Bratislava, Slovakia) domestic heating was supplied by a central public plant that pumped hot water all over its territory.

However, for most social welfare goods these distinctions are of limited relevance. They consist of services that are either individually or collectively consumed, but are excludable and hence quite susceptible to market provision. Take education and health care. Schools and universities can easily charge fees for places, and thus exclude those who do not pay for services. Clinics and hospitals treat patients individually, and can equally readily charge fees. The reason for providing these services through public finance is that many citizens could not (or would not) pay for a level of service considered appropriate for a modern society. Thus it is a political decision to give all children access to computers and the education necessary to use them competently (as in Singapore), or to provide only the poorest with state-funded health care (as in the USA). Before the modern era, the education and health care of the rich was paid for directly in fees for private professional services; that of the very poorest was paid for out of public funds, through the poor rates. In between these two were charitable bodies and mutuality groups, whose coverage was far from complete. In both the USA and the UK, universal primary education was made compulsory and given public funding long before state health care coverage was widened.

Part of the reason for this is the so-called 'externality' of most social welfare goods. If I receive a higher education, part of the benefit of this goes to me in increased earnings; this is the private return on my investment in three years at university (the opportunity costs of the time spent, as well as any fees I pay). But there is also a social benefit from my studies, because my extra skills contribute to the productivity of others, improve my citizenship competences, and increase the yield to the community through taxation.[23] In other words, my choice of higher education affects the welfare of others (positively), and I am affected by their choices. Hence governments have an interest in funding education, at least to the full extent of this social return. Since primary education is a necessary condition for all other forms of education and training, the externality in this is very high; those who fail to finish this level are far more likely to end up as costs to the community (for further discussion, see below pp. 132–3).

The case of health care is not quite the same. There is a clear externality in the sphere of infectious disease, and all illness can be a public health hazard, if sick people spill over onto the streets as destitute and dying beggars, or crazed people accosting and threatening the public. But (preventive) public health services in this limited sense – regulating the provision of hygienic conditions in public places – is a very small part of state expenditure. The externality associated with most curative medicine is small because most illnesses are survivable without specific treatment, and by far the most expensive forms of health care are required for very elderly patients, or others suffering from the illnesses that will soon terminate their lives. Hence the levels of health care funded by the state are much more variable, even in First World countries; the National Health Service in the UK uses around half the proportion of national income devoted to privately and publicly financed health care in the USA, and far less than the public systems in Germany and other European countries (see Table 4.2).[24] The social benefit of health care is a great deal less than the private benefit (which is often itself contestable).

Another difference is that all children and many adults need fairly prolonged education, but curative medicine is required only in specific conditions, and for very varying periods. Because illnesses and accidents are undesired contingencies, insurance is one way of paying for the services needed. But there are always some high-risk individuals who cannot buy private insurance at any price. Most publicly funded health services are based on the insurance principle, with the government regulating insurance companies or schemes, and enforcing the payment of contributions. One advantage of compulsory social insurance is that it creates large risk pools, and hence spreads the costs over the whole population. In the German model (and elsewhere in Central Europe) competing insurance schemes are made to compensate each other if they attract too many low risks, and not enough high ones.

Another advantage is that it overcomes problems of information and 'adverse selection'. In private insurance systems, individuals are seldom able to find out exactly what they are paying for when buying health insurance; conversely, they have an interest in concealing information

TABLE 4.2   *Total expenditure on health care, public and private, as a percentage of GDP in OECD countries, 1989*

| Country | Total expenditure: public expenditure and private households | Public only | Public expenditure's share (excluding charges) |
|---|---|---|---|
| Australia | 7.6 | 5.1 | 70 |
| Austria | 8.2 | 5.7 | 67 |
| Belgium | 7.2 | 5.5 | 89 |
| Canada | 8.7 | 6.5 | 75 |
| Denmark | 6.3 | 5.2 | 84 |
| France | 8.7 | 6.7 | 75 |
| Germany | 8.2 | 6.3 | 72 |
| Greece | 5.1 | 4.0 | 89 |
| Ireland | 8.6 | 6.4 | 84 |
| Italy | 7.6 | 5.4 | 79 |
| Japan | 6.7 | 5.0 | 73 |
| Netherlands | 8.3 | 6.6 | 73 |
| Norway | 7.6 | 7.4 | 95 |
| Portugal | 6.3 | 3.9 | 62 |
| Spain | 6.3 | 4.3 | 78 |
| Sweden | 8.8 | 8.2 | 90 |
| United States | 11.8 | 4.6 | 42 |
| United Kingdom | 5.8 | 5.3 | 87 |

Source: *Health Care Financing Review*, 1989 Annual Supplement, Schieber et al., 1991

about their health status and lifestyles. Universal compulsory insurance provides standard terms for all members, by eliminating choice on both sides.

The role of the state in the funding of these welfare goods is therefore to ensure that a (politically determined) adequate level of service is available to all citizens, partly for the sake of the social benefit, and to reduce negative externalities like crime and infectious disease, and partly to guarantee such standards to citizens who would otherwise be unable to afford them. In other words, the decision to make schooling and health care contributions (whether in taxes or social insurance payments) compulsory is partly a matter of social engineering (guaranteeing the most efficient public benefit from private actions), partly to give the assurance and security of universal protection, and partly a paternalistic measure to enforce common standards. This paternalism is open to criticism from the standpoint of efficiency and justice. Some radical critics have argued that individuals would do better to use the time and resources devoted to schooling for learning in quite other ways,[25] and that much illness is 'iatrogenic' (i.e. a consequence of medical treatment)[26] and therefore better managed by informal or non-medical forms of care.

Income transfers are the least paternalistic ways of providing welfare goods, and therefore least open to these objections. Money in the pockets and purses of citizens allows them to purchase whatever bundle of goods they most favour, and hence equalizes life chances and compensates for the higher costs associated with chronic ill health, disability or handicap. In the case of long-term care needs, for example, an additional income that is equivalent to the costs of care – domiciliary assistance, day care or residential provision – allows individuals to purchase whatever services they need, or to choose to live communally, or with family members,[27] and hence achieve an informal solution to their care needs, and manage the money in a different way among members of the group. But this is open to the objections that some vulnerable (or deranged) individuals might be unwilling to buy adequate care, with negative consequences for others; and that the most difficult, challenging individuals would not be able to buy care at any price. A semi-paternalistic solution would be to provide those in need of care with vouchers that could be used to purchase it in a variety of ways, but not for other purposes; but even this might require a needs assessment.

No state has adopted just these measures in relation to the care of disabled or frail elderly people. In some countries (such as Germany and the Netherlands) these needs are met through social insurance systems, as with health. The results tend to be rather inflexible and expensive provision, mainly through residential care. In the UK, the National Health Service and Community Care Act, 1990, requires local authorities to assess the needs and resources of applicants, and to buy 'packages of care' (mainly from commercial and voluntary sector providers) for them, while requiring them to make contributions according to their means. This has led to very restrictive rationing of services, as a way of keeping costs low.[28]

The huge bulk of income transfers are therefore made for the sake of defined contingencies – retirement, sickness and incapacity, industrial accidents, disabilities and unemployment – for the support of children (child allowances) and for the relief of poverty (public assistance, housing benefits and various forms of wage supplement for the working poor). Political decisions about these transfers (and particularly the latter ones) have been the main focus of the analysis so far. Income transfers are by far the largest element in state welfare spending in most countries of the First World, and hence attract most scrutiny from reformers and critics. But they are not 'social services' or 'collective goods' of the kind analysed in the earlier part of this section, or in the last one. They are redistributions of money to command resources (which in turn affect and are affected by the distribution of roles such as employed person, unpaid worker, or retired person). Such redistributions strongly influence the kinds of collective goods that can be enjoyed by individuals, and their capacity to participate in the groups and communities that supply them.

The new Blair–Clinton orthodoxy does not make these distinctions between collective and welfare goods and income transfers. It generalizes about broadening the scope for individual self-responsibility and private provision, without distinguishing the different effects of actions in these spheres. While its main target is 'welfare', in the narrow sense of social assistance and other means-tested benefits for the poor, it fails to take full account of the interactions between these various forms of collective and welfare systems, or the relevance of income transfers for them.

In this chapter I shall consider a number of examples of how the actions and strategies of individuals and households have unintended consequences for themselves and others. 'Self-responsible' choices within these diverse collective and state-funded systems always have outcomes that impact on others, and what is rational for the individual at the point of decision is often damaging in its collective consequences. In particular, strategies that appear advantageous from the individual or household perspective may turn out to be mutually frustrating if many such adopt them. Hence the social costs of 'self-responsible' actions and private welfare systems must always be part of the assessment of policies for welfare efficiency and social justice.

## Social and residential polarization

One of the most fundamental principles of the new orthodoxy is that individuals and households must be free to exercise choice over welfare goods, and to improve their relative position through their own efforts. Taken together with its emphasis on 'traditional family values', this implies that household members should 'put the family first' in decisions about social welfare issues, and that the institutional structure should encourage them to do so. In this, policy and political rhetoric are following rather than leading public opinion. In the Thatcher and Reagan eras, reforms through deregulation and privatization, and the weakening of trade unions and other collective actors, all encouraged individuals to give priority to the competitive advantage of their household units over reliance on public provision or mass solidarities. Research on mainstream household members' decisions over work and welfare issues showed that by the 1990s British citizens experienced a conflict between their political principles and their perceptions of what was best for their families, but justified choices which 'put the family first'.[29]

Equality of opportunity implies social and residential mobility for the sake of efficiency and equity. If promotion and reward are based on merit, then differentials in pay and status can be justified, as long as individuals have equal access to learning and training places. Indeed it is important that individuals and households should move around in search of better jobs and more fulfilling lifestyles, since this is the best way of ensuring that the most suitable people fill the posts available, and that demand is generated for the sale of the consumption items that fuel economic growth. From the new orthodoxy's perspective there is nothing unjust in all this, provided that those in 'genuine need' have access to the services that they require, and to income transfers when they fall below the poverty line.

However, as changes in labour markets have disadvantaged certain individuals, who have become trapped in unemployment, in low-paid work, in insecurity of earnings, or in long-term receipt of means-tested benefits (and hence in poverty), individual decisions over mobility have caused a concentration of such people in undesirable residential districts. Areas that were previously inhabited by a mixture of working-class people, on a range of incomes, instead become uniformly 'ghettoes' for poor households. Those who can afford to move away elsewhere do so, with the result that those left behind become immersed in a shared life of poverty and social exclusion. Such 'communities of fate'[30] then find themselves receiving the worst quality of services from both private and public sectors – deserted alike by the market and the state.[31] This in turn provokes cultural practices of resistance, seen as deviant by mainstream society and public agencies, and involves costly measures to try to control them.

Research in several countries indicates that, although many individuals and households move into and out of poverty quite quickly, a proportion get 'stuck' in it, and remain poor for many years. In the USA, the Panel Study of Income Dynamics at the University of Michigan revealed that 44 per cent of people moving into poverty would move out again after only one year, but the number who were poor at any one time consisted mainly of those experiencing longer than average spells (i.e., 4.2 years), with more than half of these poor for more than 9 years.[32] Later work from the same survey found similar rates of exit over a longer period, but that 27 per cent of those who escape from poverty one year move back to it the next, and another 16 per cent two years later.[33] Hence those who leave and return to poverty join the majority (at any one time) who are poor for long spells. The work of W.J. Wilson in Chicago reveals that this long-term and repeated poverty is now concentrated in black ghetto areas in this and other cities,[34] and that an average of 40 per cent of residents in such districts are poor.[35] Wilson relates these changes to the industrial restructurings of the 1970s and early 1980s, in which the three inner city districts of Chicago he studied experienced a depopulation of 66 per cent between 1950 and 1990, while male employment declined by 46 per cent.[36] Overall, concentrations of poverty stemmed from both migration – of non-poor black and white families from the ghettoes and of poor families into them – and the 'suburbanization of employment',[37] as industrial jobs were lost, and service ones created.

In the UK and Europe, no research has been quite so thorough in tracing local dynamics of poverty and exclusion, but the patterns discovered have been very similar. In the Netherlands, a panel study based on statistics for 1985–8 found that about half the people in poverty in the first of these years had moved out of it by the third.[38] Similar results from the British Household Panel Study were revealed when two alternative definitions of poverty were applied; about half those in poverty by either measure in 1991 had moved above that line in 1992;[39] the same authors found rates of return to poverty in the subsequent two years similar to those of the US studies.[40] This confirms the emerging picture of employment patterns in the UK, where each recession reduces the number of secure and adequately paid employments, so that those who re-enter the labour market after spells of unemployment tend to take lower-paid and less permanent positions, and to experience further periods out of work.[41] Despite the great differences in the labour market in Germany, two panel studies based on data from the 1980s show a large proportion of claimants leaving social assistance during the first year of claiming,[42] though in one of these the main reason was that they were able to establish entitlements to social insurance benefits.

What none of these UK and European studies analyse in detail is how labour market changes and poverty data interact with mobility and concentrations of poor people in certain districts. Yet it is well known that, as income polarization has occurred – especially in the UK, where the gap between rich and poor has widened most significantly since 1980[43] – certain housing areas have become focal points of poverty and disadvantage. The mass housing schemes of the 1960s and 1970s that were supposed to supply a decent standard of accommodation for working-class families have deteriorated into low-quality provision for people living on the margins of society, and mainly on public assistance.[44] Hence the strong association between the notion of social exclusion and that of deprived housing estates in the Social Exclusion Unit established by the new Labour government in Britain.[45]

It is not only in the UK that these issues have emerged as major ones for social policy. A recent study of five countries – France, Germany, Denmark, Ireland and the UK – has indicated how the programme for building cellular, pre-cast homes in giant high-rise blocks as a solution to postwar housing shortages has ended in being seen as creating undesirable environments that act as breeding-grounds for social problems.[46] Between 1950 and 1975 some 15 million new publicly funded housing units were built in these five countries, many of them in large estates on the outskirts of towns and cities. These developments are now seen as examples of utopian, paternalistic arrogance of governments, generating their own political, technical and economic momentum, creating vested interests, and thus in the process escaping organizational control and ignoring residents' feedback.[47] Hence the agenda of the 1990s – now enthusiastically endorsed by the Blair government – is to impose tighter management structures to prevent or control abuse and deviance, to enforce standards and exclude people whose behaviour is disruptive. In all the five countries in the study, policy had shifted from its original grandiose goals to ones of controlling drug dealing, violence, intimidation and malicious damage, as a way of shielding fragile communities from victimization by criminal elements.[48]

However, these phenomena were not solely the results of public housing policies, but of interactions between these and factors of labour market change and income distribution. These changes affected the whole housing market, and not only the 'problem' estates and high-rise districts. As in the USA, the worst areas suffered outward migration by higher-earning families, and were used for accommodating those groups – especially lone parents – who depend on social assistance for their incomes. In the UK, not all estates function as residual housing; in some, existing tenants purchased much of the stock, and mobility was much less.[49] Conversely, in Central and Eastern Europe, where in many cities high-rise cellular blocks made up the bulk of the accommodation, the social mix of residents offset the anonymous and sterile design of the buildings, and provided an orderly and stable environment, which has largely survived, despite the very sudden increases in unemployment and poverty in that region. This continuing stability is mainly due to the absence of alternative residential opportunities for the better-paid workers and professional classes.

The new orthodoxy therefore focuses on the consequences of residential and social polarization – concentrations of poverty, creating 'communities of fate', which lack the resources to generate formal economic activity, but are fertile environments for various kinds of informal collective action, including crime, drug dealing and protection rackets based on intimidation. Its programme is especially concerned with measures against these features of the lives of residents in these communities. It makes the case for being 'tough on crime' and practising 'zero tolerance'; but its interpretation of policies to be 'tough on the causes of crime' is highly controversial.

This programme aims to resocialize those outside the labour market, by getting them back into training or paid employment, but simultaneously to exert far stronger controls over many aspects of the life of these communities, such as imposing curfews on children, prosecuting parents whose children break the law, and clamping down on truancy from schools. These measures are necessarily expensive, and the new Labour government in Britain will have to use the money it saves from benefit cuts imposed on lone parents and disabled people to finance much of the programme against social exclusion. It is estimated that £3.2 billion will be saved between 1997 and 2000.[50]

Yet – as I have shown in this section – many of the costly mani-festations of antisocial behaviour that the programme aims to combat have stemmed from poverty-related social exclusion, brought about through the actions of mainstream citizens who move to other districts, as much as those of local authorities pursuing policies of residualizing certain estates. The price paid for desirable 'communities of choice', with their better-quality bundles of collective goods (including schools, health clinics, welfare services and civic amenities, as well as private housing and other infrastructural features), is these marginal districts, where only those who cannot afford to move to better areas now live. To penalize them further by cutting their benefits simply reinforces the processes by which such concentrations of poverty came about.

In the UK and Europe, the phenomena of the 'hollowing out' of inner cities and the 'suburbanization of employment' are not as evident as in the large cities of the USA. It is often the housing schemes on the edge of cities that are most marginal to economic life; but here the problem of transport costs – often to reach work on the opposite side of the city – becomes important. As I shall argue in the next chapter, the real issue for these districts should be how to regenerate their local economies, and mobilize their residents to action that will improve their quality of life. This will not be achieved by trying to make them take employment for which there are no economic incentives, on pain of losing their benefits.

Despite its rhetoric of 'integrated transport policy', the new Labour government plans to build half of the new homes that it claims are needed in England outside cities, in the countryside.[51] With the further growth of suburban sprawl and out-of-town shopping centres, cars become necessities (see Figure 4.1). Instead of improving public transport and using space now taken for car parking in inner cities and towns, this spread of new low-density housing gives another twist to a costly cycle of increased use of cars for routine journeys. In 1971, 80 per cent of seven- and eight-year-old children made their own way to school; by 1990 it was only 9 per cent.[52] Developers have strong incentives to develop out-of-town sites for homes, shops or car parks, rather than inner-city spaces for multipurpose uses, mixing residential, business and leisure activities.[53]

Residential polarization of these kinds is therefore costly in a number of ways. As well as escalating social problems by creating concentra-tions of poverty in deprived areas, it disperses populations over a wider area, causing high transport costs, road congestion and pollution, and lost opportunities for the revitalization of many inner-city areas. Self-responsibility and the quest for positional advantage, reflected in mobility away from run-down areas and undesirable estates, have con-tributed substantially to these costs.

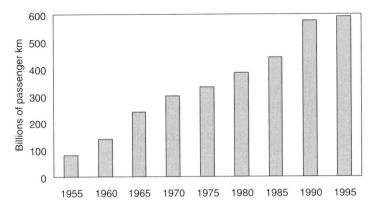

FIGURE 4.1    *Passenger transport by cars/vans, 1955–1995 (Guardian, 9 February 1998, p. 7)*

## Education, mobility and exclusion

The new orthodoxy stresses the significance of education in its strategy for social justice – 'education, education and education', in Tony Blair's summary of his policy priorities. In office, the new Labour government in the UK has been even fiercer than its predecessor in its criticisms, and more decisive in its interventions, over schools and teachers judged to be failing to realize their pupils' potential achievements. It aims to reconcile high overall standards in the state school system (and hence equality of opportunity) with the meritocratic principles of recognizing excellence and ensuring that the brightest come through to be selected for the most demanding higher levels. In this way, a comprehensive education system can deliver pupils who have been prepared for the requirements of a flexible labour market, where more sophisticated information skills will be in greater demand.

Two sets of problems bedevil these worthy objectives. The first concerns the polarization and mobility analysed in the previous section. Education can only be truly 'comprehensive' where each school is able to attract pupils with a range of abilities and social backgrounds, if one of the goals of such a system is to equalize opportunities between schools and districts. If successful schools attract the most able pupils, and better-off families move to be near these schools, then the drive for educational achievement defeats the aim of equal opportunity, and the comprehensive ideal itself. Furthermore, the attempt to promote 'parental choice', by publishing league tables of schools' successes in exam results, reinforces the informal processes of selection – by schools and parents – that sustain growing inequalities. It also gives strong incentives for less successful schools, already disadvantaged in competition for pupils and resources, to exclude 'disruptive' children, and those with special needs, in order to improve their performance. This puts extra costs on the community, as well as contributing to injustice.

As we have already seen (pp. 120–1) from the perspective of the parents, education is an *investment* giving a private return, in the form of higher pay and other future returns (such as social status, access to superior cultural goods, etc.). But from the point of view of the community this investment has a social aspect, because of the public benefit from the improved productivity and earning power it gives to the individual and others, and improved citizenship competencies, and greater yield through taxes.[54] Hence there is a common interest in equality of opportunity, as well as positional advantage for families to ensure that their children achieve their full potential.

In most European countries, state education is not organized on comprehensive lines (as in the UK); it is selective at the secondary level. But technical and vocational education is of a high enough standard for parents to be assured that those who are less suited for academic-style learning have good prospects in the labour market. For example, the German system of high schools, colleges and apprenticeships, all funded by the state, ensures that a very high proportion of school leavers get a technical or vocational training; although these occupations are not as well paid as many professional and managerial posts, their integration into a stable hierarchical order of occupations and rewards is central to the German welfare state's guarantees of security and prosperity (see pp. 218–19). This stratified social integration is inclusive in a typically continental European way, which is designed to minimize wasteful conflicts and resentments, and restrain damaging forms of competition. The fact that unemployment now manifests itself at all levels in the occupational hierarchy in Germany, including highly trained technical levels and among university graduates, indicates that this system is in trouble – but not from the costs of polarization so much as from its own rigidities and those of the labour market it supplies.

By contrast, in the UK mainstream households perceive the funding of the state educational system as giving a considerable subsidy to those who qualify for higher (university and college) levels by achieving good passes in their final school examinations. The premium consists in the rather larger proportion of the costs of higher educational investment (fees plus part of students' maintenance costs, the latter on a means-tested basis) that has hitherto been met out of public funds. Since vocational training and apprenticeships are in short supply, and not of a very high quality in many occupations, the positional advantages of higher educational qualifications have been significant, at least until recent times. So parents have been willing to make sacrifices – including costs of mobility to districts with schools achieving high rates of examination passes, or paying for private schools – to gain this premium.[55]

The fact that many have already incurred these costs, in search of this premium, explains the sense of betrayal by many middle-income parents when the new Labour government announced, as one of its first policy measures, that students would be required to meet part of their tuition fees. In terms of the goals of social justice through equality of opportunity, this seems quite fair, since it is apparent that the long-standing system of funding in the UK did subsidize higher education to a greater extent than the social return on public investment, and that students and their parents had been getting a discount on their private investment.

Since the Education Act, 1988, the British state educational system allows parents to exercise more choice – both collectively, through voting, and individually, over which school to send offspring to – and gives managers and teachers more autonomy at the school level, subject to this accountability to parents. Because local authority budgets have been devolved to head teachers and governors (with more parent representatives), parents can influence school policy, and can also vote for schools to leave the orbit of their local authority and – through 'opting out' – make their own decisions over the selection of pupils and the focus and goals of the educational programme. The Labour government's plans for passing some schools over to the management of private firms will presumably increase this autonomy and differentiation at the schools level.[56]

Hence there are several ways in which self-responsible parents can pursue strategies for positional advantage within the state educational system. They can choose to live in an area where the local school provides what they seek for their children, or move to another ('voting-with-the-feet', see pp. 114–16); they can use their new voting rights to influence collective decisions over school policy (voice); they can take available examinations and tests within the state system to try to enter a selective school, and leave the comprehensive ones (exit); or they can shift their children into private education (self-exclusion). The result is a pattern of interactions in any locality which leads to schools being organized as 'clubs' (see pp. 53–7), and managed for the benefit of their members (teachers, parents and children), but in ways that cannot take account of the interests of the whole local community, and work against the interests of the children of the worst-off parents.[57]

As 'club managers', heads and governors aim to attract a roll of pupils whose contributions (through the state funding they attract) are at least equal to the resources expended on educating them. Whether this is best achieved by an inclusive intake of children from their local district will depend partly on the available mix of high-yield/low-cost achievers and low-yield/high-cost 'problem' children; but it will also depend on the strategies of other nearby schools. If any one of these opts out of local authority control and relies on attracting many of the former group, then the others will find it increasingly difficult to sustain the inclusive strategy. If numbers of ambitious parents prefer selective schools, no comprehensive school in that district is likely to be able to offer a high enough rate of examination passes to attract such children. Once a school gets a reputation as being a 'sink' for less able pupils, staff and pupil morale suffer, and the costs for such schools escalate as (like the residential districts in which they are usually located) they are required to deal with concentrations of social problems. Any parents in the catchment area who have the resources to move away have strong incentives to do so, or to find private schools for their children.

At the lower end of the state school system, therefore, the disproportionate costs of educating children with physical, psychological and social problems fall increasingly on those schools least able to bear them. The self-responsible choices of more mobile parents concentrate these children where resources for giving them equal opportunities through a good education are least likely to be found. Furthermore, residual schools have strong incentives to exclude their most difficult children, and especially those who disrupt the orderly educational process. During the 1990s there has been a steady rise in the numbers of children permanently excluded from comprehensive schools.[58] Research shows that black boys are disproportionately perceived as disruptive, and hence excluded; indeed there is evidence that some adopt behavioural strategies to engineer their own exclusion, because their educational chances will be better if they attend special units for excluded pupils.[59] However, the majority of those who are denied access in mainstream education are at risk of drifting into other forms of activity – crime, drug use, etc. – which increase costs to the community, either through expensive special education or admission to care, and which add to their long-term risks of becoming costly clients of the social or correctional services. It has been estimated by the Metropolitan Police in London that children age 10–16 commit between 30 and 40 per cent of street robberies, car thefts and house break-ins, most of which occur during school hours.[60]

At the other end of the social scale, parents have more or less willingly borne the costs of mobility (long car journeys to a private or selective school, or paying a premium on housing near a school with good rates of examination passes) in order to get their children eligible for higher education. In the 1980s researchers estimated that for the previous 30 years in the First World the public return on the investment in each stage of education up to and including a 3-year degree was around 10 per cent, while the private return was nearer 12 per cent; yet in the UK the state was bearing most of the costs of higher education,[61] and returns to each stage were rising in the 1980s. However, since then higher education has been expanded greatly in the UK, and there are now doubts about whether such benefits can be sustained. In the USA, estimates of returns to college graduates suggested they were falling in the late 1980s,[62] and that this has continued until the mid-1990s.[63]

Indeed, in the USA, real salaries of graduates were falling as fast as those of blue collar workers, as deregulation and globalization bit in the first half of this decade.[64]

This combination of deregulation and global competitive forces exposes an ever-larger proportion of the workforce to competition from abroad. In the early 1980s it was unskilled workers in the USA and the UK who were adversely affected, and whose wages declined absolutely.[65] Later it was skilled manual workers and technicians who were affected, and now increasingly also administrative, professional and managerial staff, as services as well as manufacturing industries are relocated in lower-cost economies.

Because the returns to higher education are *positional* (i.e. welfare gains are made through advantages gained over others without access to such goods), they relate to graduates' ability to gain promotion to higher management, senior professional and other superior posts. But positional goods are vulnerable to congestion;[66] if too many young people gain degrees, they block each other's access to these superordinate jobs and the money spent on trying to attain them is wasted. As competition between parents to gain positional advantage for their offspring has intensified, so they have been willing to bear higher costs associated with longer periods of education, and of financial dependence. But employers can simply raise the qualifications required to basic posts in their organizations, and force parents to accept the increased costs of maintenance and fees for postgraduate masters' degrees and doctorates. Hence returns on investments in higher education decline, because access to promotion is limited to those with the very highest qualifications and abilities. Respondents in a qualitative study about such decisions said that their own offspring would need degrees to get jobs that they themselves had required only 'O' levels to obtain 30 years before.[67]

This falling return to educational investments helps explain the dismay of mainstream parents at the news the new Labour government will require them to contribute to the payment of undergraduate fees. Just how far the 'overqualification game' can go is shown by Germany. There, few students graduate until they are in their later 20s, and there are bars on taking up employment before 25 in several occupations and professions. But the labour market does not provide many lower-paid 'entry jobs' by which younger people can get work experience, or earn money to support themselves while studying. Now these problems are exacerbated by graduate unemployment, because the overqualified products of the educational system are too expensive to employ.

Indeed, the British research on this topic showed how strategies which are rational for an individual family in search of positional advantage for their offspring could sum together into collective outcomes which are mutually frustrating and costly. In order to finance the prolonged dependence and expensive qualifications that would give their children the best chances in the labour market, fathers who wanted to take early retirement were being required to work longer than they planned. This blocked the promotion to superior posts of younger professionals and managers, and hence access to the lower steps on the ladder to their own offspring's cohort.[68] In other words, not only were too many seeking positional advantage; the high costs of paying to give this headstart to the younger generation were forcing the older to remain in (and hence block the staircase to) exactly those positions that they hoped to make accessible to their children.

## Restrained competition and positional advantage

All this draws attention to the kinds of collective action needed to protect the benefits of higher education and other positional goods. As Hirsch pointed out in his *Social Limits to Growth*, the remarkable phenomenon of the postwar welfare state was that a whole set of occupations were given semi-professional status, and accommodated within public administration as relatively statusful, secure and well-rewarded jobs. He described this as the 'managed crowding'[69] of the era of expanding social services; large groups of 'social servants'[70] consti-tuting something like a 'new class', were gradually elevated, and their salaries and conditions protected, even as their numbers were being greatly expanded. Although this development was much criticized in the 1970s, on the grounds that it unbalanced the economy in favour of the public sector,[71] created much unnecessary or 'disabling' professional power, and gave far too much scope for collective action by trade unions and interest groups within it,[72] the whole process provides a case study for the analysis of the organizational requirements for the kind of mass upgrading in quality and status of the workforce that is sought by the Blair–Clinton orthodoxy.

What it shows is that improved education and training is a necessary but not a sufficient condition for such a collective improvement. In the new orthodoxy, equality of opportunity provides the baseline, and indi-vidual self-responsibility and mobility (through the means of lifelong learning) the dynamic for an up-skilling of the whole workforce, to take advantage of the gains in productivity that will be available in the age of information-related work.[73] But this process needs to be managed. Without restrained competition, and organized access to the institutional structures of the occupational group, the potential benefits of this improvement in the education and training of the workforce are in danger of being competed away, and the costs generated in achieving it risk being unnecessarily large and unfairly distributed.

In the nineteenth and early twentieth centuries, this process of management was provided by the professions,[74] which – like guilds before them – conserved the value of their members' expertise, by setting standards for entry, restraining competition between members, and restricting the supply of their services available on the market.[75] Professions restrained competition by complex rules, norms and cultural practices, forbidding the lowering of fees, salaries or charges, and integrating these with a distinctive ethic of service to their clientele, into a single set of cultural resources. Professional culture consisted as much in these practices of restrained competition as in those of ethically governed service; what the profession did to protect its value was part of that value, and part of the public good supplied by the profession. Tawney, for instance, following Durkheim, thought that professional groups were supplying the moral principles and social institutions that rescued society from the competition and greed of an 'acquisitive' culture.[76] Ignoring issues of power and privilege, some authors still see the professions as the means for providing the organized conservation of human capital in a global competitive environment[77] – for instance through the professional management hierarchies of the 37,500 corporations which employ 150 million people producing for the world market, of which the largest 100 companies employ around a sixth of this workforce.[78] It is argued that these provide the organizational structures in which human capital is now conserved by transnational professions.[79]

However, it is clear that the postwar upgrading and protection of occupational expertise was accomplished through welfare states, and by rather different means. The work which was expanded most rapidly in the 40 years after the Second World War was in the social services – in health, education and social work, in various kinds of public administration and community services. These newly flourishing occupations drew on the better-educated offspring of the lower middle and skilled working class, and especially on their daughters; it was women who most benefited from the growth of employment, and the higher status enjoyed by workers in these services.[80] The fastest growth in the UK took place in the early 1970s,[81] but in Scandinavia – and especially in Sweden – the process continued well into the 1980s.[82]

These occupations, as was noted at the time, were not fully fledged professions in the classical mould. Nursing, primary school teaching and social work did not have distinct knowledge bases, their skills were largely practical, and their associations were not fully self-governing. They were, it seemed, 'semi-professions',[83] which derived their occupational cultures and practices as much from the public sector institutions in which they were employed as from their own autonomous standards. It was the state that funded, organized, licensed and regulated their training programmes, that controlled their numbers through the medium of its spending departments, and that largely specified their practices through its legislation and the exercise of various kinds of political accountability and managerial control over them. In other words, the state provided the institutional context for this creation and conservation of human capital, and for the maintenance of salaries and conditions of service in the public sector. Trade unions and professional associations grew in the wake of the expansionary impetus of the state, and have since sought to sustain these gains ('protecting jobs and services', as the union slogan proclaims) in the face of budget restrictions and cuts in the harsher economic climate of the 1980s and 1990s, when market-minded governments introduced competitive principles and cost-conscious accounting into the social services sector.

It is clear that the new expansion of knowledge-based employment and the upgrading of occupational status envisaged by the Blair–Clinton orthodoxy is not to be achieved through such processes. Nation states are unlikely to be able or willing to foster and conserve a similar growth in public sector employment in the early twenty-first century, and the new orthodoxy does not promote one. Instead it sees this expansion as occurring in the private sector, as a spontaneous response to new possibilities made available by information technology and other improved communications. The growth in occupations connected with 'systems analysis' is taken as evidence for this great potential gain in human capital.[84]

But it is far from clear what the organizational vehicle for the conservation of the value of this expertise will be. Transnational corporations have an interest in some such conservation, but none in confining it to the citizens of First World countries. It would be far more rational a strategy for such companies, although their headquarters may continue to be based in the USA, the UK or France, to expand the pool of managers, professionals and technicians in those countries where they will increasingly locate production – the developing nations of the Second and Third Worlds. Hence, even though there may well be a great new growth in information-based employment, as the new orthodoxy insists, there will be no easy way that any First World government can 'capture' disproportionate parts of this. Instead, advanced economies will compete for highly paid jobs as much as for capital investment, since it will be just such people who constitute the mobile transnational workforce of the next century.

What First World governments can do is restrain the other factor tending to dissipate the benefits of human capital – competitive pressures from inside their own borders. Yet there is nothing in the main theses of the new orthodoxy to indicate a recognition of this problem. Simply expanding higher and further education, along with various forms of technical training, in the name of equality of opportunity and lifelong learning, does not address the need to conserve the value of this expertise. Of course, from the strictly market-minded perspective of the neo-liberal economist, any such measure for conservation is a distributive coalition, and a kind of conspiracy against unorganized individuals and other labour-market 'outsiders'.[85] As I have already argued (pp. 50–2), these criticisms are valid only if we take the whole world as our unit of account, since in a global context it is indeed a kind of distortion of equitable distributions to try to capture any of the value of human capital within state boundaries. But from the national perspective, it makes good sense to find effective ways of doing so, as long as policy then goes on to address any injustices this causes in distributions between groups of citizens (i.e., 'insiders' and 'outsiders').

If the new orthodoxy has any strategy at all in respect of all these issues, it is for some kind of 'partnerships' between private industry and government over the training and retraining of employees, mainly at the lower end of the labour market, and in the system of vocational qualifications sponsored by these institutions. But – unlike the situation in the era of welfare states, when the government limited the number of university places available, and had strict control over how many new entrants were funded for training to public sector occupations – it now presides over a greatly enlarged higher education system, whose output bears no institutionalized relationship to the actual demand for graduates, or the volume of information-orientated employment in the national economy. In other words, there simply is no mechanism for controlling the pressures for increased competition for positional advantage, stemming from the strategies of mainstream families identified in the previous section.

The possible range of acceptable institutional devices for restraining competition in a present-day economy has already been briefly reviewed in the previous chapter (see pp. 92–3). The point here is that, in line with the new orthodoxy's own principles of social justice, government cannot limit opportunities of access to positional advantage on grounds of class background, sex or skin colour, in the way that this was done through institutional power and prejudice in earlier times. Opportunities must be formally open to all, selection must be meritocratic, and educational and career structures must take account of factors like maternity, parental and child care needs. But, in the last resort, the negotiation of the arrangements under which particular individuals do gain superior positions, organizational power and hence positional goods, must be done under principles of social justice that are non-discriminatory, that allow access to 'late-comers', and that follow democratic procedures and processes.

Ideally, therefore, individuals should be able to move in and out of the labour market without undue penalization of their long-term prospects of promotion to positions of authority, status and higher earnings. This is not the situation at present; positional advantage is disproportionately gained by those (mainly men) who remain in similar organizations, and work their way up a ladder of incremental salaries and supervisory posts. Women, despite similar qualifications, do not usually conceive of their working lives in terms of 'career',[86] because they give priority to their 'supportive' family role, the needs of children, and the personal-developmental aspects of their working lives. But – as household income levels become less secure with the gradual deregulation and decentralization of professional and managerial employment – more women are drawn into competition for positional advantage within employing organizations, and hence increase pressure on the benefits of conserved expertise and human capital.

The only plausible way in which such competition might be restrained (consistent with the principles of social justice) would be for periods spent outside the labour market to be compensated at a rate attractive enough to allow able and well-qualified people to spend time on parenting, political work and cultural activities without experiencing undue hardship; and for the organizational arrangements over promotion and other positional advantage to allow easier entry to and exit from conventional professional ladders. The obvious institutional means for achieving this, already canvassed (pp. 93–4) would be an unconditional citizens' or basic income, sufficient to allow each individual an option to do unpaid caring, cultural, communal or political work for a period, to do part-time paid work without an undue tax penalty, and hence to trade off freedom against short-term earnings, without suffering long-term damage to prospects of a share in positional advantage. This amounts to something like 'taking turns' in the competition for organizational power and status, as well as compensating those willing to take the roles of 'outsiders' in the labour market, while not permanently disadvantaging them.

At present, there are factors which informally restrain competition for positional advantage, but these do not work in ways that are consistent with either efficiency or justice. On the one hand, there are the continuing elements of patriarchy, racism, ableism and ageism that still influence the promotion prospects of women, black people, those with disabilities and older applicants for promotion or new opportunities. At the domestic level, there are still strong expectations that women will do a disproportionate share of child care and unpaid domestic work, or at least take responsibility for organizing it and the rest of household activity. But on the other hand, the intensification of 'insiders'' workloads, and especially those with senior organizational responsibility, has increased stress levels in all types of occupation and employment, and made promotion less attractive. The upward flow of relatively junior staff into such posts is sustained by early retirements, especially in occupations like teaching and social work, which have become especially stressful and pressurized by performance indicators, assessments, regulations and the requirement to reach cost-cutting targets. But at the same time, high rates of sickness absence, often also due to stress (for instance in the police force and parts of the health service) contribute to the intensification of work, and hence to even more stress, declining morale and job satisfaction. Hard-working, conscientious staff are often most at risk from these factors, which lead to the loss of those with the greatest potential contribution to higher management posts, or advanced professional skills.

This means that the informal factors restraining competition for positional advantage work in the direction of inefficiency and unfairness, by making senior posts unattractive to all but the very ambitious and power-seeking, by damaging the morale and performance of the staff on whom good standards most depend, and by ruining the health of a proportion who become disabled by their work experiences. It is these negative features of employment that limit competition for positional goods, rather than the availability of viable alternative lifestyles, with other (non-material) advantages.

One strong argument for a radical reform of the tax-benefit system on the lines sketched in the previous chapter would therefore be that it would improve justice and efficiency, by allowing human capital to be conserved, both in the workplace (giving rise to better working conditions and improved performance) and outside it (improving the quality of life in families and communities). It is this, rather than the further intensification of competition and of work pressures, and labour market participation for its own sake, that would most contribute to social justice.

### 'Targeting' benefits and poor people's strategies

As we have already seen (pp. 99–100), the Blair–Clinton orthodoxy is particularly keen to avoid a culture of passivity and dependence developing among poor people, and to encourage them to be active and self-responsible in the labour market and in wider society. The goal of its social policy programme in the USA and the UK is to get such people, who have been excluded or excluded themselves from economic participation, to realize their full productive potential. Part of the justification of more conditional benefits, and restrictions or disqualifications for those who do not take available opportunities, is that it will increase motivation and employability, and hence allow the 'underclass' to regain some control over their lives, as well as to contribute to the economic progress of their society.

This analysis rather begs the question of what is supposed to move economic actors in a liberal polity with a predominantly market economy. I argued in the second chapter that the whole basis of a division of labour that is brought about through labour markets is that the workforce responds to opportunities to sell its skills and energies for a salary or wage, for the mutual advantage of employer and employee. It is the opportunity for this gainful exchange that is supposed to move both parties, and not any sense of obligation to benefit each other, or society at large. The politics of liberalism substitutes self-interested action for personal ties of blood and soil, and seeks to eliminate the authoritative direction of labour, except in times of war.

With the decline in Keynesian economic management of the national economy, and the impact of global market forces on the employment of less productive workers, serious problems with this model of labour markets have arisen. At first, trade unions sought to defend the employment security of all their members, and to avoid redundancies, even in the face of wholesale restructuring of traditional industries like steel, shipbuilding and coalmining, and the shift of production to countries like Korea and Taiwan. But in the 1970s and 1980s the strategies of governments and trade unions in different countries began to diverge. In the liberal polities, and especially in the UK, trade unions began to negotiate 'productivity deals', under which a proportion of the workforce (the least skilled and productive) were made redundant, in exchange for better wages and conditions for those retained. The effect of this was to transfer the costs of maintaining part of the workforce from employers on to the state. Yet the initial response of the Thatcher government after 1979 was to accelerate these processes of industrial 'shakeout', by deregulation (abolishing minimum wages and employment protections) and limiting trade union powers. The aim was to force the least skilled members of the workforce to be more mobile and adaptable, to 'price themselves into jobs', by accepting lower wages, and 'non-standard' contracts, by becoming self-employed, or moving to another area.

In Continental Europe, the strategy of governments continued to be one of cooperating with employers and trade unions to manage processes of change in the labour market. Instead of allowing wages to fall and employment conditions to deteriorate, the 'social partners' looked for ways of excluding less productive workers from the labour market by offering generous early retirement schemes through the social insurance system, and by making definitions of disability that qualified workers for similar benefits far more elastic.[87] In this way, social insurance contributions were increased, but conflict was minimized; however, over time unemployment has become a structural feature of these economies (and especially Germany and France) as redundancies finally became necessary, and young people found it difficult to get jobs.

The strategy of deregulation was taken furthest by the US government in the Reagan years. There the real wages of many groups of manual workers have been falling for 20 or more years, and the numbers of 'working poor' have continued to expand.[88] In the UK, a rather more complex pattern has emerged. On the one hand, there are large numbers of low-paid part-time service jobs, taken mainly by married women with partners in full-time employment, or by young people living with their parents. On the other, there are also many irregular, short-term, bits and pieces of employment, non-standard contracts, agency work (see pp. 48–9), and sub-contract labour, merging into self-employment. Many of these pay less than subsistence wages, or cannot be relied on to give an adequate income for a household to cover its living expenses.

The consequences of this might be called 'casualization' of the labour market, as more employers are able to hire workers for peripheral tasks (such as cleaning and maintenance) for whatever hours they are required, without regard for their subsistence needs, and as others are engaged or fired at short notice, according to fluctuating cycles of demand. The benefits system has been adapted to facilitate this process, by allowing those with children who work more than a certain number of hours for less than a certain level of earnings (fixed in relation to the number of their children) to claim family credit, which is in effect a wage supplement for low earners. Housing and council tax benefits go to other low earners who do not have children as well as to those above, and function in a similar way, as a subsidy to low-paying employers. The new Labour government aims to streamline these benefits by integrating the tax and benefit system, and converting them to tax credits, as in the USA.

However, from the point of view of social justice, there are some general difficulties about such payments. The Blair–Clinton orthodoxy praises them as being 'employment-friendly' (unlike the Continental system, which traps claimants in unemployment); as encouraging 'flexibility', in the use of labour power; and as 'targeting' those in greatest need of income supplements. But they also do three other things which are of concern to those who deal in fairness. They give a selective advantage over their competitors to employers who pay low wages; they give disincentives to increased earnings for those who receive them, because they have their benefits or tax credits withdrawn if their wages rise; and they discriminate against others who earn just above the prescribed levels, who do not qualify for supplements.

Hence the new consensus (increasingly in Europe as well as in the USA and the UK, see pp. 39–41) around the appropriateness of this form of wage subsidy (now further elaborating into new measures to induce employers to take on long-term unemployed claimants, and to sustain their incomes while they are in this kind of introductory employment) is hard to justify in terms of principles of social justice. Even if the disincentives of the so-called 'poverty trap' (the combined impact of benefit withdrawal and income tax imposition) could be greatly mitigated – as the new Labour government promises it will be under its Working Families Tax Credit proposals – there would still be objections to selective subsidies for these particular employers and employees. They are inducements for some employers to use labour power inefficiently and exploitatively, they penalize other employers who do not do so, and they cause justified resentment by those who narrowly fail

TABLE 4.3   *Social security benefits expenditure, UK, 1982–1997*

|  | **Benefit expenditure (£m)** | | | | |
|---|---|---|---|---|---|
|  | **1982/3** | **1987/8** | **1992/3** | **1994/5** | **1996/7** |
| Total benefit expenditure | 31,628 | 46,697 | 75,337 | 84,854 | 92,846 |
| Contributory | 18,210 | 25,311 | 37,320 | 39,825 | 42,337 |
| Non-contributory | 13,418 | 21,386 | 38,016 | 45,029 | 50,509 |
| Family credit | 94 | 180 | 929 | 1,441 | 2,047 |
| Income support | 4,612 | 7,960 | 14,790 | 16,377 | 14,061 |
| Housing benefit | 2,128 | 3,536 | 7,901 | 10,120 | 11,523 |
| Council tax benefit | 1,083 | 1,701 | 1,685 | 2,066 | 2,361 |
| Total means-tested benefits | 7,917 | 13,277 | 25,305 | 30,004 | 39,992 |

Source: DSS, *Social Security Statistics, 1997*

to qualify for income supplements, or are made redundant to make room for subsidized workers.

They also expose the ambivalence of the new Labour government in the UK about means testing. It was one of the ironies of the 1980s that the neo-liberal critique of the welfare state was interpreted in opposite ways on either side of the Atlantic. In the USA, public assistance – especially benefits to (mainly black) lone parents – was the main victim of benefit cuts, and 'welfare' in this limited sense the object of the greatest critical scorn. In the UK, Thatcher's regime saw a much faster growth in income support and all other means-tested benefits than in social insurance or other 'universalist' payments. Between 1982 and 1996 they rose by 505 per cent, compared with only 209 per cent (see Table 4.3).[89]

The new Labour government appears divided about the virtues of means testing. Some, like Frank Field, have been consistently critical of this method of rationing benefits. Others, like Tony Blair, Gordon Brown and Harriet Harman, though critical while in opposition, now frequently proclaim the necessity of means testing anything and everything, for the sake of selecting out those in 'genuine' need. The tax credit mechanism would be a still-complex but unified way of focusing all the means tests of the increasingly 'targeted' benefits system into a single periodic exercise, a kind of giant annual means test for all, with the filling in of each family's tax return. But it would mean that if the working household's income fell for any reason during the year, it would have to wait until the next tax return to be able to recoup this loss, and suffer poverty in the meanwhile.

Is there any way of 'targeting' the lowest earners in the economy without trapping them in poverty, creating disincentives to higher earnings, and giving subsidies to bad employers? There is, and once again it is the basic income (or citizen's income) principle. Unlike the tax credits envisaged by the new Labour government, this method gives each individual worker a guaranteed income *in advance*, and is automatically adjusted when his or her earnings rise, through the pay-as-you-earn tax system. In other words, it targets by giving income protection to all before they enter the labour market, and getting back in taxes what people can afford to pay out of their earnings, thus avoiding poverty traps. But it also avoids giving selective subsidies to bad employers, because it gives each citizen exactly the same guaranteed basic income, irrespective of their work or marital status. Consequently, no one can complain that another is getting a supplement that he or she is denied, because they themselves have the choice of living on their basic income, or of earning more and paying tax.

As we have already seen (pp. 96–8) this implies a kind of subsidy to all employers. Although this would not discriminate between them, or between workers, it might be seen as encouraging low pay in a general way. But against this, the security that an unconditional income would give to workers would allow them to refuse inefficient and exploitative uses of their labour power, and hence automatically to induce employers to allocate work more efficiently and fairly.

But the main virtue of a basic income would be to address the largest issue facing governments in their policies on benefits and labour markets. As wages for low productivity work have declined with the dual impact of globalization and deregulation, there are no incentives for members of households with no regular, decently paid earner to take the only kind of employment that is available in many districts. Low-productivity work in social reproduction tasks is an inescapable feature of all economies; but there must be some way of subsidizing the earnings of those who do it, or their incomes will decline to levels of abject poverty. Providing benefits that are conditional on unemployment, or that are means tested in any of the ways discussed above, has serious disincentive problems. It is simply not worth while for any member of a household to take this kind of employment, if they lose their benefits as soon as they renounce their status (as unemployed person, part of an unemployed person's family, disabled person or lone parent). This is why there are around 3.4 million households in the UK of working age with no working member. The work available often does not enhance their dignity or self-respect; but above all, it does not pay enough or offer enough security of earnings to attract them, given that they would lose their benefits entitlement if they took it.

The proposed tax credit system would not solve this problem either, since it would take a considerable time (longer than it does at present with family credit and housing benefits) to establish a claim and begin to receive payments. This is why the new Labour government needs the coercive and restrictive powers that it has taken under the welfare-to-work programme and the New Deal for Lone Parents. Unless it could cut the level of benefits, or disqualify claimants who refuse work or training, it would not persuade people to leave the status of claimant.

The national minimum wage may slightly improve this situation in the longer term, but the government wanted to take action to reduce the benefits budget immediately. It has to make benefits more conditional, and put more pressure on claimants, because there are no positive incentives for them to do the kind of work that is on offer, short of removing the benefits that support them. The basic income approach would save all the expenditure on surveillance, compulsion and assessment involved in these methods, because it would be unconditional, and rely on the incentives that would exist for all to do some work, even very part-time, short-term or modestly paid employment or self-employment.

From the point of view of social justice, the present situation also has a serious problem arising from the self-responsible actions and strategies of poor people themselves. Faced with the disincentives of the labour market outlined above, but also by the restrictions on benefits already implemented by the previous Major government, they have opted in considerable numbers to take short-term, part-time or one-off 'cash jobs on the side' (often called 'doing the double' in some regions[90]) without declaring their earnings to the benefits authorities. They justify these practices by pointing out that their families risk debt and destitution if they withdraw their claims to income support, because it takes so long to establish claims to family credit, and because they would also be forced to wait several weeks to get re-registered as jobseekers, or to get support as lone parents.[91] Hence they argue that as self-responsible individual actors, and especially as parents with obligations towards their children to provide 'extras' not now covered by benefits, and to pay large bills for clothes, fuel and other outgoings, they are required to do undeclared work for cash, within certain limits. There is a remarkable consistency in the amounts of such earnings seen as legitimate in different parts of the country,[92] and between claimants who have been prosecuted or investigated for fraud, and those who have not.[93]

Hence the practice of undeclared cash work has – from the evidence of these researches – become widespread and widely legitimated in the name of fairness. Claimants with children in particular see the creaking administration of the current system as penalizing them for trying to take responsibility for their families, and have invented their own rules for adapting it to the current labour market realities. In effect, although they do not justify it by the analysis I have used for introducing this new principle, they treat income support as a kind of basic income, allowing themselves to earn £30–50 per week without declaring it, but coming off benefits and paying tax if they can get better-paid or more permanent employment.[94]

The trouble with this strategy (when it is introduced in such a haphazard way) is that it reinforces trends towards casualization in the labour market. Although it is rational from the perspective of each individual and family to act in these ways, it offers marginal entre-preneurs and other opportunists the chance to employ labour power at very low rates, and use it very wastefully. Furthermore, it undermines regular work, and erodes the rates of pay of those in full-time employment. It creates conditions of 'hypercasualization',[95] in which no actor has an incentive to offer work in the form of a properly organized job, and none to take one in that form. Poor people's strategies drive down the wage rates and deteriorate the conditions already available in the work on offer. For example, in some seaside towns in winter, there is a kind of Dutch auction in rates of payment for various kinds of work, and any attempt at solidarity between workers over rates for the job crumbles through individual opportunism.[96] Unregulated and unrestrained competition of this kind damages the interests of poor people in general, as a culture of work on the side for cash develops. Customers begin to learn the interactional codes of this culture, and to become willing accomplices in these fraudulent transactions.[97]

All this would make it more difficult to introduce a basic or citizen's income system, because poor people are already compensating themselves for the restrictions on benefits attempted by successive governments. It is widely assumed that the cash economy in undeclared work explains the fact that poverty has greatly increased on the evidence of income data from the 1980s, but not from expenditure data.[98] But although the basic income principle would offer only modest gains for poor people who already use the benefits system in these ways, it would constitute a major improvement in social justice, because it would correct the injustice between those who do undeclared work and those who do not, either because they think it wrong, or because they cannot find any, or do not have the freedom to take it. Far from further casualizing employment, the basic income approach offers a way out of the cycle of hypercasualization which would allow low-productivity workers to organize themselves collectively again, and to insist on better pay and conditions, because it would give them the security of an unconditional guaranteed income.

## The debate about pensions

The new Blair–Clinton orthodoxy on social welfare is particularly keen to promote self-responsibility and commercial provision in the system of retirement pensions. It argues that the social insurance basis for supplying incomes for the years after employment is not sustainable, and must be replaced by a new system. This view is increasingly shared in Continental Europe, where social insurance provides generous earnings-related pensions that maintain differentiated incomes, commensurate with salaries during the beneficiaries' working years.[99] The new consensus is that the funding of pensions must be shifted from state to commercial provision, from collective to personal provision, and from pay-as-you-go financing to advance funding.

The rationale for these shifts is, that with the growth of the elderly population (see p. 47), and the decline in the ratio of workers to pensioners, the system by which pensions are financed by the contributions of the current working population to state-administered or state-sponsored schemes will become too burdensome to employers and employees, and will break down. The statistics on the demographics of the changing ratio of pensioners to workers are certainly striking for some Continental European countries,[100] so it is surprising that the most radical proposals for change come from the UK government, where the demographic situation is actually much more favourable, because of higher birth rates and levels of labour-market participation.

There are some grounds for concern in those countries like Germany, where contribution rates in social insurance are now very high, and Spain and Italy, where birth rates are extremely low.[101] But this should be seen as an issue for inter-generational justice, not one about the relative merits of pay-as-you-go and funded systems, or state and private provision. The fact is that there is no such thing as a cost-free pension,[102] and 'any saving for old age, whether public or private, funded or unfunded, involves the accumulation of a claim on the goods and services produced by future generations of workers'.[103] There are real issues about whether the current working generation should bear as great a burden from these claims as it currently does in Germany and other continental countries, but the 'privatization' of state pensions would not in itself reduce these costs. 'Private' pensions are as much paid for by employers and employees as state pensions, but in addition they are subsidized by taxpayers through tax reliefs. Employers' costs can also be passed on to consumers through increased prices for goods and services sold.[104] In addition, there is a serious problem in getting a funded 'personal' pension system started, because the new generation of workers would have to contribute to their own future retirement income, while at the same time paying to support the current retired population.

In the UK, the debate about pensions reform is driven by the prediction that the number of pensioners will increase from the 10.4 million at present retired to 15.5 million by the year 2030.[105] This forecast and its cost implications are disputed,[106] but continue to have a strong influence on policy formation. Conservative administrations from 1979 to 1997 found various ways to restrict state provision – by uprating the basic pension in line with prices rather than earnings; by reducing future entitlements to the state earnings related pension (SERPS); and by substituting a slightly uprated income support premium, despite evidence of low take-up among retired people. In addition, they offered strong tax incentives for taking out private (commercial) pensions, creating a far larger market in these than had existed previously.

The results of these policies were very unfortunate, especially for the 1.5 million people who were persuaded to move from occupational to private plans against their interests. At this time (the late 1980s), the number of workers enrolled in occupational schemes had been declining since the mid-1960's, and totalled less than half the workforce (around 10.7 million individuals).[107] Employers were trying to limit their own pensions spending by replacing defined benefit schemes (with provision based on previous salary and service) by defined contribution schemes (with accumulated contributions at retirement).[108] This strategy enabled them to limit their risks by stabilizing contribution rates, and to evade legislation aimed at guaranteeing adequate defined benefits. The risk of insufficient provision was therefore being transferred to employees, whose pensions would suffer if investments performed poorly or salaries were inflated. Hence personal investment in pensions and life insurance expanded rapidly during the early 1990s, from £611 billion in 1991 to £1,191 billion in 1997,[109] with many leaving occupational schemes, partly because of tax concessions, and partly through high-pressure sales tactics by the commercial pensions industry.

In the event, the Conservative government was eventually forced to announce that misselling had taken place, and the pensions regulator ordered a number of companies to pay back money they had persuaded these people to invest with them. The result was therefore that British pensioners faced a triple jeopardy – inadequate state provision, restricted occupational schemes, and fraudulent commercial plans. The new Labour government took office with promises of reform, and Frank Field openly describing the SERPS as a very poor buy – 'anyone persuaded that SERPS has a future ought to be made a ward of court' – while urging radical change.[110] But then the Chancellor of the Exchequer, Gordon Brown, announced in his July 1997 budget that he was going to abolish the right of pension funds to reclaim the advance corporation tax credits on UK dividends, thus limiting the potential investment returns generated by the Conservative government's 1988 rebates of National Insurance contributions to those 5.5 million people who had opted out of SERPS in favour of a private pension. The Independent Financial Advisers Association predicted that 3 million of its clients would return to SERPS in the early months of 1998.[111]

The present position is therefore that the basic state pension will deliver no more than 10–20 per cent of national average earnings in the third decade of the next century; occupational schemes are shrinking; and personal pensions are unable to deliver an economic return to people earning less than £10,000 a year.[112] Two-and-a-half million have earnings that are beneath the level at which they would qualify for membership of SERPS; another 1.5 million are self-employed and have no second pension; and many more women are also without coverage. Yet there is no easy solution for a government that wants to increase the proportion of individuals holding funded, personal pensions. Apart from all the other factors, mass state schemes are very efficient in terms of administrative costs; they use only about 5 per cent of total contributions revenue, compared with about 20 per cent for personal commercial pensions.[113]

In principle, however, it should be possible for commercial companies, and especially large-scale occupational pension funds, to compensate for higher administration costs by getting good returns on their investments on the stock market, especially at a time when profit rates are flourishing, and returns to capital across the board are at high levels.[114] Because of this factor, it might be argued that – in theory at least – pay-as-you-go collective schemes are preferable during a period when labour is getting a growing share of national income, and funded schemes (especially private pensions) are better when capital's share is growing. But – with the collapse of the South East Asian economies – returns to investments by these funds are likely to fall. And in practice commercial companies have (even in a favourable period) been unable to provide personal pensions yielding more than 20–40 per cent of final pay, whereas occupational schemes have been able to give around 60 per cent of the final pay (so long as job continuity has been sustained) under defined benefit rules.[115]

The Labour government is committed to the idea of 'citizenship pensions' for all who remain outside the labour market, such as unpaid carers, and 'stakeholder pensions' as a second tier, intended to be an alternative to SERPS, which is individually funded, flexible and secure, and upon which occupational provision could build.[116] It hopes to broker partnerships between commercial companies, trade unions, retailers, employers and employees, to produce large schemes with economies of scale. The unresolved issue is whether stakeholder pensions will be compulsory, given that they would require a contribution of 10 per cent by employers and employees jointly to produce worthwhile returns for low earners, and that over 46 per cent of the workforce earn less than £10,000 per year.[117]

It is therefore questionable whether these schemes for providing personal pensions through commercial companies should be the main focus of the government's policy measures. If the aim was instead to raise the level of citizenship pensions for all (on the model of the Netherlands and Denmark), then each citizen might reach a level of pension cover sufficient for adequate coverage of basic needs. They could then build upon this in their own chosen ways, including continuing to work part-time during retirement, rather than entrusting their future security to a financial services sector that is inexperienced in providing for lower-income groups.

## Conclusions

In this chapter I have analysed the scope for self-responsibility and private provision in the context of strategic action by individuals in search of their preferred bundles of collective goods. The problem for policy is not just – as the new Blair–Clinton orthodoxy argues – to find the right balance between public and private provision, but to determine the role of public power in addressing the aggregated outcomes of individual decisions. Whether this public power takes the form of national states, regional governments or supranational federations, its function should be that of steering individual strategies towards outcomes that are consistent with the common good (in so far as this is feasible, in face of capital's power to 'exit' from a national economy) and away from choices which, though rational from an individual perspective, have undesirable and wasteful social consequences.[118] Government is possible because individuals do have common interests in creating a good quality of collective goods on which to base their life together; it is necessary because without it they tend to frustrate each other in their search for individual gain and positional advantages.[119]

The thought experiment of the Black Sea property development by a private landowner was used to show that individuals can be induced to move by the provision of attractive collective goods, and that these can be supplied at optimal levels through market forces. Indeed, this 'voting with the feet' is an important feature of collective action in our globalized environment, with individuals and families drawn across borders by desire for security and a good public infrastructure, as well as by the prospect of earning higher incomes. The result is often a residential clustering together of people with like incomes and tastes; there is much evidence from the USA and Europe of a tendency towards greater neighbourhood homogeneity (in terms of residents' material resources) in the past 20 years,[120] even though populations in First World countries are becoming much more ethnically mixed.

The difficulty in all this is that private developers cannot be relied upon to supply the needs for collective goods of the whole population, or to ensure the most socially desirable mix of residents in any district. For instance, it will probably be in the interests of a landowner-developer to build cheap accommodation for the personal and collective service staff required by wealthy residents in a new and plush community, but not to provide for others with fairly modest means to live in such a neighbourhood. Similarly, it may be profitable for a commercial company to develop a new luxury health farm, employing a whole range of professionals for its staff, or a new international private school, or a secure, well-serviced residential home; but not to supply medical, educational or social care services in an impoverished district of a city.

Hence residential polarization of the kind discussed in the earlier sections of this chapter does not produce an even spread of public services, or a balanced community. It concentrates social problems in a way that exacerbates and escalates many of them, and drives up the social costs to be borne by the community as a whole.[121]

The new orthodoxy's analysis of social justice is therefore incomplete. In particular, it fails to address the consequences of strategic action within welfare states, through which individuals reinforce residential polarization by their mobility in search of positional advantage. As was shown in the example of state education in the UK, such attempts to gain superior position over others result in wasteful competition and low-return investments among mainstream citizens, and costly concentrations of socially disadvantaged pupils on the other. Middle-income parents end up by paying extra in housing costs for the privilege of living near to more successful schools, extra in fees and maintenance for extending their offspring's higher education, and extra in taxes for remedial, therapeutic and correctional care for those whose 'contaminating' effects on their children's schooling they have fled.

At the other end of the hierarchy of status and wealth, poor people have not been passive during the 25-year decline in their earnings, and the positional disadvantage that has gone with this. Residential polarization and the concentration of poverty has provided an environment in which undeclared work for cash and other illegal activities can be easily concealed. There is some dispute among researchers about the extent to which the cultural practices of poor neighbourhoods constitute a form of collective resistance, organized in the least costly way, and hence the one favoured by the most powerless and exploited in society, because it is most covert and requires least formal coordination;[122] or instead manifest individual, *ad hoc* responses to particular situations, such as debts or the threat of eviction.[123] What researchers do agree is that claimants, beggars and hustlers who take part in these practices justify them in terms of fairness, and argue that they are simply being enterprising in the only way consistent with responsibilities to themselves and their families, and compensating themselves for injustices that they suffer through the fragmented labour market and the cumbersome, restrictive benefits system.[124]

However, as was argued on pp. 144–5, these practices constitute a kind of unrestrained competition that undermines any collective solidarities and agreements between workers, and drives down the wage rates and worker protections established by trade unions and through legislation. The new orthodoxy is justified in seeking ways to limit these destructive rivalries, but it has set about this task in the most expensive and authoritarian way available to it. As I shall argue in the next chapter, it would be far better to recognize that the phenomena of the informal economy are manifestations of rational activity, in pursuit of goals relevant for the poor people who perform them, and therefore to look for ways of integrating them with the formal economy, rather than trying to abolish them.

Finally, the debate over pensions has been analysed as an example of the paradoxes of self-responsibility in a market society. The governments of the USA and the UK, along with those of Continental European countries, must now try to find an inclusive way of providing income for retirement that does not add unduly to the costs falling on the current working generation. Whereas social insurance in Europe is expensive because it provides for high levels of income replacement in societies with unequal earnings, state pensions in the USA, Canada and the UK are inadequate, and occupational pensions unavailable for a large proportion of the working-age population. I have argued that the Blair government is getting its priorities wrong in focusing on a second tier of funded stakeholder pensions, rather than seeking a modest-but-adequate citizenship pension for all.[125]

In the next chapter I shall turn to how government can pursue principles of social justice through a programme of measures that do not fall into the traps identified as besetting the policies of the Blair–Clinton orthodoxy.

# Notes and references

1 M. Olson, *The Logic of Collective Action: Public Goods and the Theory of Groups*, Cambridge, MA: Harvard University Press, 1965.

2 J.M. Buchanan, *The Demand and Supply of Public Goods*, New York: Rand MacNally, 1968.

3 F. Foldvary, *Public Goods and Private Communities: The Market Provision of Social Services*, Aldershot: Edward Elgar, 1994, pp. 30–32.

4 J.E. Stiglitz, *Economics of the Public Sector*, New York: W.W. Norton, 1986, p. 574.

5 Foldvary, *Public Goods*, pp. 63–4.

6 C. Tiebout, 'A Pure Theory of Local Expenditures', *Journal of Political Economy*, 64, 1956, pp. 416–24.

7 Foldvary, *Public Goods*, pp. 72–7.

8 K. Wicksell, 'A New Principle of Just Taxation' (1896), in R.A. Musgrave and A.T. Peacock (Eds), *Classics in the Theory of Public Finance*, London: Macmillan, 1958, pp. 72–116.

9 J. Locke, *Two Treatises of Government* (1698), Ed. P. Laslett, Cambridge: Cambridge University Press, 1967, *First Treatise*, sections 1–12.

10  E. Ostrom, *Governing the Commons: The Evolution of Institutions for Collective Action*, Cambridge: Cambridge University Press, 1990.

11  M. Taylor, *The Possibility of Co-operation*, Cambridge: Cambridge University Press, 1987.

12  Foldvary, *Public Goods*, chs 8 and 9.

13  H. Spruyt, *The Nation State and Its Competitors*, Princeton, NJ: Princeton University Press, 1995.

14  Ibid., p. 35.

15  Ibid., pp. 153–4.

16  Foldvary, *Public Goods*, pp. 57–60.

17  R. Bideleux, 'Civil Association: The British Way Forward in a Federal Europe', paper presented at the Thirteenth Lothian Conference, 'A British Leadership for a Federal Europe', London House, 11–12 December 1997.

18  A. Hurrell and N. Woods, 'Globalisation and Inequality', *Millennium: Journal of International Studies*, 24 (3), 1995, pp. 447–70.

19  B. Jordan, 'Are New Right Policies Sustainable? "Back to Basics" and Public Choice', *Journal of Social Policy*, 24 (3), 1995, pp. 363–84.

20  Foldvary, *Public Goods*, p. 13.

21  R. Bauböck, 'Migration and Citizenship', *New Community*, 8 (1), 1991, pp. 27–48.

22  J.M. Buchanan, 'An Economic Theory of Clubs', *Economica*, 32, 1965, pp. 1–14.

23  N. Barr (Ed.), *Labour Markets and Social Policy in Central and Eastern Europe: The Transition and Beyond*, Oxford: Oxford University Press and the World Bank, 1994.

24  H. Glennester, *Paying for Welfare in the 1990's*, London: Heinemann, 1993.

25  I. Illich, *Deschooling Society*, London: Calder and Boyars, 1974; *Disabling Professions*, New York and London: Calder and Boyars, 1974.

26  I. Illich, *Medical Nemesis*, London: Calder and Boyars, 1975.

27  G. Dalley, *Ideologies of Caring: Rethinking Community and Collectivism*, Basingstoke: Macmillan, 1988. B. Jordan, *Social Work in an Unjust Society*, Hemel Hempstead: Harvester Wheatsheaf, 1990, ch. 4.

28  R. Hadley and R. Clough, *Care in Chaos: Frustration and Challenge in Community Care*, London: Cassell, 1996.

29  B. Jordan, M. Redley and S. James, *Putting the Family First: Identities, Decisions, Citizenship*, London, UCL Press, 1994, ch. 9.

30  C.E. Marske, *Communities of Fate: Readings in the Social Organisation of Risk*, Lanham, VA: University Press of America, 1991.

31  R. Forrest and A. Murie, 'Residualisation and Council Housing: Aspects of the Changing Social Relations of Housing Tenure', *Journal of Social Policy*, 12 (4), 1983, pp. 453–60.

32  M.J. Bane and D. Ellwood, 'Slipping In and Out of Poverty: The Dynamics of Poverty Spells', *Journal of Human Resources*, 2 (1), 1986, pp. 1–23.

33  H. Huff Stevens, 'Persistence in Poverty and Welfare: The Dynamics of Poverty Spells: Updating Bane and Ellwood', *American Economic Review*, Papers and Proceedings, 84, 1994, pp. 34–7.

34  W.J. Wilson, *When Work Disappears: The World of the New Urban Poor*, London: Vintage, 1997, p. 12; C. Heady, 'Labour Market Transitions and Social Exclusion', *European Journal of Social Policy*, 7 (2), 1997, pp. 119–28.

35  P.A. Jargowsky, and M.J. Bane, 'Ghetto Poverty in the United States, 1970–

80', in C. Jencks and P. Peterson (Eds), *The Urban Underclass*, Washington, DC: Brookings Institute, 1991, pp. 235–73, at p. 239.

36 Wilson, *When Work Disappears*, p. 44.

37 Ibid., pp. 37–44.

38 A. Muffels, J. Berghman and H-J. Derven, 'A Multi-method Approach to Monitor the Evolution of Poverty', *Journal of European Social Policy*, 2 (3), 1992, pp. 193–213.

39 S. Jarvis and S.P. Jenkins, 'Do the Poor Stay Poor? New Evidence about Income Dynamics from the British Household Panel Study', ESRC Centre on Microsocial Change, Occasional Paper 95-2, Colchester: University of Essex, 1995.

40 S. Jarvis and S.P. Jenkins, 'Changing Places: Income Mobility and Poverty Dynamics in Britain', ESRC Centre on Microsocial Change, Working Paper 96-19, Colchester: University of Essex, 1996.

41 M. White, *Against Unemployment*, London: Policy Studies Institute, 1991.

42 W. Voges and G. Rohwer, 'Receiving Social Assistance in Germany: Risk and Duration', *Journal of European Social Policy*, 2 (3), 1992, pp. 175–91; P. Buhr and S. Leibfried, '"What a Difference a Day Makes": The Significance for Social Policy of Social Assistance Receipt', in G. Room (Ed.), *Beyond the Threshold: The Measurement and Analysis of Social Exclusion*, Bristol: The Policy Press, 1995, pp. 129–45.

43 P. Barclay, *The Joseph Rowntree Inquiry into Income and Wealth*, York: Joseph Rowntree Trust, 1995.

44 A.E. Power, *Estates on the Edge: The Social Consequences of Mass Housing in Europe*, London: Macmillan, 1997.

45 Z. Peatfield, 'Caught on the Edge', *Guardian*, 6 December 1997.

46 A.E. Power, *Hovels to High Rise: State Housing in Europe since 1850*, London: Routledge, 1993.

47 A. Giddens, *The Consequences of Modernity*, Cambridge: Polity Press, 1993.

48 Y. Dauges, *Riots and Rising Expectations in Urban Europe*, LSE Housing Annual Lecture, March 1991, translated A. Power, London: LSE; City of Cologne, *Kolnberg*, Cologne: City of Cologne Council, 1989.

49 S. James, B. Jordan and H. Kay, 'Poor People, Council Housing and the Right to Buy', *Journal of Social Policy*, 20 (4), 1991, pp. 27–40.

50 D. Hencke, 'Benefit Cuts Reap £3.2 billion', *Guardian*, 5 January 1998.

51 G. Monbiot, 'Sprawling Suburbia', *Guardian*, 7 January 1998.

52 M. Hillman, J. Adams and J. Whitelegg, *One False Move: A Study of Children's Independent Mobility*, London: Policy Studies Institute, 1991.

53 R. Rogers, Reith Lectures, BBC Radio 4, January, March, 1995.

54 Barr, *Labour Markets and Social Policy*.

55 Jordan et al., *Putting the Family First*, chs 8 and 9.

56 J. Carvel, 'Labour Revolt on Private Schools Plan', *Guardian*, 7 January 1998.

57 B. Jordan, *A Theory of Poverty and Social Exclusion*, Cambridge: Polity, 1996, pp. 137–9.

58 E. Blyth and J. Milner, 'Exclusion from School: A First Step Towards Exclusion From Society?', *Children and Society*, 7 (3), 1993, pp. 255–68. A recent report suggested that school exclusion in London had risen by 400 per cent in the past 3 years (*Hard Lessons*, Channel 4 tv, 10 January 1998).

59 P. Garner, 'Exclusions from Schools: Towards a New Agenda', paper presented at a conference on 'Changing Educational Structures: Policy and

Practice', CEDAR, Warwick University, 15–17 April 1994. In one south London borough in 1995, Afro-Caribbean boys made up 8 per cent of school rolls, but nearly 70 per cent of those excluded (P. Younger, 'Lost Boys', *Guardian*, 1 August 1995). An example of a special unit for excluded children is the Lennox Lewis College, Hackney (BBC Radio 4, *File on Four*, 6 January 1998).

60 J. Carvel, 'Truant Pupils Blamed for Wave of Street Crime', *Guardian*, 2 January 1998.

61 G. Psacharopoulos and G. Woodhall, *Education for Development: An Analysis of Investment Choices*, Oxford: Oxford University Press, 1985.

62 G. Woodhall, 'Financial Aid: Students', in *Higher Education Encyclopedia*, 2, New York: Pergamon Press, 1992, pp. 1358–67.

63 L. Elliott, 'US Reaps the Unhappy Harvest of Deregulation', *Guardian*, 20 February 1995.

64 J. Barker, 'Are Low-Wage Workers a Danger?', *The Times*, 28 July 1995; L. Elliott, 'Seventies-style Fear and Loathing Makes a Comeback', *Guardian*, 21 August 1995.

65 Commission on Social Justice, *Social Justice: Strategies for National Renewal*, London: Vintage, 1994, pp. 158–62.

66 F. Hirsch, *Social Limits to Growth*, London: Routledge and Kegan Paul, 1977.

67 Jordan et al., *Putting the Family First*, chs 8 and 9.

68 Ibid., ch. 9.

69 Hirsch, *Social Limits to Growth*, chs 2 and 3.

70 R. Bacon and W. Eltis, *Britain's Economic Problem: Too Few Producers*, London: Macmillan, 1976.

71 E. MacAdam, *The Social Servant in the Making*, London: Allen and Unwin, 1945.

72 W.A. Niskanen, 'Bureaucrats and Politicians', *Journal of Law and Economics*, 18, 1975, pp. 617–43.

73 R. Reich, *The Work of Nations: Preparing Ourselves for Twenty-First Century Capitalism*, New York: Knopf, 1993.

74 E. Durkheim, 'Individualism and the Intellectuals', *Revue Bleu*, 4th Series (10), 1898, pp. 7–13.

75 T.J. Johnson, *Professions and Power*, London: Macmillan, 1972.

76 R.H. Tawney, *The Acquisitive Society*, London: Allen and Unwin, 1921.

77 H. Perkin, *The Rise of Professional Society: England since 1880*, London: Routledge, 1990.

78 United Nations, *World Development Report, 1994*, Geneva: United Nations, 1994.

79 H. Perkin, *The Third Revolution: Professional Society in International Perspective*, London: Routledge, 1996.

80 B. Jordan, *Invitation to Social Work*, Oxford: Martin Robertson, 1984, pp. 76–80.

81 B. Jordan, *Automatic Poverty*, London: Routledge and Kegan Paul, 1981, ch. 7.

82 G. Esping-Andersen, *The Three Worlds of Welfare Capitalism*, Cambridge: Polity, 1990.

83 A. Etzioni (Ed.), *The Semi-Professions and their Organization*, New York: Free Press, 1969.

84 Reich, *Work of Nations*.

85 Olson, *Rise and Decline of Nations*.

86 Jordan et al., *Putting the Family First*, ch. 2.

87 G. Esping-Andersen, 'Welfare States Without Work: The Impasse of Labour Shedding and Familialism in Continental European Social Policy', in G. Esping-Andersen (Ed.), *Welfare States in Transition*, London: Sage, 1996, ch. 3.

88 Commission on Social Justice, *Social Justice*, pp. 158–62.

89 Department of Social Security, *Social Security Statistics, 1997*, London: Stationery Office, 1997, p. 3.

90 E. Evason and R. Woods, 'Poverty, Deregulation of Labour Markets and Benefit Fraud', *Social Policy and Administration*, 29 (1), 1995, pp. 40–54.

91 J. Millar, K. Cooke and E. McLaughlin, 'The Employment Lottery: Risk and Social Security Benefits', *Policy and Politics*, 17 (1), 1989, pp. 75–81.

92 B. Jordan, S. James, H. Kay and M. Redley, *Trapped in Poverty? Labour-Market Decisions in Low-Income Households*, London: Routledge, 1992, chs 3 and 6; E. Evason and R. Woods, 'Poverty, Deregulation of Labour Markets and Benefit Fraud', *Social Policy and Administration*, 29 (1), 1995, pp. 40–54.

93 K. Rowlingson, C. Wiley and T. Newburn, *Social Security Fraud*, London: Policy Studies Institute, 1997.

94 Jordan et al., *Trapped in Poverty?*; Rowlingson et al., *Social Security Fraud*.

95 Jordan, *Theory of Poverty and Social Exclusion*, ch. 4.

96 B. Jordan and A. Travers, 'The Informal Economy: A Case Study of Unrestrained Competition', University of Exeter, Department of Social Work, 1997.

97 BBC2 tv, 'How Much for Cash?', 30 October 1997.

98 A. Goodman and S. Webb, *The Distribution of Expenditure in the United Kingdom*, London: Institute for Fiscal Studies, 1995.

99 W. Schmähl, Comment on speech by Frank Field at the Conference on the Future of the Welfare State, Humboldt University, Berlin, 17–18 November 1997.

100 G. Esping-Andersen, 'Introduction', in *Welfare States in Transition: National Adaptations in Global Economies*, London: Sage, 1996.

101 Esping-Andersen, 'Welfare States without Work'.

102 T. Salter, 'Being Realistic About Pension Reform', *Citizen's Income Bulletin*, 24, 1997, pp. 9–11.

103 P. Johnson and J. Falkingham, *Ageing and Economic Welfare*, London: Sage, 1992.

104 Salter, 'Pension Reform', p. 9.

105 Department of Social Security, *Equality in State Pension Ages*, London, HMSO, 1993.

106 J. Hills, *The Future of Welfare: A Guide to the Debate*, York: Social Policy Research Unit, Joseph Rowntree Foundation, 1993; A.M. Warnes, *The Demography of Ageing in the United Kingdom of Great Britain and Northern Ireland*, Malta: International Centre of Ageing, United Nations, 1993.

107 J. Plender, 'Shuffle Up the Pension Path', *Financial Times*, 20 November 1997, p. 19.

108 Salter, 'Pension Reform', p. 9.

109 Office of National Statistics, *Financial Statistics, 1997*, London: Stationery Office, 1997.

110 Plender, 'Shuffle Up the Pension Path', p. 19.

111 R. Jones, 'Millions Ponder a Return to Serps', *Guardian* (Jobs and Money), 13 December 1997, pp. 6–7.
112 Plender, 'Shuffle Up the Pension Path'.
113 Salter, 'Pension Reform', p. 11.
114 Ian Gough, Response to Frank Field, Conference on the Future of the Welfare State, Humboldt University, Berlin, 17–18 November 1997.
115 Bacon and Woodrow Analysis, *Employees and Personal Pensions*, London, Bacon and Woodrow, 1993.
116 Department of Social Security, *Pensions: Consultative Document*, London: Stationery Office, November 1997.
117 Plender, 'Shuffle Up the Pension Path'.
118 B. Barry, 'The Continuing Relevance of Socialism', in *Liberty and Justice: Essays in Political Theory, 1*, Oxford: Clarendon Press, 1991, pp. 274–90.
119 A. Ryan, 'Mill and Rousseau: Utility and Rights', in G. Duncan (Ed.), *Democratic Theory and Practice*, Cambridge: Cambridge University Press, 1983, pp. 56–7.
120 G. Miller, *Cities by Contract*, Cambridge, MA: MIT Press, 1981; M. Parkinson, 'Economic Competition and Social Exclusion: European Cities towards 2000', paper given at a seminar on the Measurement and Analysis of Social Exclusion, University of Bath, 17–18 June 1994.
121 Jordan, *Theory of Poverty and Social Exclusion*, chs 5 and 6.
122 J.C. Scott, *Domination and the Arts of Resistance: Hidden Transcripts*, New Haven, CT: Yale University Pess, 1990; B. Jordan, 'Framing Welfare Claims and the Weapons of the Weak', in G. Drover and P. Kerans (Eds), *New Approaches to Welfare Theory*, Andover: Edward Elgar, 1994.
123 H. Dean and M. Melrose, 'Manageable Discord: Fraud and Resistance in the Social Security System', *Social Policy and Administration*, 31 (2), 1997, pp. 103–18.
124 Jordan et al., *Trapped in Poverty?*; Evason and Woods, 'Poverty and Benefit Fraud'; Rowlingson et al., *Social Security Fraud*; Millar et al., 'Employment Lottery'; Dean and Melrose, 'Manageable Discord'.
125 H. Parker (Ed.), *Modest-but-adequate Budgets for Four Pensioner Households, October 1994 Prices*, London: Age Concern, May 1995.

# 5

# An Alternative Programme

So far, I have criticized the new orthodoxy on welfare because its policy programme cannot deliver the measures for social justice that it proclaims as its goals. But now I must start to show that there are other ways of achieving these goals, by combining active inclusion in the common good with individual security and autonomy. In this chapter I shall outline an alternative approach to social justice in a global context, and sketch a policy programme to implement the measures that might come closest to realizing it. Everything in the first four chapters points towards the need for institutional innovation, in order to create new bridges between the elements of social justice (freedom, equality, merit and need), to encourage collectively responsible behaviour, and to bring about socially desirable outcomes.

The programme that will be sketched in this chapter is not the only feasible alternative to the new orthodoxy. I have emphasized that globalization increases reliance on markets, and emphasizes the crucial political significance of the wage relationship. A pact between world governments over competition could broaden the possibilities for income protection. But this would require international action, which will be the topic of the next chapter. In this one, I shall focus on the domestic issues for the new politics of welfare.

I have maintained that two pitfalls are to be avoided in the search for social justice. The first is a simplistic extrapolation from the morality of the family and small informal group to the civic obligations of a large polity. As I argued in Chapter 2, the search for ethical principles that apply to economic allocations is not to be confused with the attempt to justify the use of political coercion. The former seeks principled justifications for the final distribution of the basic goods of a society, and the policy programme that best approximates these, not only in its outcomes, but also in its methods of achieving them. The latter tries to lend moral force to those authoritative transactions between state officials and citizens that require the latter to act against their economic interests, and for the public good. Liberalism is rightly suspicious of all such moral theorizing, and all such transactions. It insists that ethical intuitions, however appealing, are not enough to legitimate particular instances of political coercion. The obligation to obey authority, and to cooperate for the common good, must be located in more general arguments about the justice of distributive principles, and linked to other fundamental features of a liberal democratic constitution.[1] In a free society, attempts to introduce selective coercion may also be counterproductive and costly.[2]

The second pitfall lies in the belief that social institutions must *embody* ethical principles. This is quite misleading, because – as Larmore has argued[3] – several principles apply to every kind of human social group or situation, and all must somehow be interpreted and reconciled in the search for justice. In other words, justice is not a shining prize to be awarded from on high to some political arrangements, and denied to others. It is the negotiated outcome of a dialogue over often conflicting principles, all of which apply to almost every kind of interaction; and it must be reciprocally constructed in processes of democratic compromise.[4]

The institutions in which this can most readily happen consist of informal norms and cultural practices, as well as formal rules and structures. These institutions are the most effective instruments of justice when they allow its different and conflicting principles to be *bridged*, rather than authoritatively selected.[5] It is not usually a matter of choosing which principle to apply, but one of finding legitimate ways to reconcile them. Institutions therefore should not try to embody principles, but to link them together in new ways that are recognisably fair to all. For example, this is what Sir William Beveridge (a liberal and a 'reluctant collectivist'[6]) did in his famous report on *Social Insurance*; he showed how this institution could, in the conditions of the postwar British economy and society, bridge individual liberty and collective security, by allowing citizens to build their family lives upon a firm foundation of income transfers and public services.

At various points in the previous two chapters (pp. 93–4, 98–9, 142–5) I have argued that a basic (or citizen's) income would be a more logical and feasible way of achieving the goals of the new Blair–Clinton orthodoxy, and more consistent with its own proclaimed values. It would give all citizens an equal unconditional income guarantee, adequate for basic needs, before they entered the labour market or the household. However there are real political difficulties in making this measure the basis for an alternative programme.

The first is that, despite the fact that it might be possible to 'equilibrate' work and leisure by finding exactly the right level of basic income for any economy and society (see pp. 98–9), it would still seem to break the fundamental principle of justice that no one should get benefits without making contributions. Even if it is accepted that labour contributions (and especially forced labour contributions) are inappropriate in a liberal polity, surely *some* contributions are required? Various heroic attempts have been made in recent years, notably by Philippe Van Parijs,[7] to justify the unconditionality of basic incomes, and say why idlers should be treated just the same in this respect as very industrious workers; but none has been entirely successful. The moral argument against this approach – that it rewards laziness, and gives no real encouragement to any social virtue – seems as stubbornly persuasive as ever.

Second, it is obvious that, even if a basic income is a necessary condition for social justice (because every citizen is entitled to have his or her requirements met up to a level equivalent to their fundamental needs, as Beveridge argued), it is not a sufficient condition for social justice. The case against the new orthodoxy has been made on two grounds – that it is unacceptably and discriminatingly coercive to welfare claimants, and that it is required to be so because it cannot give them adequate opportunities and incentives to participate in the common good of social cooperation.

Basic income can readily overcome the first objection, because it involves no compulsion to do anything, but on its own it cannot defeat the second. Even if every citizen had a *technical* incentive to participate (because, even at the rather high marginal tax rates that would be required to finance the payment of a generous basic income there would be better incentives for low earners than under any other proposed solutions, and because higher earners work for status, security and other non-monetary benefits as well as for their earnings), they would not necessarily have more opportunities. In fact, quite the reverse; the government and other agencies in civil society would have few motives for trying to generate employment, because the basic income would have satisfied the conditions for security and survival without any such policies.

Hence there are many political interest groups with deep suspicions about the proposal. Trade unionists fear that it would undermine their campaigns for promoting 'full employment' through more long-term public investment in public services, and attracting private investment from abroad.[8] Women are worried that it could mean that they would lose their hard-won gains, because it might contribute to a culture of withdrawal from the labour market, and a redomestication of their roles.[9] But above all, there are fears from a number of groups that the tasks of social reproduction would not be fairly shared, or might even not be done at all. Why should anyone cooperate in any sphere, if their individual subsistence were guaranteed?

All this draws attention to the strengths of the new orthodoxy, hitherto downplayed in this book. The idea that all should be encouraged to work for the common good; the notion that cooperation in productive effort is a vital source of self-respect and even for identity itself, because shared work is essential for the realization and flourishing of human potentialities; and the principle that everyone should do something to pay back what society (through the cultural transmission of its values and technical heritage, through state benefits and services) gives them – all these are indeed moral intuitions that are persuasive, and central to the bonds that could create a good, fair and cohesive society. The critique advanced in this book so far is aimed at the methods by which the new orthodoxy tries to achieve these aims, not the goals themselves.

The argument of this chapter is that an alternative which seeks to realize these goals by very different methods is both feasible and desirable. The methods proposed rely on different policy instruments, and a quite different politics of welfare.[10] Instead of enforcing obligations, they should go with the grain of individual and collective strategies. Instead of herding all minorities into the mainstream of the market economy, they should recognize that groups have potentially conflicting interests, and seek to harmonize them in more stable ways. The poor are active, and do try to improve the quality of their family lives, and of their neighbourhoods, albeit in some rather unorthodox ways that expose them to various risks, including that of exploitation. Instead of trying to outlaw and stamp out the cultural practices developed in the past 20 years, they should channel them towards consistency with the formal economy, and reconcile them with it.

At the same time, the new programme of measures should address the mutual frustration by mainstream households of each other's strategies for positional advantage. Instead of encouraging (in the name of self-responsibility and upward mobility) the pursuit of superior positions (leading to residential polarization, overqualification and delayed retirement), they should start to develop the collective means to manage crowding and ease the burdens of overstressed achievers. In a word, the alternative measures should *restrain* these rivalrous endeavours, and quell the wasteful use of energies they generate, by providing less competitive access to superior goods, and easing pressure for positions. Instead of the manic politics of productivity maximization, they should introduce a calmer culture of shared, civilized conviviality, a balanced lifestyle and sustainable development.

None of this can be achieved without a deeper consideration of the division of labour in society, and the distribution of burdens for reproducing a post-industrial community. As was argued in the first two chapters, globalization has 'domesticated' the issues of who does what in national economic life. Work comes to be disproportionately concerned with social reproduction, rather than with producing goods and services for global markets (which is done by the relatively well-paid few). The questions raised are how tasks that are rather labour-intensive and arduous (such as looking after frail elderly people) can be more efficiently and equitably divided up.

This chapter's enquiry tackles two questions – how the work of social reproduction can be most efficiently done (taking account also of production for global markets), and how to assure fairness in the distribution of rewards, roles and responsibilities in its performance. The unit for analysis here will be the nation state; in the final chapter I shall return to the issues of globalization and the relevant units for the future discussion of social justice issues raised in Chapters 1 and 4.

The first question requires me to consider the relationship between the formal and the informal economies. The latter includes the 'moral' economy of unpaid family and neighbourhood care, support networks, grassroots community action, voluntary organizations and charities. It is a sphere sustained mainly by women's commitment[11] to the value of relationships and shared responsibilities towards those at dependent stages of the life cycle, and with special needs, in interdependent groups. But it also comprises the very different economy of cash transactions, illegal exchanges, theft and violence, mainly sustained by men, and partially integrated into the formal economy of markets and their political regulation. The key issue is how these are and should be related to each other. The new orthodoxy's approach – maximizing employment and family responsibility – is examined here.

The second question calls for an analysis of the relationship between the citizenry and those officials and professionals charged with regulating the economy and society, or promoting those activities relevant for social justice. In the past, it was easy to be a bit uncritical in the use of phrases like 'the social services' or 'the caring professions'. Despite the focus on social control in Marxist and other analyses of the welfare state in the early 1970s[12] and the writings of the Foucauldian school,[13] the assumption behind much social policy discussion is of a benevolent and supportive relationship between authoritative agencies, with considerable power over the lives of citizens, and a compliant clientele, who gratefully do their bidding. In practice, the regulatory, rationing, restrictive, coercive and punitive functions of state officials and professionals have been greatly increased in the past 20 years, especially in the USA and UK, where criminal justice rather than social justice was the focus of many of the policies of the Thatcher–Reagan years, and the surveillance and control of 'deviant' minorities was a major preoccupation.[14]

Accordingly, these minorities have developed cultures of resistance practices, and strategies for exploiting systems they experienced as hostile to their interests.

The Blair–Clinton orthodoxy aims to extend many of these features of the social services in the name of social justice. It greatly expands the number of officials and professions directly concerned with counselling or compelling claimants and others towards the labour market, or training them for jobs they do not want to do, or punishing them for practising unorthodox forms of resistance. In these respects it follows the regulatory principles of Jeremy Bentham and his followers,[15] using social engineering methods to steer citizens towards behaviour desired by government, and to block off options seen as undesirable from the perspective of political authority. For example, the services proposed by the new Labour government in Britain for counselling lone parents on returning to the labour market could easily have been taken straight from Bentham's *Constitutional Code* (1843). In this they would have been given a complex Latinate title, such as Solomaternal Collaborandi; he would undoubtedly have included it among the tasks of those officials concerned with separated couples, as part of the state's 'benevolent mediation function'.[16] (Incidentally, Bentham anticipated present-day concerns about food safety, providing for a government department for 'disease and mortality from the consumption of articles of food and drink, in a state regarded as dangerous to health'[17]). New Labour, Old Bentham.

This chapter will examine the role of the enormous and complex web of government agencies that structure the tasks of social reproduction in national polities. It will argue that – if a basic income approach to the distribution of the necessities for subsistence were adopted – there would be considerable scope for re-orientating these agencies and services from controlling to supportive and promotional functions. Many of the state's regulatory activities generate evasion or resistance. But the social costs of this conflict, born of polarization, are not confined to the state sector. The price of insurance and the security measures by which the rich protect themselves from the poor is paid by private households to commercial firms. There are profits to be made from human insecurity, and all this spending shows up as growth of incomes in the national accounts.[18]

These issues cannot all be tackled through structural reforms and institutional design (the social engineering approach). The interests of groups will always conflict in various ways, and the multiplicity of conceptions of the good life will increase as societies become more diverse in their memberships, and plural in their practices. These differences have to be negotiated in political life, and claims and conflicts mediated through democratic processes. I shall argue that interest in discursive democracy[19] and the use of public reason[20] (or communicative rationality[21]) has not adequately analysed the ways in which constructive compromise and cooperation are secured. Political inter-actions (negotiation and debate) are possible only through the exchange of mutual respect, as sociological analyses show.[22] In the final sections of the chapter, I shall explore how issues of power and difference can be handled in such processes, and the potential for agreed distributions of responsibilities and resources in a democratic polity.

## Formal and informal economic activity

The traditional distinction between formal and informal economic activity presupposes (and implicitly supports) the expansion of markets, especially labour markets, and the gradual withering of household, communal, associational and non-profit cooperative production. As we have seen in Chapter 2 (pp. 50–2), part of the justification for this viewpoint is the recognition in economic analysis since Adam Smith that growth depends on the continual refinement of the division of labour, as the basis for improving workers' output, reducing costs and increasing trade. Informal activity is less specialized, therefore less efficient.[23] Furthermore, from this perspective, non-market activities are either part of a 'moral economy' that is archaic, because it is regulated by customs such as patriarchy or religious tradition, or illegal, and hence distort optimization by unfair competition.

An alternative economic view of informal activity that has gained ground in recent years is that it represents a rational response to the comparative costs of different methods of producing goods and ser-vices. The view of household and communal production as a distin-guishable 'moral' economy, in which actors are not guided by principles of rational choice, has been strongly criticized by both economic theorists such as Becker[24] (who showed that household decisions over choices of partners, when to marry and have children, and so on, could be explained as instances of choices by agents maximizing utility under constraint), and empirical researchers like Popkin[25] (who analysed the allocation of time and resources between communal and market-orientated production in peasant societies in terms of spreading risks and minimizing costs). In other words, much informal activity can be shown to follow a similar rationale to that of the formal economy. Goods and services are produced cooperatively and consumed collec-tively because it is too costly to organize a division of labour, or to partition and price the products, or because sharing amongst members is regarded as a benefit rather than a cost.[26]

Similarly, the informal economy of 'shadow' work that is undeclared to tax and benefit authorities, or done by immigrants in breach of their entry visa conditions,[27] unlicensed street trading in public places, or the unauthorized trade in branded products or unpackaged goods, are all rational responses to signals (prices, costs, opportunities, constraints) in the formal economy, and occupy 'niches' or hidden corners, which are actually *created* by the rules governing official, legal exchanges. Markets are, of course, politically constructed, and often their rules and institutions reflect political rather than economic norms (health and safety regulations, equal opportunity rules, minimum wages, immigration controls, taxes and social insurance contributions). These necessarily 'distort' purely economic allocations, and in this sense it is informal actors who are behaving as rational maximizers in the narrower economic sense. These laws and collective agreements thus make openings for unofficial entrepreneurs. Some neoclassical economists argue that the shadow economy reveals the over-regulation of the market by the state, and the over-provision of benefits for the unemployed and other welfare claimants.[28]

This shadow activity has been called the 'paid informal sector', to distinguish it from the 'moral economy' or unpaid sector described above.[29] The paid informal sector is distinguished from the criminal one of force, theft, fraud and trading in illicit (e.g., drugs) or misappropriated goods by the fact that it is legal apart from being unregistered and hidden from the state's authorities.[30] But this distinction is quite difficult to maintain, because of the close connections between some paid informal activities and criminal ones. For example, the sex industry includes some kinds of prostitution that are legal in everything except the avoidance of tax, and others that involve serious offences, such as abduction of foreign nationals, confiscation of passports, and coercion under threats of violence.

A good example of how the paid informal economy merges with criminal activity is the whole informal sector in South Africa. This huge volume of activity grew up in black townships there during the *apartheid* era, when racialized laws governing 'group areas' for living, and controlling black employment opportunities and movements through white districts (the pass laws), led to the emergence of a range of unregistered services. These included whole transport networks (African taxis), the production and sale of liquor, and street trading in white as well as black areas. It is plausibly argued that the growth of the informal sector was a major factor in the breaking down of *apartheid*, because the formal economy was so artificially regulated by *apartheid* laws, that acted as a fetter on the growth of new businesses, and goods and services for which there was a big demand, that black economic actors simply broke through these legal barriers, and created new relations between each other and white citizens that defied these rules.[31] The law was then forced to follow by repealing many of the *apartheid* regulations.

However, the paid informal economy in the largest black townships and squatter camps was always closely related to both subversive political activity (like the intimidation of police and government informants) and organized crime. After the collapse of the *apartheid* regime, and the electoral victory of the African National Congress (ANC) government, the policy issue became one of how to integrate black paid informal activity into the (predominantly white-controlled) formal economy. The policies adopted by the ANC government will be discussed in more detail below (see p. 185). But one of the problems besetting this policy is the persistence of very high crime rates, and especially organized gang activity and violence, in the townships and the squatter camps.[32] Policies that try to integrate, legalize or channel the informal sector towards the formal stumble on the issue of distinguishing between informality and crime; and policies for suppressing criminal activity risk harming the informal sector.

This shows that, in certain circumstances, the formal economy can come to depend for its comparatively efficient functioning on the informal. In the case of South Africa, this was because of the relative sizes of the black and white populations. Being in a large majority, black people's economic activities were a very important part of the whole economy, even when they were much poorer than whites, and excluded from most well-paid jobs. During the 1980s, the growth in the South African economy all occurred through the rise in black incomes, and much of this through activities that were formally illegal, like street trading, or were enabled through an illegal transport system (African taxis), breaches in the pass laws and group areas acts.[33] Even as *apartheid* was crumbling, white businesses depended on the growth of black custom for their expansion; advertising and product branding switched towards sales to the black population, often through illegal outlets.

The extreme case of this dependency of the formal on the informal was, of course, the Soviet system of central planning. There the cumbersome political regulation of production and distribution worked so inefficiently by the 1980s that the whole economy only functioned through informal barter between enterprises, and illicit distributive cliques that got the products to their clients. Indeed, where planned systems of production used raw materials so wastefully that they actually *subtracted* from their value, criminals who stole these, and informal entrepreneurs who used them for their own purposes, were in fact increasing economic efficiency by their actions.[34] This situation still prevails in parts of the former Soviet Union. However, here again the difficulty of disentangling the paid informal from the criminal sector is obvious. Such 'businesses' necessarily rely on mafia protection for their property rights and to enforce their 'contracts';[35] the rule of law cannot be fully established so long as this situation persists.

But other, less extreme examples of this phenomenon are available from cities or regions of First World countries. For instance, in Japan the long-established pattern of 'core' employment in large firms and peripheral subcontractors with far lower wages and less security, has been further refined into layers of subcontractors, with a lowest layer of 'informalized' family firms 'where females do unpaid, or only partly paid, work *outside* the household'.[36] In the USA there are now core and periphery firms, rather than workers. The USA now has recorded immigration of around 700,000 per year (mainly from Central and South America and Asia) and 'migrants often carry jobs with them. The creation of 25 million jobs in the USA over a period with little if any net job creation in western Europe from 1972 to 1986 is inexplicable without this supply-side contribution of the migrants'.[37] In the garment industry, a pre-modern family structure characterizes the workshops, 'in which women typically do unpaid work in the (informalized) public sphere'.[38] The same phenomenon is found in Turkish clothing and plastics workshops in Hackney, where small family firms employ unpaid family labour, and larger ones undocumented migrant workers, in the past from Turkey, but more recently from Poland.[39] In these examples it can be seen that the paid informal sector and the unpaid household sector become hard to distinguish, but that both contribute strongly to the growth of employment and trade in local and regional economies.

It is widely assumed that paid informal work is concentrated among marginal populations, and especially among those who are right outside the formal labour market, and usually claiming benefits. However, various attempts to estimate this sector,[40] and research data from the USA, UK and other European countries,[41] all indicate that the largest volume of such activity is done by people in formal paid work, in their 'spare' time – as it was in the former communist countries, and especially in Hungary, where most workers had a second job in the informal economy.[42] The important distinction here is between work which individuals choose to do as a second employment (which may be rewarding or satisfying for non-monetary reasons, or taken to pay for some expensive taste, such as saving for a foreign holiday) and work which is taken to meet basic needs. The paid informal work of mainstream citizens is far more likely to be of the first kind; that of marginal people (like illegal immigrants and claimants) of the second.[43]

Hence it is the poor and marginal who do the worst-paid and most dangerous, unpleasant, stigmatized and menial work – paid informal work being the limit case of exploited and unprotected casual labour. As Williams and Windebank, in their review of this sector, have commented:

> This informal labour market . . . is segmented in similar ways to the formal labour market, so far as gender, ethnicity and socioeconomic factors are concerned . . . The result is that there exists a structure to, and social stratification of, the paid informal sector which mirrors employment.[44]

The economists and sociologists who have researched the paid informal sector in the USA, UK and Europe are agreed that, in spatial and social terms, it does not provide an adequate standard of living,[45] mitigate inequalities to any significant extent,[46] or provide a means to economic development or welfare mechanism for deprived populations.[47] The British research suggests that claimants do see it as a way of compensating themselves for the injustice of the restrictive social policies pursued by Conservative governments between 1979 and 1997,[48] and expenditure surveys, when compared with income data, hint that this may be one of the reasons (along with growing debt) why poor people – and especially the self-employed – spend more than they officially receive.[49] But even with this additional resource they are still relatively much poorer than they were in the 1970s by expenditure measures.

In Chapter 2 (pp. 64–5) I defined exploitation in terms of the wasteful use of labour power, which could be more efficiently deployed in other uses in the economy if the exploited worker were able to devote his or her time and skills to another task. This definition took no account of the informal use of labour power, either in unpaid or paid activity. If indeed, as economists and anthropologists of the rational choice school have argued,[50] the moral and formal economies are not incommensurate, and economic actors do allocate their energies between them according to a single utility function, and calculation of the least costly way of satisfying it, then we should include all these aspects in my discussion of exploitation, and the policies to remedy it. For example, an ethnic minority immigrant woman who lacks access to the formal labour market because of discrimination is not less exploited if she works unpaid in her husband's workshop than if she works for a similar number of hours unpaid in his home; and an East European woman forced to be a prostitute by an unscrupulous racketeer club owner in the Netherlands or Belgium is not less exploited because he pays taxes on his earnings than if he does not.

Yet it is extremely difficult to devise a way of measuring exploitation that takes account of alternative uses of labour power between such radically different sectors as the most technologically sophisticated industry, the cash economy of 'moonlighting' and 'doing the double', and the private world of unpaid household work, child and elderly care. The analytical Marxist John Roemer argues that an individual or coalition is exploited if they would be better off if the assets relevant to their productive relations (e.g., capital or skills) were shared out equally, and each individual or coalition then withdrew with their share of these assets from the institutional arrangements in which they participated in the system.[51] Conversely, an individual or coalition is an exploiter if he, she or they would be made worse off by this partition and withdrawal. If it could be shown that some people had an interest in sharing and withdrawing, then others must be using power of some kind (including ideological power) to make sure this option was not open to them, because as exploiters they had an interest in continuing the system.

In principle, this test could be applied to any system of production, any assets and any productive relations, including the household and the informal economy, though in practice it is difficult to apply to the *combination* of all. Take the case of women married to wealthy men and themselves working in interesting and fulfilling professional jobs, but for pay that does not reflect the full value of their education and training[52] – hence 'outsiders' in terms of the distinction made on pp. 65–6, compared with their partners' 'insider' status. Suppose now that these women employ cleaners who are married to unemployed men, and working for cash to pay for 'extras' like clothes for their children.[53]

It could well be that, by Roemer's test, the professional women are exploited in relation to their formal labour-market participation, in systems of producing goods and services (i.e., as 'outsiders' in relation to the male 'insiders' in their employing organizations). But they are probably exploiters in relation to their cleaners, because they are paying them well below the rate which would be required to draw them into work if they were not receiving benefits. And the cleaners themselves might be exploiters in relation to the system of benefits itself, since they are doing much better than single parents, who cannot do cash work because they cannot leave their children with a partner, as the cleaners can.

Hence the lone parents might form a coalition to withdraw to their own system of cooperation with their share of benefits from the income support system, but the professional women would not make common cause with either of the other two groups to withdraw from domestic collaboration with men, even though *all* women in this example are exploited in relation to men, in the labour market, in the household, and in the paid informal economy. So the reason that there could not be a single coalition of women who are exploited in the labour market, the household and the benefits system is that the professional women have a stake in their husbands' 'insider' assets through their partnerships[54] (hence their 'supportive' approach to 'putting the family first', and rejection of redistributive politics or egalitarian collectivism of any kind[55]), while the cleaners have a stake in their partners' benefits and their cash work 'on the side', and hence would not want to share with the lone parents. So the unpaid work of household partnership, despite being the patriarchal origin of women's shared exploitation, also divides them into coalitions with conflicting interests. The professional women are primarily stakeholders in their partners' job assets; their cleaners too have a stake in partnership, if only for the prospect of their men's future employment; and the lone parents are left to the mercies of the government's agencies.

The cross-cutting relations between the formal and informal economies are therefore a very important complicating issue for distributive
justice in every imaginable society. Clearly this raises issues of both
inequality of resources and inequality of power. Social justice is not
solely concerned with redistributing income, or giving improved
services to disadvantaged groups. It is also concerned with holdings of
wealth, roles and responsibilities in all spheres of the productive and
reproductive process, and with the rules that govern every aspect of
social relations. It should address how these rules (both formal, such as
laws, and informal, such as norms and traditions) get changed, and who
has an interest in changing them.

One final example will illustrate this point. The feminist critique of
patriarchy focuses on men's ability (through holding disproportionate
wealth and power in the private and the public spheres) to impose a
patriarchal regime on women. But in a global context First World
women, now having access to better-paid jobs in the public sphere, can
employ Second and Third World women as nannies and *au pairs*, often
without the proper immigration requirements being fulfilled. In the
USA, for instance, several politicians have been denied high office when
it emerged that they had employed illegal immigrants as nannies in
their households. Differential wealth and power now affect the closest
of domestic relations between citizens of one state and those of another,
and the paid informal labour market of shadow work allows
immigrants from poorer countries to earn more than they could get
by working at home, but much less than they would get if they were
national citizens, legally employed under a proper contract.

## Social justice and the politics of welfare

The analysis in the previous section raises the following important issue
that has not been so far tackled in this book: even if we can decide, by
careful philosophical argument, based on good empirical evidence, how
social justice might be best achieved through institutional change, who
would have a political interest in achieving it? If the present rules
governing social relations, and their distributive outcomes, are shown to
be unfair, is there any realistic chance of bringing about a more just
society? Who would have an interest in changing the rules, and how
much political support could they muster?

The new Blair–Clinton orthodoxy is a reforming political movement,
that aims to change society. In the UK particularly, Tony Blair has
modernized the Labour Party, and now wishes to modernize the
country.[56] At the time of writing this, he is touring the country on a
mission to persuade his party and the electorate that reform of the

welfare state is necessary, and to gain support for carrying it through. The new orthodoxy is a creed to mobilize this support, and remoralize society and the economy, not to justify the status quo. Although it is still unclear – and the Prime Minister is very coy about speculating over – who will be winners and who losers in the process of reform, there are strong hints that those unwilling to change their behaviour and their attitudes on self-responsibility, work and private commercial provision will suffer. The state welfare system is to become a safety net for the most needy, and not a universal provider.

The new politics of welfare seeks to mobilize those who resent the amount they pay in taxes (in the UK according to the government, £80 per week for the average-income household) towards the income-maintenance system, and are concerned that what they pay is not benefiting those they regard as most deserving. The fact that almost half of the benefits budget goes to retired pensioners, and almost half the rest to people classified as disabled, gives the reforming mission a political problem, since these are conventionally the most 'deserving' groups of claimants, and since all can realistically expect to draw one or both of these themselves at some time during their lives. This raises the second problem for the new orthodoxy – that the middle class do have a stake in the welfare state, and stand to lose if benefits become more 'targeted' on the poorest, as the safety net analogy implies. Hence it is not surprising that the first restrictions and reductions in benefits were for lone parents, the classic needy yet stigmatized group, the poorest yet the most ethically controversial, and the one least organized to voice political protest, or to make an impact on electoral politics. In the USA, social insurance payments have not been cut; both the Reagan and Clinton administrations focused on the far smaller social assistance ('welfare') programmes for the poor, and especially for black women.[57]

The new politics of welfare does appeal strongly to principles of social justice but – as we have seen in Chapters 2 and 3 – to a version of social justice that is strongly rooted in the ethic of hard work in paid employment, and to the narrow mutuality of the family, rather than the wider society. Implicitly it mobilizes moral disapproval of other lifestyles, and especially those of poor people suspected of using benefits as a springboard for paid informal work, or claimants of disability benefits who are not as incapacitated as they seem. What it does not do is invite citizens to question present distributions of wealth and power, or how these interact with formal and informal work roles to shape interests in the present earnings differentials, variable work conditions and distribution of tax burdens. In this sense, the new orthodoxy acts as part of the ideological reinforcement of existing inequalities of wealth and power as well as income, and to suppress other possibilities for changes in the rules that might lead to a closer approximation to social justice.

But this does not imply that an alternative politics of welfare is impossible. If the arguments were framed in slightly different ways, they might point to quite different policy measures, and mobilize political interests behind these reforms instead. The difficulty is that such arguments would have to realign the coalitions of interest formed during the 1980s, under Margaret Thatcher and Ronald Reagan, which Tony Blair and Bill Clinton now mobilize behind their policy programmes. This would be a far more ambitious project than the present one, though necessary in the long run, if parties of reform and progress are to avoid costly mistakes, leading to long-term unpopularity, or even unelectability.

Democratic electoral politics is about organizing for majority endorsement of a programme, and in the process of organization, wealth and power play important roles. Reformist politics, that seeks to change rules and modify institutions, has to draw attention to the undesirable consequences of current arrangements, even ones which seem to offer relative security and positional advantage. The new orthodoxy has highlighted problems in the welfare state, and in this process has called into question the security that some mainstream voters see in their stake in current welfare systems (like state pensions). But it has not provoked a review of how the current distribution of assets such as wealth, control over corporate resources, or 'insider' jobs, linked to maleness and whiteness, give advantages, and how these in turn affect the distribution of resources and responsibilities in our society.

Could there ever be a majority mobilized behind an equal distribution of the advantages at present given by these assets? Roemer's test implies a slightly different question: how could institutional arrangements be changed so that they generate a distribution of income (as a proxy for welfare) such that the fewest possible citizens are exploited, to the least possible extent? One way to interpret this is that the reform should aim to ensure that, in every system of cooperation (formal and informal) that makes up an economy and society, the maximum number of members participate by choice, in their own interests, rather than out of constraint (unchosen participation).

We might define chosen participation as that which someone has an interest in doing under the current distribution of assets, and constrained participation as that which someone does, even though they would have an interest in the egalitarian redistribution of assets relevant to this system of social relations, and usually because they have no access to the resources they need other than through this system.[58] So for instance, the professional women's participation in the insider–outsider division of labour in formal employment is constrained in this sense, as is the cleaners' in low-paid informal work. And if the lone parents 'voluntarily' enlisted in New Deal measures to retrain or take short-term work, under pressure from prospective reductions in benefits, this would also be constrained participation.

The challenging questions for advocates of the basic income principle are whether it would be the measure that would maximize chosen
participation in all these spheres, by generating the most efficient
feasible productive relations under minimally exploitative conditions;
and whether a political coalition could ever be mobilized in support of
it, given the present pattern of interest-group organization, and the
current politics of welfare.

Of course it is not possible to give a conclusive answer to either of
these questions, but I shall argue for a positive one to both. Chosen
participation implies that individuals make rational decisions about
with whom they will live and bring up children, as well as where they
will work, and how they will spend their incomes. In order to be able to
make such choices, they require some fundamental autonomy, so that
they can recognize alternatives and select between them. In a First
World country, for the majority of the population any such autonomy
stems from resources that they derive from their parents in the first
instance (nurture, a roof over their heads) and from the state (education,
including a contribution to the costs of further or higher education).
Secondly, it is derived from skills they learn, and that they can use to
earn wages and salaries. And thirdly, it is derived from property rights,
given by or inherited from their families, accumulated during their
working lives, and taking the form of purchases from savings, or of
claims against state benefits funds.

The new orthodoxy argues that the task of welfare reform is to ensure
that a significantly larger group of citizens gain this basic autonomy
through participation in the labour market. But this is a wildly unfeasible
project. In the first instance, in Europe the proportion of the working-age
population who are in employment has never been over two-thirds. In
1965, when the 'golden age of full employment' was at its peak, and
labour had its largest share of national income, only 65.2 per cent of the
working-age population of the current European Union had a job. Most
of these were men, and in full-time employment. By 1992, this had fallen
to 60.8 per cent,[59] despite the enormous increase in participation by
married women, most of whom work part-time. It is extremely unlikely
that any set of policy measures can reverse this trend. But – even more
significantly – the proportion of employment paying wages and salaries
sufficient to sustain subsistence, whether for a family or a single person,
has declined also, under the pressure of globalization, and with the
falling share taken by labour out of total income. Even in economies with
relatively high participation rates like the USA and the UK, most
households need two or more earners to subsist, and even with these the
resources devoted to subsidizing the low wages of the working poor (by
tax credits, or means-tested supplements like family credit and housing
benefits) have grown substantially over the past two decades.

In other words, despite the best efforts of the Thatcher and Reagan
administrations in the 1980s, neither skills nor property rights give

TABLE 5.1   *UK recipients of social security benefits, 1996*

|  | **National insurance benefit (000)** | **Income support (000)** |
|---|---|---|
| Retirement pensioners | 10,451 | 1,764 |
| Unemployed claimants | 397 | 1,495 |
| One-parent families | – | 1,059 |
| Incapacitated claimants | 1,066 | 786 |

*Source: DSS, Social Security Statistics, 1997*

assets that can provide basic autonomy for the majority of the population during their working age or in retirement. This can be very easily demonstrated. If savings-based property rights were sufficient to give autonomy, then the majority of those who became unemployed or disabled, or who retired, would not qualify for means-tested benefits. In fact, the majority of men who are unemployed for over a year in the UK do claim and receive income support, as do the majority of those receiving incapacity benefits[60] (see Table 5.1). Another 17 per cent of pensioners qualify for means-tested assistance, and it is estimated that a further 1.2 million could be eligible if they claimed it.[61] As far as skills are concerned, although a minority of men receive wage subsidies through the state when they are in work, a majority of women are forced to claim public assistance of one kind or another (income support or family credit) when they become lone parents.[62] Hence we can see quite clearly that participation in the formal economy for the majority is constrained rather than chosen, and that this must influence participation by women in the household also, since so few of them can afford to leave their partners without recourse to benefits which are stigmatized and inadequate.

It is therefore women who stand to gain most from a redistribution of resources such that the maximum proportion of the population have basic autonomy, and can therefore participate in the household, the informal public sphere and the labour market on chosen terms. This in itself would be a strong argument for basic income – that it would give women this autonomy, by guaranteeing them a subsistence income in their own right. But taken together with the fact that a significant minority of men lack such autonomy by virtue of their skills and private property rights, the case for basic income becomes much stronger. In so far as each individual would then have an unconditional income (unlike the contingency entitlements of the present system, with increased pressure to seek work or demonstrate incapacities, and the disincentive effects of means-tested benefits that are withdrawn with increased earnings or savings), this increase in fundamental autonomy would be a major contribution to the equalization of power and reduction of exploitation in every sphere.

I have already indicated why this common interest in the implementation of the basic income principle is not made visible in the electoral politics of countries like the USA and the UK. As I showed in the previous section (pp. 167–9), individual interests are not aggregated into common interests in this simple arithmetic way.[63] Women married to men with 'insider' jobs, occupational pension rights and perks, calculate their interests as members of households with a stake in the existing rules and distributions, from which their families gain positional advantage. Even families of households with two or more low incomes reckon that they do better under the present system (if not in income then in status and access to other welfare-enhancing resources), and resent the taxes they pay to support claimants, rather than supporting an egalitarian redistribution of basic autonomy of this kind. Thus disadvantage in the labour market is concentrated in those households where no one is in employment, or which only have a single low-wage earner, which alone perceive themselves as clear winners from such a scheme.

The new Blair–Clinton orthodoxy is serious about addressing this situation in the name of social justice. It tries to mobilize interest groups (including business federations and employers) behind the idea of combating exclusion, especially in deprived neighbourhoods, by getting workless households back into the labour market. The goal is quite legitimate, but the means are flawed. With only a slightly different 'spin' on its message, the new orthodoxy could advocate the basic income principle, in the name of just the same goals.

1   *An employment-friendly system.* Because it would give far less disincentives to employment than either means-tested income support (which has an unemployment trap in relation to low wages) or means-tested wage supplements like family credit and housing benefits (which are withdrawn as earnings rise) it would promote employment, by giving all on average and below-average earnings equal incentives to work. Assuming higher tax rates on the higher earners (as at present), their higher salaries would ensure that, in absolute rather than percentage terms, their incentives would as now be greater, not less, than those on average earnings or below.

2   *A savings-friendly system.* Because the basic income is not means-tested, it encourages savings, even by small savers. This allows them to accumulate private property rights, and to be self-responsible over all their needs above those met by the guaranteed subsistence provided through the basic income.

3   *Equality of opportunity.* Because the basic income is given at exactly the same rate to all citizens of working age, and extra supplements are given only in relation to the higher costs of living associated with chronic illnesses, disabilities and handicaps, it promotes

equality of opportunity of all citizens, regardless of sex, skin colour, religious affiliation, or any other factor.

4   *Targeting those in genuine need.* Because the basic income would be automatically 'taxed back' from all who enter the labour market, or who have property incomes, and receive payment, it would be targeted directly on those with lowest incomes. It would achieve this without the stigma and disincentives of means tests and without the problem of take-up with benefits that have to be claimed under special conditions.

The interest groups likely to oppose these arguments would be those with the greatest stakes in the present distributions of opportunities and resources, viz. working-age men with large property holdings or claims, or 'insider' job assets, and the perks that these include. Their stake in present distributions is well disguised. Although they argue that they are entitled to their high rewards, since they hold their positions on merit, work harder and take more responsibility than any other economic actors, they in fact enjoy a far greater range of freedoms and choices than any other. Their participation in the economy is chosen, to the extent that most can retire relatively early, and still enjoy a good proportion of their present incomes, and a secure future.

Although they are taxed at a higher rate than others, this still leaves them with considerable income advantages, and they also get the benefit of a large number of tax allowances, both against work expenses of various kinds, and against savings and long-term investments. Those now in middle age received generous tax relief on mortgage payments, to the extent that – with price inflation – they virtually got their houses free.[64] Even if income tax rates remained exactly the same as now (i.e., an effective marginal tax rate on higher earnings equivalent to the present rate plus national insurance contributions), they would be rather worse off than at present, because of these other benefits that they enjoy by virtue of disguised tax allowances and exemptions. It is for this reason – that they gain more from the existing welfare state arrangements than poor people do – that they would oppose a change to an equal basic income for all.

However, it would be possible to make the political case for a basic income reform of the welfare state even to this group in quite convincing terms. The following arguments would appeal directly to their interests – and hence indirectly to those of their household partners and their offspring.

5   *Slowing down the pace of change.* As argued in Chapter 3 (pp. 93–4), a basic income approach to reform of the welfare state would delay the impact of globalization on 'insiders'' job assets, by restraining competition from 'outsiders' (women, young people, the

unemployed and excluded). In so far as all European countries adopted this principle, it would also restrain competition from relevant foreigners. Far from being a radical proposal for accelerating change, it could be presented as a way of slowing it, by offering 'insiders' a principle of justice through which they could compensate 'outsiders' for their disadvantages, and still retain some advantages of their own, on the grounds that this would benefit all, by conserving the value of the human capital of the nation state.

6   *Minimizing wasteful use of resources and rising social costs*: The basic income would restrain destructive competition in a more effective and less wasteful way than any other system available to government. By offering citizens 'time out'of the labour market for cultural or political pursuits, for investment in higher skills or improvements to their homes, for looking after the next generation, or people with special needs, or simply for travel, recreation and personal development, it would maximize chosen participation and minimize constrained activity. If this meant that less labour was supplied than the economy needed for efficient functioning, the basic income would inevitably have to fall to a level that would once more increase formal labour supply. On the other hand, in combination with other measures (see below) the basic income would reduce socially wasteful transaction and enforcement costs. Because it would be provided automatically, it would cut the rising budget for staff in income maintenance who assess, scrutinize, maintain surveillance, counsel, warn, admonish, disqualify and prosecute claimants. Above all, it would contribute to a fall in criminal action against the better-off by resentful, poor people, conscious of injustice, and with no other obvious means to compensate themselves for their grievances. Since the criminal justice budget is the most rapidly rising element in public expenditure in both the USA and the UK, this would be a very important argument in favour of basic income to higher-rate taxpayers.

In all these ways, a reforming government could appeal to the interests of potentially hostile voters to argue for a basic-income reform of the tax and income maintenance systems. Indeed, it might be easier to persuade them of this than to bring off the changes currently promoted by Tony Blair in the UK. As we saw in the first chapter (pp. 22–3), reform must somehow save taxpayers' money, get more of the poor into work, and give those in genuine need at least as much or more. In order to pull this off, the new Labour government is forced to contemplate cuts in the rights to state benefits of better-off citizens (Harriet Harman's 'affluence tests'), or significant reductions in the benefits of those – such as disabled workers or lone parents – not judged to be in 'genuine need' (which increase the insecurity and fear of a much wider group). Hence the repeated refrain of 'hard choices', and the time borrowed in early 1998 to persuade the public of the need for change, and rethink how exactly to accomplish it at least political cost.

## Liberal justice, contributions and the costs of basic income

However, I have still not directly addressed the two supposedly crucial objections to the basic income principle – that the unconditional guarantee of subsistence to those who do not supply labour to the formal economy (and perhaps not to the informal economy either) is unjust, and that it would cost taxpayers too much. In this section I shall discuss both these objections, and their implications for the politics of welfare.

First, although – for reasons to be analysed below – it is not obvious why liberals should object to the principle of an unconditional basic income, it is obvious why authoritarian socialists should do so. Particularly in its Stalinist version, authoritarian socialism used the power of the state to squeeze the idleness of the rich under capitalism out of the economic system. It substituted the exploitation of skill and expertise for capitalist exploitation of labour power in general,[65] confiscated large parts of the value added by skilled workers in the productive process, and invested it in ever more gigantic industrial plant, to employ more unskilled, low-productivity workers. The danger is that policies for increasing labour market participation for its own sake might have a similar effect under the new orthodoxy, because work-creation can become an end in itself, to be pursued irrespective of inefficiency and cost.

In the liberal tradition, there is no objection to those with property incomes doing no paid or unpaid work, or those who have accumulated enough pension claims retiring early. Despite the notion that all home-based women are busy in unpaid domestic chores and child care duties, no one raises a criticism of a well-to-do wife who hires a cleaner and a nanny to do these things for her. Yet even liberals experience moral qualms about voluntary unemployment among benefits claimants, and about rich mothers getting child benefit payments. There is something about the receipt of money from public funds that offends the sense of justice built into the liberal tradition, as was shown in Chapter 2 (pp. 55–6).

In the previous section, six impeccably liberal reasons – that it is employment-friendly, savings-friendly, promotes equality of opportunity, targets those in genuine need, slows down the pace of change that threatens existing distributions, and minimizes waste – were given for the basic income principle. Other approaches might be found that could accomplish any one of these aims better, but none that does them all simultaneously, and reconciles them to each other. To this can be added that the basic income principle promotes individual autonomy and minimizes coercion, which is (or should be) the fundamental value of political liberalism. The only requirement that it fails to meet is that all should be required (under penalty) to contribute to systems of cooperation from which they benefit.

Since when was this a principle of *political* – as opposed to moral – liberalism? As I argued in Chapter 3 (pp. 81–2), the hallmark of the liberal tradition is that rights of citizenship are strong and unconditional, and obligations weak and conditional. If this is true for civil and political rights, why should it not be so for social rights also? The supposed evil of the citizen who might not choose to work for the common good is much less, according to liberal principles, than the very real evil of forced labour and other losses of the rights of freedom.

Against this, it can be urged that social justice demands that distributive principles be grounded in clear normative arguments for particular outcomes, rather than simply in the avoidance of possible wrongs. But this again is a distortion of the liberal view. Because of its strong emphasis on personal and property rights, liberal social justice insists that individual resource entitlements by ownership – even if these are historically grounded in force or fraud[66] – are respected as far as possible, and that taxation is kept to the minimum consistent with efficiency and justice. This implies that market distributions are accepted unless there is clear evidence that they are unjust; and this is certainly how the new orthodoxy tackles issues of distribution. So if it is possible to show – as I believe it is – that basic income redistributions are in the long run likely to be less demanding, in terms of taxation and state expenditure, than the programme of the new orthodoxy, then this in itself should count as a liberal argument (of a Hayekian kind) for basic income.

There are, of course, many possible normative arguments for the principle of giving every citizen a guaranteed sum, equivalent to their subsistence needs, before they enter the labour market or the household. The strongest is the one for universal equal autonomy, which was developed in the previous section. Without this, the freedom of exchange that is supposed to characterize the labour market is an illusion. The constrained participation of the majority is simply emphasized by caricature in the forced labour of workfare and welfare-to-work participants.

How are we to understand, from a normative perspective, the common pool from which the basic income is distributed? What are the normative grounds for collecting it, and then distributing it equally to all members, rather than paying it according to merit of some kind, or demonstrable need? The clearest way of understanding the moral nature of this common fund (or any other collected out of compulsory contributions from the factors of production) is that it represents the unearned technical legacy and heritage of past labour, skill, ingenuity and invention, that accounts for such a great part of the productivity of capital and labour in a First World economy.[67] Only a very small portion of the value of the present output of the economy is directly attributable to any factor in today's productive processes. The greater portion is contributed by the inheritance of technology, organization, wealth, tradition and ordinary know-how that comes to present employees and employers from the past. There is no way of distributing this according to ancestral merit, nor is it obvious how needs (other than those special costs associated with the daily life of someone with a chronic illness or handicap) constitute a valid claim upon this fund. According to liberal principles, it seems just to pay an equal share to all.

If anything, the principle of equal autonomy points to a rather generous basic income for each citizen, drawn from such a common fund. But liberal economy and efficiency can devise a compromise between the normative demands of justice, and the practical requirements of prosperity. This is the 'equilibrating principle', defined on p. 98. The basic income should be at just that level which allows the labour power supplied to be efficiently used for socially necessary purposes, as a higher provision would lead to some tasks not being done, or being done less efficiently, and a lower one would involve the inefficient, wasteful use of labour power, and hence a form of exploitation of those workers' energies and skills.

What indications are there of how much this level of basic income would cost – in tax rates – in a society like the UK? The first thing to say about this question is that it is slightly misleadingly framed. The basic income is a pure transfer, and involves less expenditure of resources – staff time, buildings, materials – than any other conceivable system of income transfers. It is not like a redistribution of goods and services, or a collective infrastructural good (see p. 120). Hence it does not reduce the total volume of resources available for the production of goods and services, as taxes raised for those kinds of public expenditures do.

Secondly, there have been many attempts to calculate the amounts required to provide an adequate basic income for all, and estimates of the tax rates associated with them vary between the alarmingly high (around 70 per cent in some analyses[68]) and the extremely modest (less than current British tax rates in more libertarian proposals[69]). The most careful and responsible calculations have been made by Hermione Parker and Holly Sutherland,[70] based on detailed study of household budgets and the real costs of various needs (unlike actual social welfare provision) and the attempt to minimize sudden gains and losses in a transitional period between the final provision of basic incomes and the present system. Parker and Sutherland aim to set out various options for transition to a basic income scheme that improve incentives for

TABLE 5.2 *Value (£/week) of income tax allowances plus child benefit, compared with TBI of £20 plus earned-income tax credit of £7.25, 1997–1998*

| | Existing system | | | |
| --- | --- | --- | --- | --- |
| | **20%** | **23%** | **40%** | **TBI 97** |
| Single | 15.56 | 17.89 | 31.12 | 27.25 |
| Married couple (1 wage) | 20.84 | 23.17 | 36.40 | 47.25 |
| Married couple (2 wage) | 36.40 | 41.06 | 67.52 | 54.50 |
| Unmarried couple (1 wage) | 15.56 | 17.98 | 31.12 | 47.25 |
| Unmarried couple (2 wage) | 31.12 | 35.78 | 62.24 | 54.50 |
| Couple + 2 ch (1 wage) | 40.89 | 43.22 | 56.45 | 87.25 |
| Couple + 2 ch (2 wage) | 56.45 | 61.11 | 87.57 | 94.50 |
| Single + 2 ch | 46.94 | 49.27 | 62.50 | 73.30 |

Assumption: In two-earner couples, each spouse/partner has same marginal tax rate.

*Source:* Parker and Sutherland, *How to Get Rid of the Poverty Trap* (1998), Table 1, p. 12.

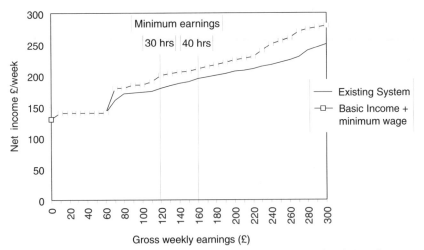

FIGURE 5.1 *The poverty trap, April 1997: existing system compared with TBI of £20/week and minimum hourly wage of £4.00 (married couple with two children under 11) (Parker and Sutherland, How to Get Rid of the Poverty Trap, 1998, Fig. 3, p. 13)*

those at present excluded from labour markets, but do not leave individuals and households suddenly exposed to new risks, or significantly worse off than they are at present. Their proposals are broadly revenue-neutral in the short to medium term, though obviously there are gainers (mainly single-earner households with children, and women generally) and losers (mainly higher-income households, and men).

Table 5.2 illustrates the effects of a small Transitional Basic Income (TBI) of £20 per week for every man, woman and child, to replace tax allowances (with the exception of residual age allowance) and which is deducted from existing social security benefits (except that National Insurance retirement pension, incapacity benefit and widow's pensions are reduced by £15 instead of £20). Figure 5.1 illustrates the consequences of this TBI plus a minimum wage of £4 per hour.

These distributive consequences stem from their assumptions (for instance, about the need to retain a means-tested housing benefit as a residual feature of the system, for a small minority of households with low earnings and high housing costs) rather than from intrinsic features of the basic income principle itself. It could be introduced in a number of alternative ways, with different effects on groups of taxpayers and beneficiaries.

## Community development and social control

It is now appropriate to turn to the other main criticism of the basic income principle – that even if it is justifiable in its capacity to give equal autonomy to all citizens in a society, it is undesirable because it cannot supply the motivating factors that would lead them to do the work that is necessary for social reproduction, or provide them with the opportunities to contribute to the common good in the ways required for human flourishing.

I have already indicated at the start of this chapter that I believe this criticism to be justified, but not good grounds for rejecting the basic income approach to distributive issues. The basic income is a necessary but not a sufficient condition for social justice, because it needs to be backed up (or underpinned) by other measures that will motivate active contribution and participation, and provide opportunities for fulfilling work. This is especially so after a 20 year period when the organization of work, and the incentives for doing it, have been demotivating for a section of the population, who have become disconnected, deskilled and disaffected, and have turned to other ways of achieving their ends and developing their capacities.

In the remaining sections of this chapter, I shall consider the measures that might be taken under an alternative approach to address these issues. In this section, I shall analyse how local authorities, voluntary agencies (non-government organizations) and grassroots community groups might work together to improve the quality of life of people living in districts that have been deserted by the market and the state, in order to achieve economic regeneration and social support. In the next, I shall outline the essential features of a new politics of welfare, in which responsibilities are negotiated rather than imposed, and the division of

labour – in households, as in the public sphere – results from democratic dialogue and compromise, rather than a struggle for power and
domination.

The communitarian rhetoric of the Blair–Clinton orthodoxy on
welfare is its least developed element in policy terms. It emphasizes
family values, self-help, voluntary associations and civic responsibility
in an 'age of giving'.[71] It draws its inspiration from the writings of
communitarians who are backward-looking in their appeal to the
traditional ethics of small-town virtue, and particularly of the social
control exercised by neighbours and extended families over young
people,[72] and the mutuality and self-responsibility practised in the
working-class associations.[73] The closest links between this rhetoric and
the policy programme of the new orthodoxy are in law and order
measures like curfews,[74] tagging, neighbourhood watch schemes and
police liaison groups. It sits uneasily with the pluralism of present-day
communities and their cultures, with migration, multi-ethnic societies
and transnational groups, and with the public–private globalism of the
Internet and satellite TV.

This is not the only possible form of communitarian theory, or the
only possible policy programme that such ideas can inspire. The radical
agenda[75] builds on the existing network of informal groups and grassroots community associations in marginal neighbourhoods, and seeks to
mobilize their communal resources and release trapped energies; but it
demands important institutional changes for its realization,[76] to enable
informal economic activity to feed into the development of the neighbourhood's resources. It concerns itself with crime and order, but seeks
local support in building alternative activities and facilities for disaffected youth.[77] It addresses the social exclusion of residents in
deprived areas by trying to extend their scope for informal collective
action in their own interests, rather than trying to coerce them into
activities that serve the interests of mainstream citizens.

The new orthodoxy's approach to social exclusion is to reintegrate
members of deprived communities and deviant groups into mainstream
society through the formal labour market, and to crack down on crime
and undeclared cash work through policing and fraud surveillance
squads. These approaches cut right across the social relations of
marginal housing estates, and the informal collective action practices of
excluded people. In particular, they fail to recognize any potential for
economic regeneration of these districts, or mobilization of these people,
in the informal activities in which they are already engaged. The new
orthodoxy is a project for remoralization through compulsory integration, taking no account of the rational resistance of these people to such
measures, or of the positive potential of their cultural practices.

The informal culture of marginal communities poses problems for
social policy because of its diversity and apparent contradictions. On
the one hand, there is collective action for mutual aid and support,

mainly by women, and especially by lone parents.[78] This provides a degree of cohesion and stability in such communities, and survives against the odds, often with little back-up and no resources from official agencies, but sometimes with an input of expertise and infrastructural provision by voluntary agencies. On the other hand, and often linked to such networks by domestic partnership and kinship, there are circuits and groups of people (mostly men) involved in drug dealing, theft and undeclared work for cash,[79] resisting the controls of the official agencies, and scorning the rules and structures of the formal economy.

Yet both these aspects of the culture of deprived communities can be understood within the same theoretical framework as economically rational responses to recent changes in the formal labour market and in social policy.[80] Increased investment by poor people in their local networks of support, and increased unauthorized income-generating activities, reflect respectively restricted access to state welfare resources, and the decline in opportunities and incentives for formal employment. Attempts to suppress the illegal aspects of these practices tend to raise social costs. In the UK since 1993, despite official crime statistics showing a fall in the number of offences, the prison population has grown by almost 40 per cent, and is set to rise still more.[81] In the state of California, spending on criminal corrections now exceeds that on higher education, and the prison building programme threatens to consume the whole state budget; there are more black men in prisons in the USA than in universities, and each place costs more.[82] On the trends of the 1990s, by the middle of the next century, everyone in California will be either a prisoner or a prison guard, neatly solving the welfare-to-work problem. The new politics of welfare becomes the politics of enforcement,[83] and the attempt to restrict spending on social services ends up in increased expenditure, but on correction and control.

As we have seen in the earlier sections of this chapter (pp. 164–7), paid informal economic activity by poor people is rational because it provides income-generating opportunities at low cost, often (when subsidized by benefits) with better returns than are available in the formal labour market. The costs of taking short-term, low-paid employment are high, because claimants lose their entitlements, which take a long time to re-establish when they have to claim again.[84] Because plenty of paid informal work is available, the costs and risks of taking this are low, since it is difficult to detect in an environment where it has become normal practice. A network of information and exchange around such work grows up, and a culture of acceptance of these practices, with denunciations confined to instances of personal spite and rivalry, or perceived greed in exceeding informal limits on hours and earnings.[85] This culture of resistance (or survival) merges at one end into the informal support systems of the female network (which include child minding by lone parents for each other while they do undeclared cash work) and legal exchanges, such as trade in animals and fish that counters the cycle of formal economic participation and unemployment in households.[86] It merges at the other end with crime and hustling, and one problem for policy is how to promote the positive features of some aspects of this culture, and discourage the negative ones.

The informal culture of paid work is able to respond flexibly to short-term changes in the micro-economy, including needs within such neighbourhoods that are not met by commercial enterprises, most shops having withdrawn to more promising locations. By producing and selling goods and services in a tightly bounded locality, its activity is protected against competition from outside the area. Ironically, therefore, this extreme form of local protectionism is more effective than that which most firms and family businesses in the formal economy are able to foster, because informal economic actors have an effective monopoly of certain supplies in areas that are no-go ones for formal providers.[87]

Furthermore, the economies of such districts are inevitably more communal than those of mainstream communities, because a large element of barter and exchange of labour services enters into daily transactions between households, and especially between members of kinship groups, as well as among men who do paid informal work together. The spirit and practice of such exchanges was captured in a quotation from one member of a close-knit community of poor people, speaking to a researcher about her husband's network of friends who help improve each other's houses:

> I mean, they don't sort of keep up and score, you know. I mean Gordon might come out and borrow, say, three things in one week and he [husband] might go out and like, borrow the one, you know what I mean. I mean there's no equivalent to it.[88]

In addition to this informal system of exchange and barter, collective consumption is a more conspicuous aspect of life in these communities than in mainstream (and especially suburban bourgeois) ones. Residents attach considerable importance to social and recreational clubs, to parties and other communal gatherings, and informal groups – despite the dearth of suitable buildings and facilities for these activities.

In the 1960s and 1970s, before the residential polarization described in Chapter 4 (see pp. 124–6) took full effect, the practice of community development in poorer districts, which was borrowed from the developing world by theorists who had studied and worked in Africa and Asia,[89] was seen as a promising way of improving the relative situation of these communities, and preventing marginalization and deviance. Although the movement for community development is still strong in many First World countries[90] (and stronger in Scotland and Northern Ireland than elsewhere in the UK[91]), it has not fulfilled its potential as a way of mobilizing the poorest members of society, partly because of the conflict orientation of many of the early practitioners in the late 1960s and early 1970s,[92] and the subsequent nervousness of official agencies and local politicians.

In the 1990s, the idea of *partnerships* between local authorities, social welfare agencies and collective actors in the informal economy has been explored in several countries, including Canada[93] and Italy,[94] and now it is being taken up by English local authorities, partly in response to budget constraints over the provision of social and infrastructural services.[95] The principle of partnership is that local people in deprived areas play a much more active role in defining their own needs, and in providing the services to meet them, than under traditional, paternalistic arrangements, based on technocratic planning and political bargaining, together with professional expansionism, and the standardized public provision of welfare goods.[96] Sometimes these developments have taken place *within* local authority departments, such as community education or social services,[97] and sometimes *between* them, as a separate community development strategy,[98] with the active involvement of non-government organizations, self-help groups and churches in the district.

The most ambitious example of this approach is in South Africa, which has an enormous informal economy in black townships and squatter camps, and also a very high rate of violent crime (see pp. 164–5 above). There new initiatives in the training of social workers, and in policies within public services, aim at shifting the focus of practice towards income-generating projects and cooperatives among poor people, in order to build a stronger informal sector, and foster a more cohesive civic culture.[99] By mobilizing and linking together the skills of disadvantaged people and the local authorities' resources, these policies hope to build bridges with the formal economy. These initiatives acknowledge that the formal economy cannot absorb the enormous pool of underemployed black labour, and that the (formerly illegal) entrepreneurial projects and casual employment of these communities can provide an important source of economic and civic regeneration. Informal economic actors are also included as stakeholders in new institutions for re-negotiating the rules and rights of post *apartheid* social justice in spheres such as housing, planning and development.[100]

Some such principles are implicit in new approaches to economic regeneration and social provision in the UK; for example, the Emmaeus Foundation emphasizes economic independence and productivity in its centres for homeless people,[101] and the government guidelines and principles for Single Regeneration funding require public bodies to consult and form partnerships with groups and organizations for community action in the 'social economy' (including housing and community development projects). There are a number of centres where partnerships between local government, business and informal-sector actors have been attempted.[102] But all this is made much more difficult if the central thrust of government policy is to replace informal activity by

formal employment, or training for it, and if the rules of benefit systems
are tightened to penalize paid informal work.

Indeed, the new orthodoxy makes an even stricter distinction
between the economic activity by which men and women are supposed
(or required) to earn family income, and the social support by which
they help each other, enjoy a shared quality of life, and address the
problems of their neighbourhoods. In deprived communities like these,
such distinctions make little sense. They cut across the grain of social
relations, and the links between male and female networks that sustain
community life.

I am suggesting here that the policies and practices of government
agencies in the UK tend to impede the mobilization of regenerative
energies in decaying neighbourhoods. Official practice has become cut
off from radical ideas of community development – in mainstream
education, housing, health and in the personal social services. Since the
mid-1980s, they have become more concerned (under the influence
of legislation to decentralize budgets and encourage a managerial
approach to cost-conscious decisions and value for taxpayers' money)
with competing for resources and positional advantage, with meeting
efficiency targets, and with responding to the price signals of the new
quasi-markets they inhabit. With these priorities, individuals from
disadvantaged neighbourhoods come to be perceived as costly and
disruptive, and hence liable to be excluded from school (see pp. 132–3),
struck off doctors' lists,[103] evicted or prosecuted.

A particularly clear example of this is found in social work policy
and practice. It might be thought that some of the issues identified in
this section would provide an opening for social work to extend its
scope, and broaden its approach to communal problems, as has
happened in South Africa since the fall of the *apartheid* regime. Instead
of focusing narrowly on the special needs and problem behaviours of
individuals and the care of dysfunctional families, it could reach into
the wider tasks of empowering citizens to respond proactively to social
issues, and mediate between community initiatives and formal welfare
systems.[104] Elsewhere in Europe (for instance in Germany[105]) some such
developments are taking place. But in the UK, social work has become
trapped in a hard place, and is not taking advantage of this potential
opening.

Far from broadening its concerns, most recent legislation, policy and
practice has tended to narrow them.[106] The management of individual
care plans, purchased from commercial providers, has become the
dominant model of social service. On the other hand, the problems of
deprived communities have increasingly been seen in terms of the
organizational management of risk, dangerousness and correction – as
issues of assessment, control and punishment. These changes privatize
and familialize issues of care, and criminalize issues of poverty and
insecurity.[107] As British society has become more divided and

conflictual, social work practitioners have been drawn back into the administrative sphere, as assessors, managers and monitors of care, and enforcers of the law and standards of behaviour.[108] When not involved in arm's-length, office-based work (such as court reports), their direct, face-to-face encounters with clients have been rationed to focused therapeutic or authoritative interventions.[109] All these developments have pulled social workers away from the perception of themselves as brokers of the informal sphere, who humanize and particularize the public provision of welfare, and help strengthen community networks of social support, and towards the authoritative enforcement of legal rules and societal norms.

In practice, therefore, it is difficult to draw social workers or their departments out of contractual relationships with the voluntary sector, a policing relationship with deprived communities, and a high-handed, power-laden practice style, and into dialogue and partnership with other local authority departments and residents' groups over community development issues.[110] Yet the current style of practice is increasingly recognized as wasteful and redundant, as well as sometimes unjust. For instance, in the field of child care, research has shown that an increasing proportion of resources go on investigation of (often anonymous) complaints of child abuse; yet in only 15 per cent of these are the children considered to require protection, and in only 4 per cent are they removed from their parents under court orders.[111] Studies in Australia[112] and elsewhere indicate that, as child protection systems are established, complaints go up as much as 140 per cent in four years; yet the number of proven incidents of significant harm to children remains almost constant, with the largest number of these being minor injuries and emotional trauma.

What happens in a divided and unequal society is that complaints are made about poor families, lone parents and members of ethnic minority groups.[113] Social workers spend their time and their expensive skills in trying to assess the risks in thousands of such cases, yet few resources are left over for giving the services they have been trained to offer. The social control element in social work – as in other social services professions – becomes the dominant element in professional activity, and the enabling and preventive aspects of the work become neglected. Social workers take on the role of Monty Python's Spanish Inquisition, rushing to investigate one complaint after another, never expected when they arrive, and seldom missed when they depart.

If it is true that those who have developed cultures of resistance to the expectations of mainstream society and its official agents would not easily slip back into that mainstream simply by virtue of being given a basic income, it is also manifestly the case that the skills and goodwill of many professionals could be better deployed in motivating, enabling and supporting such people than they are at present. Partnerships between official agencies and poor people always involve difficult negotiations of power differentials, and the policing role can never be wholly absent. But the present orientation of British social work intensifies these difficulties.

In this section, I have argued that there are grounds for concern that, taken in isolation from other policy measures, the basic income would do little to address the social exclusion and lack of opportunities of particular groups and communities in First World societies. Because they have experienced some 20 years of neglect and hostility, the residents of districts where poverty is concentrated have adapted culturally and strategically to their exclusion, in ways that will not be easily changed. Conversely, the British social services have also adapted to a divided society, and to the changed opportunities and constraints of the public sector. They have become more orientated towards the tasks of risk management and social control,[114] and towards the interests of the welfare 'clubs' they organize – their school, health clinic, housing estate or residential home. It will take an equally large cultural and behavioural change to shift them from the policies and practices associated with these systems of social control and budgetary management.

The change required would reorientate them towards the support and development of collective action by poor and excluded people, for the improvement of the quality of their shared lives. It would be concerned with the rebuilding of the social and physical environment of those neighbourhoods; with constructing and maintaining new collective facilities, and new groups to act within them; with supporting and channelling entrepreneurial initiatives; and with strengthening existing networks of care and assistance. I have elsewhere raised the question of whether basic income, if it came now, is already too late for people who have adapted to the ghetto, the prison, the children's home or the meaningless drudgery of the welfare-to-work programme.[115] The incentives offered by a basic income plus low-paid work would be small compared with the opportunities and rewards of drug dealing and crime. The challenge for the social services would be to make more visible the individual benefits and shared advantages of participating in existing and new networks of voluntary and paid collective activity, to regenerate common lives of communities of fate.

## The politics of negotiation and compromise

In the previous section I have, like the Blair–Clinton orthodoxy itself, focused on the most extreme examples of social exclusion – the concentrations of poor people in deprived districts. But the issue of how a basic-income society would motivate and organize its citizens to do the socially necessary tasks of the community in an efficient and fair way is far wider than this. It embraces all the work at present done on an unpaid basis in households, and all the paid personal services rendered by poorer people for those who are better off, as well as the infrastructural tasks that keep society healthy, mobile and efficient, and the care provided for its most vulnerable and dependent members.

These issues focus on the questions that have been implicitly raised throughout the book so far. In Chapter 2 I pointed out that the globalization of industrial production and trade meant that issues of social justice now become more focused on the division of 'domestic' (national) labour over tasks of social reproduction. These concern questions of power and justice between men and women, white and black, rich and poor. They ask why women should still do most of the unpaid work of the household and take responsibility for the organization of child care; but they also ask why lone parents should be made to clean Harriet's toilet (see pp. 37), and why black people should find it harder to get promotion at work, and be more at risk of losing their benefits or being sent to prison than white.

The new orthodoxy has three characteristic ways of dealing with these issues. In the first place, it refuses to recognize any that stem from fundamental inequalities of wealth and power, such as those between rich employers of domestic servants and those who take such work. Second, it argues that flexible labour markets can resolve all the problems that might be raised, because well-trained and hence employ-able labour power can find its most appropriate place in the division of labour under equality of opportunity. And third, where incentives fail (as they do across a wide range of low-paid insecure work) it relies on the power of the state to enforce conformity with the demands of the market, by requiring unemployed and other claimants to train or take such work, or punishing them for resisting these requirements.

It could well be argued that the line I have taken in this chapter is insufficiently radical on issues such as these. As was indicated in Chapter 1 (pp. 16–17), the project of social justice is a liberal reformist rather than a revolutionary one. Although the basic income approach to distributive questions has been dismissed as utopian and unrealistic by some on the left as often as it has been hastily sidelined by others who worry about whether they could still be able to get their toilets cleaned, there is certainly a case to be made against it, for failing to address underlying issues of wealth and power in society, that would continue to influence the division of labour after a basic income was introduced. In this section I shall argue that for liberals – those who want to minimize coercion in social relations, and especially the use of compulsion by political authority and its official agents – the kind of society envisaged by a basic income is the best approximation to social justice available in the immediate future.

Throughout the book I have argued that the new orthodoxy leads to a politics of welfare that is moralistic, authoritarian and intolerant; that divides the working class on lines of perceived 'deservingness' and moral worth, and mobilizes the self-righteous and judgemental majority against those they neither know nor understand; and that it drives up enforcement costs, and ends by spending most of the welfare budget on control, surveillance, compulsion and correction. This is not social justice; it is not even liberalism. It is no wonder that the term 'liberal' now has a connotation of 'soft on crime' and 'too generous to the (black) poor' in the USA. The new politics of welfare is a departure from the best traditions of that country, as well as a worrying revival of some of the worst traditions of politics in Europe.

Also implicit in my analysis throughout is the notion that issues about the division of labour and responsibility for the tasks of social reproduction could be negotiated between self-responsible and morally autonomous actors, if each had an independent income for subsistence through a state-organized basic income scheme.[116] This suggests that such agents could reach voluntary agreements on these fundamental questions for social justice in the political environment created by a single social policy measure, reinforced by a set of other public services for giving practical assistance to the most vulnerable individuals, and support to the most deprived communities. Are there any grounds for such optimism about a politics of negotiation and compromise, given the remaining inequalities of power and wealth in society that would survive the implementation of a basic income scheme?

This question touches on a whole strand of recent political theory that is concerned with the conditions for, and practice of, a democratic form of dialogical reasoning over issues of potential conflict of interest between individuals and groups in a complex, multicultural society. At the most abstract level, there is the work of Rawls on public reason,[117] and Habermas on communicative rationality;[118] at a more policy-orientated and practical level there is Dryzek's work on 'discursive democracy',[119] and that of Ostrom and others[120] on the management of environmental resources. All these theorists seek ways of analysing the processes through which free agents can reach agreements about such issues without the intervention of the public power, in a civil society that lies behind the formal political process and the official organs of the state's machinery,[121] and which feeds into the practice of representative democracy in that formal political sphere.

What these theoretical developments have in common is the idea that there is a distinctive form of public reasoning about potential conflicts (arising either from competition for resources, or from cultural or religious differences), through which such issues can be successfully managed in a 'win–win' way, resulting in a binding agreement or consensus about the outcome. This form of reasoning is put forward as an alternative to the instrumentalist one used in conventional liberal democratic politics, where interest groups mobilize for competition, and conflicts are either won by the most powerful forces, or else arbitrated by other instrumentalist experts (who in turn are bearers of their own interests, for instance in expansion of their professional activities). Hence they distinguish not only between the two kinds of rationality appropriate for politics, but also between the two spheres in which such politics take place – the 'systems' and the 'lifeworlds' in Habermas' work.[122] They therefore oppose social engineering solutions to policy issues, and try to protect a realm for discursive, dialogical resolution of such issues.[123]

Critical theory in this tradition is much preoccupied with the limitation of public power and expert management, and with the creation of conditions favourable to the exercise of reflective deliberation and intersubjective dialogue between competent members of a political community. If this approach were accepted as well-founded, it would have important implications for the structural features and political conditions necessary for the success of a basic-income project. But I shall argue in this section that the distinction between instrumental and communicative rationality is somewhat misleading, and that the practical resolution of conflicts of interest can accommodate differences in power, including those between officials and ordinary citizens that are characteristic of many problems of social justice.[124]

There is an alternative (sociological) account of how communicative interactions create a social order with inbuilt common interests in sharing and restraint of rivalry (what Hume called 'benevolence'[125]). Goffman's analysis of interaction ritual focuses on the reciprocal claims of social value ('face') within which meaningful communication is accomplished.[126] In ordinary conversations, the processes of making, giving and saving 'face' construct an everyday, informal order of identity and mutual trust, that keep up 'normal appearances'[127] and sustain the sense of mutual obligation, predictability, moral necessity and indeed 'reality' itself.[128] This informal order is improvised, as it were, by members of interactive communities who cooperate to sustain this sense of order and purpose, and confirm its standards to each other, even when their disparate actions and cultural practices reveal radically different interpretations of its requirements, in line with their divergent interests.[129] This informal interaction order of everyday exchanges that sustains cooperation and community is responsive to the needs of identity and communication, but is always accountable to the formal, institutional order of power, political structure and the instrumental, strategic relations of the economy.[130]

It is in this very different sense of reciprocity (compare pp. 55–61) that this value is highly relevant to sustainable forms of social justice. The informal (and indeed inevitable) reciprocity of exchanges of value between unequal partners in a dialogue or negotiation is the way that differentials of power are 'normalized' in everyday life. The powerful need to legitimate their authority to the subordinate, who in turn have opportunities to subvert power by turning these justifications against those who use them[131] – as the Central European dissidents used the vocabulary of human rights against those regimes that had signed the Helsinki Agreement, but done nothing to implement its terms. Of course, cooperation under circumstances of unequal power and wealth is fragile, and trust can be easily destroyed.[132] However, the whole project of democratizing society, and extending the notion of partnership to power-laden spheres like social services provision[133] relies on this notion – that unequal partners can construct common interests through dialogue and negotiation.

It follows that, in a liberal democracy where the division of labour and responsibility for the tasks of social reproduction must be made up of voluntary exchanges, either in labour markets or in agreements between public agencies and civil society organizations, or in the private sphere of households and voluntary associations, that this informal order of reciprocity, cooperation and trust must provide a very important element in the creation and maintenance of a sustainable regime. Social justice is in this sense a discursive creation, just as the sense of fairness and mutual obligation is achieved through everyday interactions between domestic partners,[134] even when power and resources are not equally divided between them. However, the autonomy provided by a basic income should allow the parties in such negotiations that degree of independence to minimize coercion, and to give the disadvantaged scope gradually to press for better terms, by using the legitimatory repertoires of the more advantaged against them.

The aim of the liberal compromise between parties with different interests is the mutual acceptance of an agreement. Bellamy argues that this is to be distinguished from a bargain between traders, or a deal between trimmers who ignore issues of principle.[135] Liberals do not approve of compromise based on expediency; a principled view is necessary to separate a just solution from one based on power alone. Trading is based on rules necessary for gainful exchange, not ethical principles of right. It involves no ethical judgements about outcomes. Trimming evades issues of values, and can construct agreement when no principles are at stake. But liberal compromise requires negotiation for a mutually satisfying solution, when there is a collective problem – for example of distributive justice over benefits or burdens – to be solved. The art of compromise involves recognizing situations where the only possible solution is the second-best option for all parties, or some procedural compromise, like a lottery.[136] But above all, compromise relies on the practice of reciprocity and mutual respect in negotiation, and encourages members of a political community to accommodate each other's values and principles.[137] It appeals to common ground that can only be constructed in dialogue, and not settled in advance; and to some underlying principles of justice, tradition and common interest. This form of compromise is a good in itself, because it supplies the sense of empowerment and inclusion, even though none of the parties can achieve all their goals.

What this implies is that the strict division between the instrumental rationality of the 'systems world', of professional expertise, of public policy and political authority, and the communicative rationality of the 'lifeworld', of community, and discursive democracy is untenable. The issues about justice in the division of labour and responsibility for the burdens of social reproduction can and should be tackled through a constant negotiation between the representatives of all interest groups and cultural traditions. A just solution to conflicts of interest, like an efficient division between paid and unpaid work, cannot be stipulated in a constantly changing situation, according to standards that are themselves variable, and interpreted by the negotiating parties.

The basic income principle can supply the conditions most favourable for this democratic dialogue to reach a conclusion that is agreed to be fair for all. But such agreements must inevitably be provisional and subject to perpetual challenge and modification in the light of changing circumstances. Social justice in these issues is never final.

## Conclusions

This chapter is inevitably little more than a sketch of the alternative programme for social justice available to present-day politicians, and the kind of politics of welfare it could enable. There are many questions raised by this analysis that cannot be answered in the scope of a book of this length, and that demand more detailed research or debate elsewhere.

Inevitably there will be some readers left dissatisfied with the answers I have given to both the major challenges to the central policy proposal rehearsed here. On the one hand, the risks of introducing an entirely new principle of income maintenance for people of working age (children, old people and others outside the labour market get citizens' incomes in several countries) may seem disproportionate to the benefits, especially when the need to soften the impact of gains and losses in the transitional process means that the appealing simplicity of the basic income becomes compromised by surviving elements of selectivity, for instance in housing benefits. On the other hand, the ways I have tried to answer concerns about the motivation for doing socially necessary work, and how individuals will be held to account for their contributions to the common good may seem unacceptably vague and nuanced. Finally, many radicals might argue that the measures proposed do not do enough to redistribute wealth and power, or to address the injustices of racism, sexism and other forms of politically reinforced prejudice and discrimination.

In concluding this chapter, I can only restate the requirements of a politics of welfare for the sake of social justice that is both liberal and democratic. While the outcomes of such policies must be justifiable according to some ethical principles of distribution (which often conflict with each other), they must also reflect fair processes and procedures, which minimize coercion, and above all discriminatory coercion, that forces minorities to act (or refrain from acting) according to their choices and their interests, and instead to act for the good of the majority (or powerful sections of the majority). I have argued that the new orthodoxy's policies fail this test in a number of ways.

The moral principles relevant for social policy are not to be uncritically derived from the morality of everyday interactions. For instance, it is generally held among ordinary people that fathers should contribute to the costs of bringing up children, unless they are living in a partnership in which, under a fair agreement with their partner, they take the major share of unpaid child care, and hence earn little or nothing. But it does not follow from this that public policy should seek to compel fathers to contribute to their children's upbringing, through court orders punishable by imprisonment in their breach, or through compulsory deductions from wages. Providing an adequate unconditional basic income for each woman and each child might be a better way of securing the livelihood of the nurturing unit, and at the same time ensuring that the couple negotiate over paid and unpaid work roles from positions of relative autonomy.

Indeed, this sphere of public policy gives an example of the failure of the new orthodoxy's programme, when put to a practical test. In the UK under the Conservative government – but with the support of the parliamentary Labour party – the Child Support Agency was established in 1991 to force parents (mostly fathers) to make contributions in these ways. This measure privileged biological parenthood over social parenthood, ignoring the realities of income and poverty in lone parenthood and second marriages and the negotiated nature of family obligation.[138] It attempted to change behaviour by coercion without regard for popularly constructed notions of social justice.

The outcome was that, despite a parliamentary party political consensus in favour of the measure, the new law and administrative regulations were strongly resisted in the country, both by collective action and by individual defection from liabilities. Lone parent mothers and their children joined demonstrations by separated and divorced fathers against the CSA, and complained that they were worse off under its regime. The numbers of extra payments achieved were negligible, but administration and enforcement costs rose steeply. In the end, the amounts paid were not worth all the political trouble caused, and all the extra public expenditure.[139]

There are general lessons to be drawn from this experience. Drawing the line between private responsibilities and civic obligations is never easy, but the attempt to enforce moral duties that belong in civil society, and especially in the sphere of families, is seldom effective or equitable in its outcomes. It seems likely that much the same difficulties will be encountered in the New Deal for Lone Parents, and in the welfare-to-work programme.

The informal negotiation of work roles in households, voluntary associations and communities, and the invisible hand of market incentives, may seem uncertain instruments of social justice, especially to authoritarians who have changed from old-style socialist producti-vists to new-style Blairites. But if one goal is to save the wasteful use of taxpayers' money, these methods have much to recommend them, especially when they come so much closer to consistency with liberal (and market) principles than the enforcement measures currently being contemplated.

In this chapter, I have taken the nation state as my unit of account. This has led to several oversimplifications of the issues concerning systems of cooperation, and their distributions of benefits and burdens. In all the previous chapters I have emphasized the mobility of people across borders, and the necessity to take account of transnational exchanges in the discussion of social justice issues. Even though social reproduction can be meaningfully analysed in national terms, these factors should be taken into account.

Accordingly, in the final chapter I shall return to the theme of globalization, and consider how transnational mobility – both legal and illegal – affects the ideas of a basic income society, and a politics of compromise.

## Notes and references

1  B. Barry, *Justice as Impartiality*, Oxford: Clarendon Press, 1996.
2  H. Dean, 'Undermining Social Citizenship: The Counterproductive Effects of Behavioural Controls in Social Security Administration', paper given to ISSA Second International Research Conference on Social Security, Jerusalem, 26 January 1998.
3  C. Larmore, *Patterns of Moral Complexity*, Cambridge: Cambridge University Press, 1987.

4  R. Bellamy, 'The Politics of Compromise', paper given at the Oxford Political Thought Conference, St Catherine's College, Oxford, 8–10 January 1998.

5  B. Jordan, 'Basic Income and the Common Good', in P. Van Parijs (Ed.), *Arguing for Basic Income: Ethical Foundations for a Radical Reform*, London: Verso, 1992, pp. 155–78.

6  V. George and P. Wilding, *Ideology and State Welfare*, London: Routledge and Kegan Paul, 1976.

7  P. Van Parijs, *Real Freedom for All: What (If Anything) is Wrong with Capitalism?*, Oxford: Oxford University Press, 1995.

8  TUC, Labour Party Liaison Committee, *Partners in Rebuilding Britain*, London: Trades Union Congress, 1983.

9  M. McIntosh, 'Feminism and Social Policy', *Critical Social Policy*, 1 (1), 1981.

10  B. Jordan, *The Common Good: Citizenship, Morality and Self-Interest*, Oxford: Blackwell, 1989, ch. 8.

11  B. Campbell, *Goliath: Britain's Dangerous Places*, London: Methuen, 1993.

12  P. Corrigan and P. Leonard, *Social Work Practice Under Capitalism*, London: Macmillan, 1978; D. Statham, *Radicals in Social Work*, Basingstoke: Macmillan, 1978.

13  M. Foucault, *Discipline and Punish: The Birth of the Prison*, Harmondsworth: Allen Lane, 1977.

14  B. Jordan, *A Theory of Poverty and Social Exclusion*, Cambridge: Polity, 1996, ch. 6; J. Handler and Y. Hasenfeld, *We the Poor People*, New Haven, CT: Yale University Press, 1997.

15  S.E. Finer, *The Life and Times of Sir Edwin Chadwick*, London: Methuen, 1952.

16  J. Bentham, *Constitutional Code*, in J. Bowring (Ed.), *The Works of Jeremy Bentham*, London: Tait, 1843, vol. 9.

17  Bentham, *Constitutional Code*, II, xi, 5, p. 439.

18  E.J. Mishan, *Economic Myths and the Mythology of Economics*, Brighton: Wheatsheaf, 1986.

19  J. Dryzek, *Discursive Democracy*, Cambridge: Cambridge University Press, 1990.

20  J. Rawls, 'The Domain of the Political and Ideas of the Good', *New York University Law Review*, 64, 1989a, pp. 234–5.

21  J. Habermas, *The Theory of Communicative Action* (1984), Boston, MA: Beacon Press, 1987, pp. 233–55.

22  E. Goffman, *Interaction Ritual: Essays on Face-to-Face Behaviour*, Harmondsworth: Penguin, 1972.

23  J.M. Buchanan, *Ethics of Economic Progress*, Norman, OK: University of Oklahoma Press, 1994.

24  G.S. Becker, *The Economic Approach to Human Behaviour*, Chicago, IL: Chicago University Press, 1976.

25  S. Popkin, *The Rational Peasant: The Political Economy of Rural Vietnam*, Chicago, IL: Chicago University Press, 1979.

26  D.C. Mueller, *Public Choice II*, Cambridge: Cambridge University Press, 1989; D.A. Starrett, *Foundations of Public Economics*, Cambridge: Cambridge University Press, 1988; Jordan, *Theory of Poverty and Social Exclusion*, chs 2 and 5.

27  T. Hammar, *Democracy and the Nation State: Aliens, Denizens and Citizens in a World of International Migration*, Aldershot: Gower, 1990; B. Jordan and D. Vogel, 'Which Policies Influence Migration Decisions? A Comparative

Analysis of Qualitative Interviews with Undocumented Brazilian Immigrants in London and Berlin as a Contribution to Economic Reasoning', *Des Arbeitspapier* 14/97, Centrum für Sozialpolitik, Bremen, 1997.

28  K.G.P. Mathews, 'Reward for Currency and the Black Economy in the UK', *Journal of Economic Studies*, 9 (2), 1982, pp. 3–22; A. Sauvy, *Le Travail Noir et L'Economie de Demain*, Paris: Calman Levy, 1984.

29  J. Windebank and C.C. Williams, 'What is to be Done about the Paid Informal Sector in the European Union? A Review of Some Policy Options', *International Planning Studies*, 2 (3), 1997, pp. 315–27.

30  J.J. Thomas, *Informal Economic Activity*, Hemel Hempstead: Harvester Wheatsheaf, 1992.

31  J. Kane-Berman, *South Africa's Silent Revolution*, Johannesburg: South African Institute of Race Relations/Southern Book Publishers, 1997.

32  A. Duval Smith, 'Fear Enforces Jungle Law in Cape Town's Badlands', *Guardian*, 13 January 1998.

33  Kane-Berman, *South Africa's Silent Revolution*.

34  E. Luttwak, 'The Good Bad Guys', *Guardian*, 31 July 1995.

35  E.L. Feige, 'Underground Activity and Institutional Change: Productive, Protective and Predatory Behaviour in Transition Economies', in J.M. Nelson, C. Tilly and L. Walker (Eds), *Transforming Post-Communist Political Economies*, Washington, DC: National Academy Press, 1997, pp. 21–34.

36  S. Lash, 'The Making of an Underclass: Neo-Liberalism *versus* Corporatism?', in P. Brown and R. Compton, *Economic Restructuring and Social Exclusion*, London: UCL Press, 1994, pp. 157–74, at p. 162.

37  Ibid., p. 163.

38  Ibid. See also A. Phizaklea, *Unpacking the Clothing Industry*, London: Routledge, 1990.

39  F. Düvell and B. Jordan, *Undocumented Immigrant Workers in London*, Interim Report on ESRC Research Project, Exeter: Exeter University, 1998.

40  P. Harding and R. Jenkins, *The Myth of the Hidden Economy: Towards a New Understanding of Informal Economic Activity*, Milton Keynes: Open University Press, 1989; Thomas, *Informal Economic Activity*.

41  C.C. Williams and J. Windebank, 'Spatial Variations in the Informal Sector: A Review of Evidence from the European Union', *Regional Studies*, 28 (8), 1994, pp. 819–25; Thomas, *Informal Economic Activity*.

42  F. Fehér, G. Márkus and A. Heller, *Dictatorship Over Needs*, Oxford: Blackwell, 1983.

43  Windebank and Williams, 'Spatial Variations in the Informal Sector'.

44  Ibid., p. 318.

45  C.C. Williams and J. Windebank, 'Black Market Work in the European Community: Peripheral Work for Peripheral Localities?', *International Journal of Urban and Regional Research*, 17 (1), 1995, pp. 6–29.

46  E. Mingione, 'New Urban Poverty and the Crisis in the Citizenship-Welfare System: The Italian Experience', *Antipode*, 25 (3), 1993, pp. 206–20.

47  R. Waldinger and M. Lapp, 'Back to the Sweatshop or Ahead to the Informal Sector?', *International Journal of Urban and Regional Research*, 17 (1), 1995, pp. 6–29.

48  B. Jordan, S. James, H. Kay and M. Redley, *Trapped in Poverty? Labour-Market Decisions in Low-Income Households*, London: Routledge, 1992.

49 A. Goodman and S. Webb, *The Distribution of Expenditure in the United Kingdom*, London: Institute for Fiscal Studies, 1995.
50 Becker, *The Economic Approach*; Popkin, *The Rational Peasant*.
51 J.E. Roemer, *A General Theory of Exploitation and Class*, Cambridge, MA: Harvard University Press, 1982, part III; Jordan, The Common Good, ch. 4.
52 B. Jordan, M. Redley and S. James, *Putting the Family First: Identity, Decisions, Citizenship*, London: UCL Press, 1994, chs 6 and 8.
53 Jordan et al., *Trapped in Poverty?*, chs 3–6.
54 Jordan, *The Common Good*, ch. 6.
55 Jordan et al., *Putting the Family First*, chs 5, 8 and 9.
56 T. Blair, interview with H. Young, *Guardian*, 17 January 1998.
57 A. Waddan, *The Politics of Social Welfare: The Collapse of the Centre and the Rise of the Right*, Cheltenham: Edward Elgar, 1997, pp. 174–8.
58 Jordan, *The Common Good*, p. 60.
59 European Commission, *Employment in Europe*, Luxembourg: Office of the Commission of the European Communities, 1993, p. 52.
60 Department of Social Security, *Social Security Statistics, 1997*, London: Stationery Office, 1997, pp. 4, 26.
61 R. Baird, 'Why Not Enough People are Feeling the Benefit', *Guardian* (Jules and Mung), 17 January 1998, pp. 16–17.
62 Department of Social Security, *Social Security Statistics, 1997*.
63 Jordan, *The Common Good*, ch. 6.
64 M. Ball, *Housing and Economic Power: The Political Economy of Owner Occupation*, London: Methuen, 1983.
65 Roemer, *General Theory*.
66 A. Smith, *The Wealth of Nations* (1776), early draft version, quoted in W.R. Scott, *Adam Smith as a Student and Professor*, Glasgow: Brown, 1937, pp. 326–8.
67 C.H. Douglas, *Economic Democracy* (1919), Sudbury: Bloomfield, 1974; G.D.H. Cole, *The Next Ten Years in British Social and Economic Policy*, London: Macmillan, 1929; B. Jordan, *Rethinking Welfare*, Oxford: Blackwell, 1987; F. Hutchinson and B. Burkitt, *The Political Economy of Social Credit and Guild Socialism*, London: Routledge, 1997.
68 P. Van Parijs, 'Competing Justifications for Basic Income', in P. Van Parijs (Ed.), *Arguing for Basic Income*, London: Verso, 1992, pp. 3–46.
69 A. Duncan and P. Hobson, *Saturn's Children: How the State Devours Liberty, Prosperity and Virtue*, London: Sinclair-Stevenson, 1995.
70 H. Parker and H. Sutherland, 'Why a £20 CI is Better than Lowering Income Tax to 20 per cent', *Citizen's Income Bulletin*, 19, 1995, pp. 15–18.
71 T. Blair, speech to Labour Party Conference, *Guardian*, 22 October 1997.
72 A. Etzioni, *The Spirit of Community: The Reinvention of American Society*, New York: Touchstone, 1993; N. Dennis, *Rising Crime and the Dismembered Family*, London: Institute for Economic Affairs, 1993.
73 D. Green, *Rediscovering Civil Society: Welfare Without the State*, London: Institute for Economic Affairs, 1995.
74 J. Carvel, 'Labour Targets Lazy Parents', *Guardian*, 16 January 1998.
75 D. Donnison, *A Radical Agenda: After the New Right and the Old Left*, London: Rivers Oram Press, 1991.
76 G. Hughes and A. Little, 'Radical Communitarianism in Europe: Social Policy and the Politics of Inclusion in the Work of Jordan and Gorz', Political Studies Association, Proceedings of Annual Conference, 1996, pp. 341–72.

77  G. Hughes, 'Communitarianism and Law and Order', *Critical Social Policy*, 16 (4), 1996, pp. 17–42; B. Jordan and J. Arnold, 'Democracy and Criminal Justice', *Critical Social Policy*, 44 (5), 1995, pp. 171–80; D. Donnison, *Politics for a Just Society*, Basingstoke: Macmillan, 1997, ch. 7.
78  Campbell, *Goliath*.
79  Jordan, *Theory of Poverty and Social Exclusion*, chs 4 and 6.
80  Ibid., ch. 4.
81  Home Office, *Prison Statistics 1997*, London: Stationery Office, 1997.
82  D. Donnison, *Politics for a Just Society*, Basingstoke: Macmillan, 1998.
83  Jordan and Arnold, 'Democracy and Criminal Justice'; Jordan, *Theory of Poverty and Social Exclusion*, ch. 6.
84  Jordan et al., *Trapped in Poverty?*, ch. 4.
85  Ibid., ch. 7; K. Rowlingson, C. Wiley and T. Newburn, *Social Security Fraud*, London: Policy Studies Institute, 1997.
86  Jordan et al., *Trapped in Poverty?*, ch. 7.
87  S. Leather and B. Jordan, 'Food Poverty: Do Labour's Policies Make Sense?', Exeter: Social Work Department, Exeter University, 1997.
88  Jordan et al., *Trapped in Poverty?*, p. 245.
89  T.R. Batten, *Communities and their Development: An Introductory Study with Special Reference to the Tropics*, Oxford: Oxford University Press, 1957.
90  A. Barr, 'Empowering Communities – Beyond Fashionable Rhetoric?', *Community Development Journal*, 30 (2), 1995, pp. 121–32.
91  Donnison, *A Radical Agenda*.
92  J. Benington, 'Community Work as an Instrument of Institutional Change', in *Lessons from Experience*, London: ACW, 1972.
93  H. Lustiger-Thaler and E. Shragge, 'Social Movements and Social Welfare: The Political Problem of Needs', in G. Drover and P. Kerans (Eds), *New Approaches to Welfare Theory*, Aldershot: Edward Elgar, 1993, pp. 161–76.
94  O. de Leonardis, 'New Patterns of Collective Action in "Post Welfare Society"', in Drover and Kerans, *New Approaches*, pp. 177–89.
95  Kirklees Metropolitan Authority, 'Working in Communities', Huddersfield: Kirklees Metropolitan Authority.
96  P. Beresford, *Meeting the Challenge: Social Work Education and the Community Care Revolution*, London: NISW, 1996, pp. 20–30.
97  South Glamorgan County Council, Children and Families Division, 'Users' Involvement Strategy', Cardiff: South Glamorgan County Council, 1994.
98  Plymouth City Council, 'Unitary Plymouth: Plan for Community Development', Consultation Paper, Plymouth, 1997.
99  F. Mazibuko, 'Social Work and Sustainable Development: The Challenges for Practice, Training and Policy in South Africa', paper given to Joint World Congress of IFS and IASSW, Hong Kong, July, 1996.
100  Ibid.
101  Emmaeus, UK, *Understanding Emmaeus*, Cambridge: Emmaeus Foundation, 1997.
102  R. Douthwaite, *Short Circuit*, London: Green Books, 1996; R. Hambleton and H. Thomas (Eds), *Urban Policy Evaluation: Challenge and Change*, London: Paul Chapman, 1995; K. Popple, *Analysing Community Work: Its Theory and Practice*, Oxford: Oxford University Press, 1995; D. Vanner, 'Local Economic Strategy and Local Coalition Building', *Local Economy*, 10 (1), 1994, pp. 33–47.

103 Jordan, *Theory of Poverty and Social Exclusion*, p. 180.
104 B. Jordan, *Social Work in an Unjust Society*, Hemel Hempstead: Harvester Wheatsheaf, 1990.
105 Freie Hansestadt Bremen, 'Regeneration Project Osterholz-Tenever', Application, Urban Pilot Project, Bremen, 1992.
106 N. Parton, D. Thorpe and C. Wattam, *Child Protection, Risk and the Moral Order*, Basingstoke: Macmillan, 1997.
107 J. Arnold and B. Jordan, 'Beyond Befriending or Past Caring? Probation Values, Training and Social Justice', in B. Williams (Ed.), *Probation Values*, Birmingham's Venture Press, 1995, pp. 75–92.
108 J. Clarke (ed.), *A Crisis in Care: Challenges to Social Work*, London: Sage, 1993.
109 R. Hadley and R. Clough, *Care in Chaos: Frustration and Challenge in Community Care*, London: Cassell, 1996.
110 M. Mayo, *Communities and Caring: The Mixed Economy of Welfare*, Basingstoke: Macmillan, 1994.
111 J. Gibbons, 'Relating Outcomes to Objectives in Child Protection Policy', in N. Parton (Ed.), *Child Protection and Family Support*, London: Routledge, 1997, pp. 78–91.
112 D. Thorpe, 'Policing Minority Child-Rearing Practices in Australia: The Consistency of "Child Abuse"', in Parton, *Child Protection and Family Support*, pp. 59–77.
113 Ibid., p. 70.
114 Parton et al., *Child Protection, Risk and the Moral Order*.
115 B. Jordan, 'Basic Income: Is it Too Late?', paper given at Nuffield College, Oxford, May 1996.
116 Jordan, *Common Good*, ch. 2.
117 Rawls, *Political Liberalism*, New York: Columbia University Press, 1993.
118 Habermas, *Theory of Communicative Action*.
119 Dryzek, *Discursive Democracy*.
120 E. Ostrom, *Governing the Commons: The Evolution of Institutions for Collective Action*, Cambridge: Cambridge University Press, 1990.
121 D. Ivison, 'Excavating the Liberal Public Sphere', paper given at the Oxford Political Thought Conference, St Catherine's College, 9 January 1998.
122 Habermas, *Theory of Communicative Action*.
123 Dryzek, *Discursive Democracy*.
124 B. Jordan, 'Democratic Community and Public Choice', in E.O. Eriksen and J. Loftager (Eds), *The Rationality of the Welfare State*, Oslo: Scandinavian University Press, 1997, pp. 76–97.
125 D. Hume, *A Treatise of Human Nature* (1745), Ed. L.A. Selby-Bigge, Oxford: Clarendon Press, 1888.
126 E. Goffman, *Interaction Ritual*.
127 H. Garfinkel, *Studies in Ethnomethodology*, Englewood Cliffs, NJ: Prentice-Hall, 1967.
128 R.A. Hilbert, *The Classical Roots of Ethnomethodology: Durkheim, Weber and Garfinkel*, Chapel Hill, NC: University of North Carolina Press, 1992.
129 J.C. Scott, *Domination and the Arts of Resistance: Hidden Transcripts*, New Haven, CT: Yale University Press, 1990.
130 A.W. Rawls, 'Language, Self and Social Order: A Reformulation of Goffman and Sacks', *Human Studies*, 12, 1989b, pp. 147–72.
131 Scott, *Domination and the Arts of Resistance*.

132 B. Jordan, 'Service Users in Child Protection and Family Support', in Parton (Ed.), *Child Protection*, pp. 212–22.

133 Beresford, *Meeting the Challenge*.

134 Jordan et al., *Putting the Family First*, ch. 6.

135 Bellamy, 'Politics of Compromise'.

136 B. Goodwin, *Justice and the Lottery*, Cambridge: Cambridge University Press, 1986.

137 Bellamy, 'Politics of Compromise'.

138 H. Dean, 'Paying for Children: Procreation and Financial Liability', in H. Dean (Ed.), *Parents' Duties, Children's Debts*, Aldershot: Ashgate, 1995.

139 J. Millar, 'Lone Parents', paper given at a Conference on the Future of Welfare States: German and British Perspectives, Humboldt University, Berlin, 17–18 November 1997.

# 6

# Conclusions: Freedom and Solidarity in a Global Economy

This book started from the paradox of the new politics of welfare – that prospects for social justice looked bleak in the global context of nation states' reduced scope for economic management and redistributive allocations, yet the project for moralizing economic activity and mobilizing electorates in support of reforming values seems more lively and urgent than at any time since the Second World War. The analysis of the previous chapters suggests that this may be no paradox at all. The new politics of welfare could simply be the nation state's adaptation to global realities – the programme through which national governments seek to adjust electorates' expectations of public social provision, to reshape perceptions of the possibilities of meeting needs, and to close down options for dependence and strategic action within welfare states.

   The new politics of welfare 'puts work at the centre of the welfare state'. I have tried to show how this reflects the fact that globalization has put the wage relation at the centre of politics. It would be a fair criticism of my alternative programme in the previous chapter that global capitalism could accommodate or even benefit from it – that basic income would allow new possibilities for flexibility and growth, and community work would bring ideological control closer to the people. It would be possible to use the evidence I have produced to argue for a restoration of class politics on a global scale, and the extension and export of the corporatist or social democratic compromise to the newly industrializing countries, as a more feasible alternative to capitulation to the power of remobilized capital.

I shall not address these criticisms directly in this chapter, but I shall try to take account of them in my analysis of global social justice issues. The new politics of welfare is primarily, I have argued, a programme for national renewal. The case against its mobilization of national sentiments and energies is partly independent of the alternative strategy. But I shall also argue that a transnational version of the Continental European welfare state is unlikely to be a strong political rival to the new orthodoxy in the next century.

Three questions that have been raised at various points in the analysis so far remain unresolved, and will be the focus of the final chapter. The first is the set of issues arising from the increased transnational mobility of people. There is the potential for 'private communities' whose collective goods are supplied by markets. There is the emergence of transnational communities of individuals who are linked across borders, and who supply their own non-market goods through networks of support that do not rely on states. And there is the increase in numbers of those attracted by the bundle of public goods provided by the state itself.

At one end of this continuum of mobile individuals are wealthy people, who live an international life of relative luxury, relying on packages of goods and services provided by commercial companies (hotels, condominiums, health farms, private schools, holiday villages and security-guarded gated communities) in various locations. Next to them come groups of business and professional people (like myself) who increasingly spend part of any year working in other countries, are members of international networks, firms and organizations, and rely on a global infrastructure and local services (such as public transport) for their work and lifestyles. At the other end are transnational ethnic groups, such as the Kurds, dispersed by political persecution in the Middle East to countries all over Europe, and the Romanies of Central Europe, now appearing in the West as refugees from racism, exclusion and economic marginalization. As in the past dislocations that created the diasporas of the nineteenth and earlier twentieth centuries, the issue for them and others is partly also economic – systematic disadvantage in their countries of origin – and partly the experience of cultural racism in their desired countries of settlement.

In between these clusters of migrating people are others, for all of whom the collective goods of particular locations are relevant for their decisions to move across borders. Even though they are seldom primarily motivated by the public provision of welfare states, and make little or no use of social security in the first instance, economic migrants from Third World countries and from the former communist states of Europe do want the benefit of a well-organized, secure and prosperous society with a good public infrastructure of services of all kinds, they do want access to a community which includes others from their own countries, and they do make use of some social services, notably health care.[1] And refugees from those countries, even if the primary motivation for their flight is persecution, and they have little choice about in which state to seek asylum, do benefit from at least one public good – peace and the absence of persecution – if they are lucky enough to find it.

All these mobile individuals defy the logics of welfare states and national systems of redistribution in the name of social justice, all of which are in some sense membership-based. The arguments used for ethically orientated allocations and political principles of inclusion can seldom be extended to them, and neither the new orthodoxy on welfare nor the alternative programme outlined in the previous chapter, takes full account of their needs and claims.

The second group of issues stems from the emergence of new transnational regimes and subnational units, which seem to signal new forms and levels of political authority. This gives rise to the possibility of multiple and differentiated sovereignties in the same territory (see p. 116), and the erosion of the system of international relations based on the monopoly power of sovereign states within their territories. While neither the emergence of a single world order and a regime for international governance, nor the breakup of the existing pattern of states into regional authorities, seems likely in the foreseeable future,[2] both international regimes and regional authorities are gaining power at the expense of nation states in the present era, and this has important implications for the politics of welfare and social justice.

It is as yet unclear whether these developments indicate a further stage in the collectivization process,[3] under which each administrative unit's collective action problems over social welfare in each era are resolved by the formation of a larger unit, and new more inclusive institutions for pooling risks and resources. If this process – evident from the beginning of modern times – were to continue in the present one, then the European Union will become the focus for the new politics of welfare, and the most important instrument of social justice. But it remains to be seen whether issues of social justice will be more prominent at that level, and new settlements relevant to relations between generations and classes in society struck there, or whether they will come to be concentrated in disputes and struggles within the newly semi-autonomous regions of Europe (like Scotland and Wales), which will develop their own distinctive distributive principles and policy measures.

The third set of issues concerns the responses of nation states to the first two. On the one hand, the reduced effectiveness of national governments in economic management and social allocations, and the emergence of supranational and subnational authorities, challenge the power of national governments to mobilize their populations in new patriotic movements of national renewal. On the other, increased immigration and mobility, bringing foreigners (like Mohammed Al-Fayed in the UK) to positions of prominence and influence, and making refugees and their minorities highly visible, offend national stereotypes and self-identities. The 'imagined communities'[4] of blood and soil nationalism, and the ideology of cultural unity, all come to clash with the realities of economy and society. New issues of religious tolerance and multiracial coexistence challenge liberal democratic institutions, and demand more plural political processes.

The spectre of xenophobic national political movements, of neo-Nazism and neo-fascism, has loomed and faded in the past decade, just as its progenitors did in the 1920s.[5] These movements have never quite broken through into the political mainstream (unless Jörg Haider's ambiguous party's successes in Austria are counted as such a success), but they are ever-present as a threat and a reproach to democratic politics, and they have shifted the parties of the mainstream in the direction of restricting immigration and asylum opportunities, and worsening the conditions for these groups within the population. As in the interwar period, authoritarian nationalism is opportunistic in its responses to particular issues and specific conditions, seeking to escalate temporary issues, local disturbances and sudden fears. It has no fixed ideology or support, but recruits from the disappointed and disillusioned of all classes and political backgrounds, and exploits all kinds of insecurities.

The combination of factors reviewed so far produces a potentially unstable political environment, especially in the newly democratizing countries of Central and Eastern Europe and the former Soviet Union, and in the newly industrializing countries of South East Asia. Immigrants and resident ethnic minorities can become the targets of a politics of resentment and violence. The combination of globalized economic development and nationalistic political mobilization can contribute strongly to this instability. For instance, in the South East Asian region, the impact of the collapse of the Korean economy, the shakiness of the Japanese financial sector, and the weakening of the currencies of almost all these countries in international trading, have all put in jeopardy the 3 million immigrants working in countries other than their own. As national governments invent campaigns for patriotic self-denial (accepting wage cuts and refraining from purchasing foreign-produced goods) they simultaneously launch programmes to repatriate these migrant workers, leading to sudden flows of population, and disruption to the lives of millions.[6] At the same time, the mass flight of Czech and Slovak Romanies to Britain and Canada indicates the relevance of the politics of welfare for these issues. In those countries, the selective blindness of official agencies – from the police to social services departments – to racism and the exclusion of this ethnic minority group has

now been reinforced by selective expulsions and the differential treatment of their asylum claims by the receiving countries, and particularly
the UK.

The new politics of welfare does not appeal directly to nationalistic
sentiments of this xenophobic kind; but it does deal in moral categories,
such as 'genuine need' and 'reciprocity', that stand as proxies for
'deserving' and 'belonging'. There is a real danger that a moral majority
might – as in parts of the USA – turn its wrath against racial minorities,
just as in Britain it has turned its back on the material plight of many
asylum seekers, who survive without any income support from the
state, and without access to work in which they could earn their
subsistence.

Globalization theory is ambiguous about whether national governments are to be seen as helpless bystanders in the context of world
development,[7] or as rogue elephants who threaten the evolution of
transnational regimes and more equitable distributions through the
growth of transnational exchanges of all kinds. The debate is not a new
one, and has many echoes of the later phases of the last Great Transformation,[8] when the institutions of free trade and liberal democracy
were destabilized by the very political forces they released, and authoritarian nationalism seized the chance to introduce violently
oppressive forms of economic and social protectionism, in the name
of the defence of national sovereignty and national capitalism against
the threats of internationalism and socialism.

It seems unlikely that nationalism will be peacefully laid to rest in
the first half of the twenty-first century. Its resurrection in the former
Soviet Union and the Balkans indicates the contrary. The new politics
of welfare is a self-proclaimed programme for national revival and
renovation, with all citizens urged to contribute to national prosperity
and development, and those that hold back authoritatively required by
authoritarian means to do so. The principles of social justice are
manipulated for national popular mobilization.

Conversely, the new orthodoxy on welfare has nothing much to say
about the transnational issues to be discussed in this chapter. Its
programme is based on prescriptions for linking efficiency and justice in
a national economy, conceived of as a single system of cooperation (see
Chapter 2). It leaves immigration and supranational justice out of the
account.

But the same criticism could justifiably be made of the alternative
proposals set out in Chapter 5, for a programme to supplement the
basic (or citizen's) income scheme. The analysis of the principles at stake
is complicated by immigration and issues of equity between citizens of
different countries. Indeed, these factors cast severe doubt on whether
the distribution of benefits among citizens of a nation state, according to
criteria that exclude non-citizens, can be justified. Hence it is questionable whether a politics of compromise and negotiation over the

division of labour in tasks of social reproduction is compatible with a citizenship-based redistributive system; and whether the latter is consistent with the pluralistic forms of liberal democracy appropriate for a global context. The attempt to deal with global issues of justice in terms of the concept of universal social rights of citizenship is criticized in this chapter, and a more satisfactory framework sought.

In the last resort, the issues raised in these concluding sections are of a different kind from the ones discussed in previous chapters. There is an existing order of distributive justice (and injustice) within present nation states, and especially in First World welfare states. The new politics of welfare is a movement for reforming these systems. But there are no institutions for redistributing resources for the sake of global justice, and none in prospect. The global perspective exists as an alternative standpoint from which to evaluate the outcomes of national systems that claim to meet the criteria of social justice. Mass migration exists as a challenge to these systems, and an issue that they must find ways to address. This chapter tries to fill a gap in the new politics of welfare, and to point to weaknesses that could further distort the outcomes of its policy programme, and endanger the liberal institutions in which it locates is agencies.

## Migration and welfare states

This book has attempted to set out something like an action theory of welfare states, and to analyse the issues of social justice that this generates. It has addressed social policy issues in terms of the interactions between individual choices and strategies, the formal systems, policies and rules of public agencies, and the informal norms and practices of groups and associations. It has tried to explain how the mass solidarities created in the postwar period are tending to fragment into narrower mutualities, and how individuals (usually with similar incomes and/or similar risks) choose to join together in associations (or 'clubs') for mutual advantage or protection, excluding others from the goods they supply each other. While the formation of such groups reflects opportunities for cost minimization and value maximization for their members, it is not necessarily efficient or equitable for society as a whole.[9]

Migration has played an important part in both the historical process of collectivization,[10] and in the current process of fragmentation.[11] De Swaan has shown how migration intensified collective action problems over the poor relief provided by towns and cities, and hence accelerated regional, and eventually national solutions to problems of social welfare and social control.[12] But in the present age, migration also plays an important role in political pressure to exclude groups from welfare systems, and to form associations based on narrower mutualities. The politics of migration contributes to a perception of welfare goods as congestible (see p. 119) and hence to a politics of conflict and exclusion over such goods. This in turn leads to further self-protective action by groups facing similar risks, and thus a spiral of fragmentation (as in the American health care system) is set in train.

First World welfare states make spaces for migrants from other countries, but do not resolve the issues of equity they raise. Markets in high-quality infrastructural and collective goods create the possibility of 'private communities' of wealthy citizens and immigrants within national borders. Some migrants enter welfare states, and find opportunities to work within them, precisely because they are not eligible for the various forms of employment and social protection available to national workers. These short-term contract and undocumented migrant workers do not enjoy full political or social rights, and are most likely to take unprotected or less protected forms of work at low wages. The higher the (official) wages of national workers, and the better their systems of social protection, the more opportunities there are likely to be for short-term contract work and shadow undocumented labour.[13] National workers (through their trade union federation) often collude with the open and covert recruitment of foreign labour to do certain unpleasant and badly paid jobs, for instance in the construction industry and seasonal agricultural work, thus protecting their privileges and advantages.[14]

Germany provides an example of these processes in the period since full employment was achieved in the late 1950s. With the completion of the German 'social state' at this time, and the rise in labour's share of national income,[15] *Gastarbeiter* schemes allowed migrant workers to be admitted from Southern Europe and Turkey, many of whom were eventually granted permanent residence and work status, and settled with their families as 'denizens'[16] (i.e., with full social but not political rights of citizenship). But the second wave of immigration in the late 1980s and the 1990s has occurred in conditions of rising unemployment among the resident population (including among the new generation of denizens who do have social protection), and has consisted of short-term contract and undocumented workers from Central and Eastern Europe (especially Poland), who have no social rights.[17] Hence, although Germany has around 4 million registered unemployed people, it also employs some 1.9 million guest workers, mainly from Turkey and the former Yugoslavia, and another 150,000 contract workers from Central Europe, as well as countless undocumented workers from that region and further afield.[18]

From the standpoint of a prospective migrant now living in one of the Central European countries and unemployed, and contemplating the possible gains and losses[19] of trying to work in Germany, several factors come into consideration. Many Polish families already have members living in Germany, for instance because they managed to escape the communist regime in the late 1980s (around half a million, mostly highly educated Poles reached Germany in this period[20]), or because they discovered German ancestors and 'returned' to Germany as *Aussiedler* in the 1990s, and hence now have full citizenship rights there (around half a million from Poland alone). Having family members already in the country minimizes the costs and risks for those who follow,[21] and having a whole network of families and Polish organizations all over Germany allows large numbers of immigrants to be absorbed,[22] including undocumented workers who are able to move freely within this network, and use its infrastructure of information contacts, and cultural resources.[23] Alternatively, the would-be immigrant can enrol with one of the contractors who supply labour there under an official government scheme, or one of the unofficial brokers who satisfy the covert demand for emigration from Poland on the one hand, and shadow, short-term workers on the other.[24]

In the UK the situation for the would-be immigrant from Poland is slightly different. The option of travelling through a broker agency is open, especially for those wanting to do undocumented work, for example in a hotel in London,[25] though the agent arranging the flight and work placement would take a large part of his or her wages. Alternatively, for better-educated and better-resourced individuals, there is the chance to travel as a tourist, and then enrol as a student, but do undocumented work while staying. Although the British immigration authorities are far more vigilant at the border than their German counterparts,[26] the UK economy relies on large volumes of international tourism, and on attracting great numbers of overseas students, especially to learn English as the international language of commerce. Many so-called 'language schools' function as visa brokers, charging their 'students' fees to register them for immigration purposes with the Home Office, and hence extend their stay and allow them greater opportunities for undocumented work.[27]

Although welfare states create these opportunities, both through policy (in the UK, for instance, by allowing special immigration status to Central Europeans working as au pairs), and through the unintentional creation of spaces for shadow work, they cannot easily accommodate their manifestations into citizenship rights or political accounts of social justice. Welfare states are conceived as closed systems, with boundaries that distinguish members (supposed to be both contributors to and beneficiaries from collective goods) from non-members. Distributive justice requires some moral basis of kinship or fellow-feeling, or some other grounds for favouring the claims of some and excluding others, in the division and sharing of the resources of the membership group.[28] The distributive logic of closure is threatened by economic migration, and that of national social justice by strategic action to gain access to welfare goods. While shadow immigrants who do undocumented work justify their illegal activities by saying that they are only doing work that the national population is unwilling to take, and that the latter can rely on social security payments not accessible to them,[29] they do in fact use some welfare provision, notably the health services,[30] and when they are able to gain the status of legal residents (for instance, through marriage to an EU citizen, or getting hold of a passport for an EU country) they do then claim their entitlements to earnings supplements such as housing benefits.[31]

The politics of welfare must somehow address the issues raised by these phenomena, because ordinary voters are aware of many of the issues, and because authoritarian nationalistic parties constantly play upon them with alarmist propaganda, dwelling on the threat to national culture and racial purity, the loss of national identity, congestion of welfare goods to the disadvantage of citizens (especially over housing claims), and the links between race and immigration and perceived problems of rising disorder and crime. But in addition to this problem for liberal democratic politics, there are also real issues for social justice in the growth of migration of all kinds. In so far as this reinforces the fragmentation of welfare states, and the proliferation of a plurality of narrower mutualities, as well as the increase in kinds of social exclusion, it demands a broader view of inclusive social justice, and the possibility of transnational collective action. But in terms of the everyday pressures of competitive party politics, it tends to contribute to a spiral of enforcement rhetoric, in which mainstream parties compete over processes on the tough line they will take on immigration controls and the deportation of illegal immigrants, similar to and linked with that which affects the politics of law and order and criminal correction.

This raises the question of whether issues of social justice and social inclusion could be located in an ethical context of human rights, rather than one of membership through citizenship of nation states. In such a scenario, the transfer of distributive justice to the realm of human rights or *world* citizenship would mark a new stage in the ethical progress of humanity and of civilization, to forms of solidarity beyond nationality and ethnicity, achieving both universality and freedom from state coercion.[32] The libertarian, market-orientated version of such a project might take a form similar to that discussed in Chapter 4 (pp. 114–19) – Lockean individual moral sovereignty, Wicksellian consensual contributions to collective goods, and the erosion and eventual collapse of sovereign territorial states in the face of a growth of private, market-supplied self-governing communities. But such a project would face many of the social policy dilemmas of the Holy Roman Empire between the late middle ages and Bismarck's German unification. Private communities for the rich would take the place of wealthy cities under that regime, with between them huge tracts of impoverished countryside still under feudal (or in contemporary terms, coercive state) rule, and forests inhabited by outlaws and bandits outside political authority (as late as the eighteenth century there were as many as 3 million of these in Germany[33]). The freedom and self-government of the few would be paid for by the exclusion, serfdom and political oppression of the many, in an acceleration of developments already visible in the new politics of welfare.

The alternative version of this project emphasizes the ethics of inclusion and distributive justice rather than the freedoms of the global marketplace. Its goal is 'post-national' citizenship, based on human rights and subnational cultural associations.[34] This view reminds us that 'citizenship has historically been definable in various ways outside of the modern nation state, from city states to empires with their dual or plural structures of membership, legal identity and rights'.[35] The idea of a transnational civil society and public sphere, together with 'world citizenship' (in the sense of a human rights-respecting world community) would give rise to political movements and struggles for transnational regimes of regulation and institution-building. As a step towards this, European citizenship is seen as a manifestation of a new political culture and communication networks.[36] Social rights in the EU come about through case law at the European Court of Justice, which adjudicates on the social rights of workers, and especially migrant workers.[37] Thus migration becomes the focus of a form of citizenship residing in something other than nationality and statehood, and social rights of citizenship become transnational in this process.[38]

The point about this second version of the argument is that it claims that new transnational institutions will transform both political authority and membership in the directions of inclusion and social justice. In the next section I shall examine the evidence that the European Union is a step of this kind, and that it can facilitate distributive measures to these ends. In the final sections I shall return to the concepts of citizenship and social rights, when I review the links between nationalism and the new politics of welfare, and consider possible transnational alternatives to both these political movements.

## Regimes of regulation and deregulation: the European Union

After the Second World War, the international settlement resulted in the compromise of 'embedded liberalism', under which trade and capital flows were to be gradually liberalized from the position of protectionism and autarky that characterized the prewar and war situations. In return for tolerating the change and dislocation that this would bring over time, national governments were enabled to put into effect the new potentialities for economic management and social protection that had been developed during the same period, in the shape of welfare states.[39] Over the next 50 years, however, liberalization has reached the point where national differences in domestic regulatory and protective structures affect international transaction flows, especially in the 'intangibles' (trade in services) that now make up about a quarter of all such transactions. Since these are traditionally more regulated than trade in goods, international trade policy regimes (such as the various rounds of the General Agreement on Tariffs and Trade) now require domestic restructuring; the international deregulatory imperative affects national economic institutions, and the barriers between national policies and international agreements break down. Along with the growth of global corporate organizations that internalize production and exchange by trading transnationally among subsidiaries, this challenges core assumptions about how national governments pursue sustainable growth and social stability through embedding economic relations.[40] At the end of 1997, the sudden crisis for the South East Asian 'tiger' economies (which seemed best adapted for these new global conditions) reminded all governments that no particular domestic regulatory institutions are secure under the competitive pressures of international market forces.

In this chapter I shall consider the ambiguous development of the European Union in this context. There is little agreement among the many analysts who study its evolution and trajectory about its nature or purpose, and still less about its likely destiny. Is it a faltering (or even failing) attempt at creating a superstate, which is seeking by its sheer size to succeed in embedding economic relations in a stable set of social institutions on the Continental European model (i.e., a Greater Germany by another name)? Or is it a transnational regulatory regime for one world region, providing the constitutional and legal framework for what may be quite a different set of institutional arrangements, including further deregulation? Linked to these questions are ones about the future of European social policy. Will the role of the EU in social policy be one of gradually increasing importance, or will it play a part in dismantling the Christian Democratic welfare states that have been the distinguishing feature of European social policy?

The first view of the European Union's history is that it was always a project for a United States of Europe, but that the momentum for creating this federal superstate is running out as the century draws to a close.[41] The original inspiration for this project stemmed from the failure of the system of European nation states to protect their citizens during the years between 1914 and 1945; the goal of federation was to guarantee peace and stability, as much as to sustain prosperity and growth. But in this the EU has become a victim of its own interim success. Already – before the federal dream is realized – the idea of a war in Western Europe is unthinkable, and since so many of the founders' economic goals have been achieved, the system of sovereign nation states has been reprieved. The illusion of continuing independent sovereignty, and the difficulties in achieving the next stage of integration, are enough to lead the members to settle for the present half-measures as a second-best solution, in order to avoid the political costs and complications of the full programme. With the proposed expansion into Central and Eastern Europe at the beginning of the next century, the EU will become too heterogeneous, and the decision-making process too difficult, to overcome the stubborn reservations of countries like the UK. The project has been overtaken by globalization on the one hand, and regionalism on the other.

On this account, British caution and pragmatism, for so long seeming to be the cause of missed opportunities of the full benefits of committed membership, is, in the final reckoning, justified. British reservations over the democratic deficit, and doubts about the practicality of unification, go back to the conferences of the early 1930s;[42] instrumental, selective cooperation on economic issues, but always with an eye to national interests, has been the hallmark of British policy ever since. The irony is that the Europe of this British vision – a close cooperation between sovereign nation states, allowing the UK to retain its trans-atlantic links and world role – seems to be roughly what is now emerging.

The second view is that, although a federal superstate is neither feasible nor desirable, 'in so far as Western Europe operates within a common framework of supranational law regulations and policies, it is already a supranational federation of sorts, even though it is far from becoming a centralized, unitary, territorial state'.[43] The British view, most powerfully expressed by Margaret Thatcher, has been that 'the larger Europe grows, the more diverse must be the forms of cooperation it requires'.[44] A superstate risks reproducing the defects of the nation-states system on an even larger scale than before.[45] But the rules governing the Single Market, environmental policy, conditions of work and mobility, under the ultimate jurisdiction of a supranational Court of Justice, already constitute the regulatory regime of a supranational federation.[46] During the 1960s and 1970s, the primary and direct effect of EC law was established, and the inter-state treaties that established the Community were given constitutional status. The Court of Justice became the supreme court and constitutional watchdog of the Com-munity, with a new legal order imposed on individuals as well as member states.[47]

Bideleux argues that the EU 'is becoming a post-Hobbesian "civil association", a politically neutral framework of rules, regulations and laws permitting public agencies, enterprises and voluntary associations and citizens to pursue their own ends, in so far as these do not interfere with the equal rights of others to do likewise'.[48] The project has been and remains a typical eighteenth-century Enlightenment one (an élitist movement for a civil legal order) rather than a typical nineteenth-century democratic, popular, nationalistic one; hence it does not seek to safeguard liberties by democratic processes, but by balancing these with a constitutional order protecting individual rights. The rules regime of the EU insists on maximum certainty, equity and transparency of all rules governing economic, social and environmental matters, and that they should apply equally to all. In this sense it reinforces individual liberty, and becomes (in a globalized and regionalized environment) an alternative – and arguably more reliable – safeguard for civil and political liberties than (diminishing) national democratic control and accountability.[49] This can be regarded, following Oakeshott, as a form of 'civil association', as a coherent set of mutually supporting liberties, arising from and representing a dispersal of power in society, through the rule of law, freedom of association, property rights and freedom of speech.[50] Such a rules regime, which maximizes liberty and minimizes conflicts, already exists, and complements the member states' functioning at a national level, creating a resilient framework for common policies, and causing national laws to conform increasingly to European ones. In this view, the blandness of documents like the Amsterdam Treaty reflects the routinization of regulatory federalism, and is a sign of its success, not failure.[51]

If the EU should be seen as taking its place at the world regional level, as the European complement to international regulatory regimes like the World Trade Organization, the Organization for Economic Cooperation and Development, the International Monetary Fund, the World Bank and the United Nations, providing a framework of supranational law that protects liberties and contains power and gives redress, then its benefits stem as much from deregulation as from regulation. This conforms with the widespread observation that the EU has proceeded much faster with the 'negative integration' agenda of market-making than with substantive 'positive integration' through economic management and social protection.[52] It also helps explain why some of the more backward, over-regulated member states, like Ireland and Portugal, have benefited most from membership. On this analysis, the main gains for the applicant countries of Central Europe will come from access to a rules regime that allows freedom of exchange and of individual initiative, not their share of redistributive largesse through the Structural Funds. The fact that the Czech Republic, Hungary, Poland and Estonia all have GDP per head in a range of 20 to 11 per cent of EU average[53] indicates that even the enlargement in prospect for the first wave would give rise to serious distributional conflicts. The present beneficiaries of the Structural Funds – Spain, Portugal and Ireland – would try to block the claims of the post-communist countries, and a zero-sum game would ensue. Hence from this perspective these funds should be abolished as a necessary condition for successful enlargement.

The question therefore arises about what – given this fundamental divergence of views about the nature of likely future trajectory of the

EU – the role of social policy in its regime should be. Under 'embedded liberalism', we might summarize this role as follows:

1   to provide non-economic norms and institutions for exchange, to manage competition and conflicts of interests between groups and classes, and hence to 'embed' economic relations in society;
2   to slow down the impact of economic change on vulnerable groups, and to protect communities and cultures;
3   to establish channels of communication between the state and civil society, giving mutual feedback, and allowing dialogue about change.

This view follows the analysis of Karl Polanyi,[54] who saw some such policies as necessary for reconciling freedom with solidarity under global capitalism, since without them unrestrained market forces would destroy the whole fabric of society. But in this light it is interesting to observe that the legislation constituting 'Social Europe' – the Charter of the Fundamental Rights of Workers, which became the Maastricht Social Chapter – focuses so exclusively on workers' rights as what are to be defended. It is, in the main, an 'insiders' charter' in this sense, though it does deal in equal opportunity (for example for women and part-time workers, as well as people with disabilities), alongside its major themes of freedom of movement, fair remuneration, working conditions, employment-related benefits, collective bargaining and vocational training.[55]

Even those who emphasize the emerging role of the EU in social policy acknowledge that individual rights of social citizenship are still underdeveloped.[56] The European Court of Justice has required almost all national social rights to be extended to EU citizens living in a member state, but the exception to this is 'welfare rights', apparently construed as most means-tested benefits.[57] Equality of treatment for men and women, including equal pay for equal work, is another Court decision enforcing individual entitlements on national governments.[58] The Structural Funds and Common Agricultural Policy are redistributive measures, but relate to backward regions and the agricultural sector, rather than individual protection against market forces – though the latter might become a direct income grant, rather like a basic income, but going only to farmers.[59] But there are also formidable barriers to the expansion of the social policy dimension of the EU.[60] Its political institutions inhibit such initiatives, as UK resistance under Margaret Thatcher and John Major demonstrated. The likely focus for such policy consensus – a Christian Democratic or Social Democratic form of corporatism – would be difficult to mobilize, because of doubts about the competitive stamina of the Continental model. The sheer heterogeneity of the EU population – especially following enlargement – makes redistribution across national borders problematic and a source of potential conflicts. And national welfare states are jealous guardians of this function, since they are increasingly unable to deliver on other policy dimensions.

Hence what prevails is the more limited aim of protecting EU workers (rather than citizens), and a programme for defending the privileges of 'insiders' through a regime of employment rights on the Continental model, while protecting exclusive European citizenship through stricter immigration controls and stronger implementation of the Schengen Agreement. The new politics of welfare may appeal to the European Commission in its emphasis on labour-market flexibility, employment-friendly social protection, and the promotion of individual self-responsible provision.[61] In these respects, it is likely to try to shift Continental governments towards programmes which edge their social policy regimes closer to the US and UK models, in the name of greater consistency with its deregulatory agendas, with global trade regimes, and with the obligations-orientated, participative version of citizenship canvassed in the new orthodoxy.

This raises the question whether Continental national governments – and especially the German government – will be willing to reform their welfare states in these directions, or whether they can plausibly argue that their difficulties in the 1990s are merely a temporary phase of adjustment (exacerbated by factors like German reunification and the budgetary restraint requirements of the creation of the European Monetary Union). If they can convince themselves and each other that this is the case, then those who anticipate an expanding Social Europe may turn out to be right, especially since the post-communist countries of Central Europe have largely adopted Christian Democratic forms of welfare institutions in the German model, despite the influence of American and British advisers who advocated leaner, meaner welfare provision. On the other hand, there is evidence in the opposite direction in the rapid growth of social assistance programmes in all countries of the EU in the 1990s,[62] and even more rapid expansion in the post-communist countries of Central Europe.[63] If these developments signal the 'Americanization' of European welfare states,[64] then the new politics of welfare and its policy programme of reform will follow close behind.

## The future of the Continental European welfare state

In many ways it is surprising that the new politics of welfare has arisen in the USA and the UK rather than in Continental Europe. In those countries, the demographic situation facing welfare states in the next century is much less favourable. For example, in Germany 24.5 per cent of the population will be over 65 by 2025, whereas in the UK it will be

TABLE 6.1 Total fertility rates within the EU by calendar
year, 1970–1995

|  | 1970 | 1980 | 1995 |
|---|---|---|---|
| EU 15 | 2.38 | 1.82 | 1.43 |
| Austria | 2.29 | 1.62 | 1.40 |
| Belgium | 2.25 | 1.68 | 1.55 |
| Denmark | 1.95 | 1.55 | 1.80 |
| Finland | 1.83 | 1.63 | 1.81 |
| France | 2.47 | 1.95 | 1.70 |
| Germany | 2.03 | 1.56 | 1.25 |
| Greece | 2.39 | 2.21 | 1.32 |
| Ireland | 3.93 | 3.25 | 1.86 |
| Italy | 2.42 | 1.64 | 1.17 |
| Luxembourg | 1.98 | 1.49 | 1.69 |
| Netherlands | 2.57 | 1.60 | 1.53 |
| Portugal | 2.83 | 2.18 | 1.40 |
| Spain | 2.90 | 2.20 | 1.18 |
| Sweden | 1.92 | 1.68 | 1.73 |
| UK | 2.43 | 1.90 | 1.71 |

Source: Chris Shaw, Harri Cruijsen, Joop de Beer and
Andries de Jong, 'Latest Population Projections for the EU',
Population Trends, 90, 1997, table 1, p. 20

only 19 per cent.[65] In Italy and Spain, which had among the highest
rates in 1970, the fertility rate of women stands at 1.17 and 1.18 respectively, compared with 1.71 in the UK (Table 6.1); in Germany 30 per
cent of women bear no children. Secondly, participation rates in the
formal economy are lower, and unemployment higher, in those
countries. Thirdly, several have crises in their social insurance funds,
with growing gaps between revenue and payments. And fourthly, they
contribute a far higher proportion of GDP to public expenditure on
health care than in the UK, and attempts to limit this aspect of state
expenditure have had only limited success.

There are several reasons why a politics of radical welfare reform
has not got started in any of these countries (with the partial exception
of Denmark since the 1970s[66]). Demographic issues have not been raised
in Germany because of the memories of population politics in the Nazi
era, and this applies to other countries also. Institutional reforms are
difficult to carry through because, unlike in the British model, many
social policy measures are administered through independent tripartite
bodies, and these corporatist systems create strong organized interests
in existing systems. Particularly in the case of health insurance and
health care, the professional groups with investments in current
standards and distributions are very powerful and resistant to change.

But the biggest obstacle to a politics of radical reform has been
the success of this kind of welfare regime right up to the 1990s, and the

interlocking elements in the institutional systems which delivered this success. This is most easily illustrated from the case of Germany. The problems of the German social model can be best understood as stemming from its industrial system's difficulties in competing with new, flexible patterns of production in the Far East and in North America,[67] which undermine a number of elements in its former strength. The German economy was envied for its set of interlocking labour-market institutions that encouraged firms to follow high-quality, high-value-added strategies.[68] The German bank-industry relationship allowed managers to include the interests of workers in their business plans; it promoted long-term investments, and gave them opportunities to pursue in-depth training programmes. Craft apprenticeships supplied the labour force necessary for this strategy, and young people were willing to work hard at school and to forgo short-term earnings for the sake of a place in one of the upper echelons of the hierarchy of skills. Pay was settled at the sector and regional levels, and the system of works councils gave employees a voice in companies' decisions, promoting trust relations, and restraint in collective bargaining.

From this summary it is clear that the productive system and the institutions of the labour market interacted to ensure high skills and high quality in the industrial sector. With the investment of employers and employees in the craft training system, efficiency and equity were simultaneously secured. Efficiency was served by low transaction costs, and the active monitoring by employer organizations that limited free-riding.[69] Equity was achieved by giving access to a prosperous and well-regulated career, with a quasi-professional status, based on high-quality training and collective self-discipline. Craft unions were central to the success of these institutions, giving organized labour its distinctive associative status,[70] and promoting order and cohesion.

So long as this model gave Germany high growth rates, low unemployment and high social provision, its internal coherence made it virtually unchallengeable. But when faced with competition from the alternative of flexible or 'lean' production,[71] this same coherence has become an obstacle to radical reform. The new challenge was from work organization and practices (developed mainly in Japan) that integrated design and manufacture, avoided shortages and stockpiles, built total quality control into production, used team work and job rotation to reduce monotony, and pursued cooperative industrial relations through quality circles and other participatory methods.[72] These changes reduced the need for expensive craft training and worker autonomy. They largely abolished the distinction between the German 'high road' of a high skill, high value-added strategy, and British attempts to compete in terms of lower wages and other costs, calling into question the craft system and all its institutional underpinnings,[73] and placing a higher emphasis on flexible individuals and groups, willing to adapt to uncertain events through competence-based training.

Because of the interlocking nature of the German institutional system, all aspects of this strategy come under simultaneous pressure. The bank–industry relationship encourages long-term planning, but not flexibility or the entrepreneurial flair of small business innovation. Work organization and production processes cannot readily respond to the challenge of flexibility. Instead, what has happened is that employers lay off older workers through traditional early retirement schemes (see p. 140), and take on temporary low-paid employees for less than one year, paying them 610 Deutschmarks per month, and avoiding social insurance contributions. There are now 5.6 million Germans employed in such jobs, resulting in 16.8 billion Deutschmark losses for insurance funds.[74] Hence (by the back door) German industry is taking the 'low road' of cost competition through evading social costs and collective agreements, but doing so in a way that increases the crisis of the welfare model.

This indicates a further weakness in the whole set of interlocking institutions. Most of the workers employed under these short-term contracts are young; these jobs do not give them pensions contributions. In general, the birth cohorts now in retirement, or about to enter it, made low contributions to social insurance funds, and will receive high benefits. The birth cohorts of the generation entering the labour market must pay high contributions with uncertain prospects for their retirement pensions. There is growing resentment of this among young people.[75] From one perspective on equity the situation can be justified, because it gives high replacement rates to older workers on retirement, but from the perspective of equity between birth cohorts, the young are entitled to feel unfairly treated. In other countries (such as Sweden) the trust of the new generation in the abstract systems[76] of Continental welfare states is waning.

Finally, the health insurance system in Germany has also come under strain in recent years. As globalization and the problems of the industrial model have led to higher unemployment, and high social costs associated with this have led to lower investment activities, so demographic change has added to the costs of health insurance, and required higher contributions. Thus there is a vicious circle of fewer jobs, higher contributions and less money for the health insurance funds, leading to a 4 billion Deutschmark deficit in the first half of 1997.

The German state system insures more than 90 per cent of the population through 500 statutory schemes, regulated by law. Contributions are equally divided between employers and employees, and go to purchase care from health professionals of a high – some would say luxurious – quality, including access to extended 'cures' for chronic conditions, often provided in residential spa complexes. The problem of rising costs and stagnating or falling revenues has stimulated reform, notably in 1992, and the introduction of a stronger element of co-funding,[77] and competition between health insurance schemes, with individuals being given more scope to move between them. They in turn have more freedom to negotiate contracts with health care providers. These reforms have been claimed to have checked the rise in expenditure – which has even fallen in 1997 for the first time – but against a background of political demonstrations against the new measures.

The significant feature of all these debates and discussions is the difficulty of addressing any one aspect of the new dilemmas without tackling all of them. This helps explain why no political party has opted for an agenda of radical welfare reform, and risked unpopularity with large sections of the mainstream population with stakes in the present system. Instead, they have penalized marginal groups, like students in Germany, or long-term unemployed people, whose benefits have been cut in France, while maintaining rhetorical loyalty to the present institutional structures, and promises to increase employment levels through restoring faster growth. In so far as reforms are under even specialist discussion, they mainly concern the introduction of greater flexibility through the reduction of working time (including an increase in part-time work), wage subsidies for small firms using labour-intensive processes, retraining schemes, sabbaticals and the introduction of tax credits and other supplements for low-paid workers.[78]

It is too soon to predict whether the problems of the Continental model will prove insuperable, or whether radical reform movements will eventually arise within these states. What does seem unlikely is the idea that these institutional systems can be somehow translated to the European level, and hence made more impregnable by virtue of their scale and scope. There is simply no economy strong enough to sustain a European federal welfare superstate of this kind, and no dynamic capable of generating the revenues that could supply a redistributive commitment of this kind. The idea of some such institutional structures seemed feasible in the 1980s, when the UK economy was still in the grip of an untried radical transformation, and Germany was still riding high on the long-term success of its model. But now that Continental corporatism is under greater question (and experts in Japan are reading books on lessons from the British economy), no such movement seems likely to arise to press its claims.

Instead, the best that can be hoped for by supporters of the Continental model is that a coalition of economies in the same regulatory EU framework can more effectively defend their national welfare states, by refusing to compete down wages and conditions, or to cut social costs significantly. This would be a concerted refusal to take part in globalization's 'beauty contest' of national governments' attractions in trying to appeal to international investors, at least in terms of cost-cutting of the kind indulged in by British Conservative governments. The EU would therefore constitute a kind of restraint on competition of this kind between national welfare states, rather than a welfare superstate which pooled its social-services resources.

This helps to explain the emphasis on workers' rights in the existing EU rules, decisions and charters. If the main aim is to avoid welfare cost competition and 'social dumping',[79] then the focus should be on protecting the continuing privileges of labour-market 'insiders', and the status hierarchy of embedded labour-market positions that they still construct. But this then raises further questions about the growing numbers who are excluded from the labour market, and who increasingly fall through social insurance provision, and into social assistance safety nets. This issue is even more prominent in some of the post-communist countries of Central Europe which are seeking admission to the EU.

Hence the central debates raised by the new orthodoxy on welfare reappear in a European context, and eventually demand attention. If the Continental model of welfare states cannot realistically offer levels of labour-market participation achieved in the USA and the UK (even though it can offer its populations better protection against poverty), then it must seek other ways of combating social exclusion, encouraging some form of contribution to the common good, and increasing social cohesion. All the issues about social justice raised and analysed in the first five chapters of the book apply equally to the prospects for Continental welfare states. The further progress of the EU offers limited scope for avoiding or postponing a political solution to these problems.

## Citizenship and social justice

The choices facing EU member states are often discussed in terms of the alternatives of 'Fortress Europe', with a politics of ethnic citizenship, race and social exclusion,[80] or inclusive democratic citizenship, and a politics of international civil society and human rights.[81] In this section, I shall try to link the discussion of issues of immigration (pp. 207–11) with that of transnational institutions and the future of European welfare states in the previous two sections. I shall argue that the concept of citizenship is an unsatisfactory one within which to analyse issues of social justice.

This is relevant for the new politics of welfare, because the Blair–Clinton orthodoxy promotes active and self-responsible citizenship and the ethic of contribution to the good of the community. As we have seen (pp. 59–60), recent theory of citizenship has likewise refocused attention from individual rights to the activities, qualities and obligations of members.[82] But it has also sought to extend human rights in a transnational context, hence divesting the concept of citizenship of its connotations of national exclusiveness, and fitting it for an era of cultural pluralism and economic globalization.[83] Implicitly or explicitly, it appeals to a notion of 'world citizenship' and the implementation of something like the economic development rights first recognized by the United Nations in 1986, in the form of transfers between rich and poor countries.

I have also argued (pp. 53–5) that exclusion is not an incidental and avoidable feature of the collective life of groups and associations, but an essential and defining characteristic. The duties and virtues required of members constitute their contributions to collectivities, and are supposed to mark them as worthy of benefits; conversely they justify excluding non-members. In this sense, far from combating exclusion, the 'active citizenship' of greater civic involvement necessarily generates exclusive membership and excluded individuals. For example, the Blair–Clinton orthodoxy is more concerned to generate participation in the formal economy as a means of including and mobilizing unemployed claimants than it is about the fate of those who are disqualified for benefits or who drop out of government training schemes. At the time of writing, the new Labour government has not repealed the disqualification for benefits of asylum seekers who do not apply at the point of entry. The emphasis on active contributions actually increases the numbers of those excluded from welfare claims through programmes of compulsory inclusion.

There are various ways in which the theory of citizenship can try to counter this. The 'civil society argument' for active citizenship[84] suggests that people become good citizens by active participation in associations, through which they supply the kinds of collective goods they value, in ways that are most appropriate for them.[85] Some who advocate 'associative democracy' of this kind emphasize the need for a regulatory framework which guarantees that members have a voice in such associations' decisions, and bans discrimination and oppression in their rules.[86] The collective life of the community is then enriched by the democratic responsibility which members share for working together to produce distinctive forms of cooperation and collective benefits (including welfare services). But if the poor are excluded from such voluntary civic involvement because they lack the skills or resources to make the relevant contributions, and their own voluntary collective action brings them into conflict with the agencies of the state (see pp. 143–5), then public power comes to be used to force them to participate in the formal economy, and adjust their behaviour to the requirements of mainstream society. In a basic income society, this would not involve compulsion, but could take the form of guiding collective action towards more orthodox methods, inclusive practices and equitable outcomes (see Chapter 5); but in the Blair–Clinton orthodoxy it involves more coercion and exclusion, or more constrained participation under the close supervision of state officials. And the more that poor people and minorities are excluded from the collective life of mainstream civil society, the more their obligations as members of a national system of cooperation (rather than their needs) become the focus for their dealings with the state's agencies. In the new politics of welfare, active citizenship thus entails the selective enforcement of members' duties.[87]

Another line of argument against the one that I have taken is that active citizenship and civic involvement increases the 'social capital' of a society,[88] and in this process contributes to a culture of inclusiveness and cooperation, as well as spilling over into the economy and the system of governance in ways that benefit all, including the poor. Hence higher participation in voluntary associations and clubs is reflected in lower transaction costs, greater enterprise and initiative, more flexibility and adaptability, and better government, because it generates trust in social relations.[89] This implies that civic involvement produces a culture of generalized reciprocity (see p. 56), in which citizens are willing to invest in formal and informal cooperation without an immediate return,[90] to share facilities with others through democratic systems of management,[91] and spontaneously to redistribute resources in ways that are responsive to each other's needs. This last aspect might explain how the cultural spillovers from civic involvement and participation could result in voluntary reallocations that prevented need, and avoided individuals becoming marginalized and losing their places in cooperative, communal networks.

This argument for inclusive community through active participation works in a completely different way from that of the Blair–Clinton orthodoxy's new politics of welfare. Community of this kind combats exclusion by its capacity to trust individuals who cannot reciprocate immediately, by sharing resources within which all have common property rights, and by its willingness to redistribute for the sake of need rather than entitlement or merit, as well as its responsiveness to outsiders or even strangers[92] in distress. In this sense, inclusive community would be the hallmark of, and a very desirable outcome from, a society that adopted the basic income principle. But it would be inconsistent in many ways with a politics of welfare that emphasized the balanced reciprocity of measured contributions and formal obligations, and a programme of enforcement under threat of exclusion from collective benefits.

The culture of inclusive commmunity is therefore a desirable feature of a society seeking social justice, but it cannot be relied upon as the basis for a policy programme in search of justice. It is a very important feature of the informal collectivities under which marginal people – such as many immigrants and other vulnerable individuals – survive on the edges of society, and receive assistance from strangers or from voluntary organizations. But it is not promoted by the kinds of policy programmes adopted by the new orthodoxy on welfare.

The final possible counter to the arguments I have developed in this section is that transnational citizenship rights of the kind that are emerging through the EU,[93] and ultimately human rights, can provide institutionalized rights of inclusive membership, that combat the exclusive features of national citizenship. In so far as transnational rights for immigrants increase vulnerable individuals' security by giving them access to collective protection they clearly do reduce their risk of various kinds of social exclusion. But I shall argue that they do not constitute a new kind of transnational citizenship that is free from the exclusive elements in national versions, and that universal human rights cannot provide the basis for an inclusive form of citizenship.

The notion of citizenship necessarily appeals to the rights of members of an association of some kind (including any size of political unit), and hence implies exclusiveness. Even if all citizens of each EU member state had transnational rights in other member states, there could still be many non-EU citizens resident in the EU as 'aliens', without citizenship rights. Whether it is defined nationally or transnationally, citizenship has built into it this inescapable element of membership. Conversely, human rights imply universality, and apply to all, irrespective of the existence of political units of any kind, or their membership of any particular unit. Human rights are derived from universal principles of justice, that apply to relationships between human beings everywhere, whatever kind of society they happen to be living in.[94]

Human rights supply a standpoint from and standards by which we can assess particular aspects of social relations in any society. In principle, a polity could perfectly institutionalize a system of human rights, such that all its citizens were enabled to behave justly towards each other. Hence the citizenship of that country would embody human rights, because its social relations perfectly reflected the requirements of universal ethical principles. But such a polity would still have to determine how to respond to the rest of a non-human rights respecting world – for instance, whether to allow millions of asylum seekers from such unreconstructed states to enter and benefit from the collective goods of its regime.

Immigration raises two quite separate issues of public policy in a polity concerned with social justice. How can a state (or transnational unit like the EU) make rules about entry from abroad that are fair for foreigners and for citizens, allowing outsiders to come and work and eventually become full citizens? And how can those who live as legal residents or citizens, but are distinguishable by skin colour, beliefs, customs and practices from groups within the 'indigenous' population, be accorded all the rights and respect due to them, and included in an active, participatory role that is appropriate to their legal status as members?

It is seemingly impossible to find a single set of coherent principles with which to address both these groups of questions. The first cluster raises issues of justice about those outside a particular system of cooperation and collective goods wanting to get in. The second is about the rules of such a system of cooperation and collective goods, and how it deals with cultural diversity, and the fact that some members have joined more recently than others. Clearly the attempt to generate a single set of principles of justice appropriate to both sets of issues points in the direction of open borders, and the extension of human rights to the world as a whole.[95] But in a situation where there is still differentiation in economic development and in the rights regimes of various states and regions, there will always be conflicts between the requirements of the two sets of rules.

In other words, human rights seem to demand not merely non-discriminatory access to the country of one's choice, but also open access, given the Lockean notion of individual moral sovereignty discussed on p. 115. But once we take account of a whole series of (non-commensurable) claims for collective goods that are congestible, or limited in their supply from members (including those who have only recently gained citizenship), then a case for restricted immigration and entry rights can be readily made. Arguments from universal principles of justice between diverse human beings and arguments from membership of established, organized exclusive systems of cooperation pull in different directions, and there seems to be no fair way of arbitrating between them. In practice, governments make rules that express some kind of compromise, such as Germany's relative generosity in admitting asylum seekers, but restrictiveness in granting full citizenship rights on the basis of ethnic origin, or the UK's increasing restrictiveness in admitting both refugees and New Commonwealth immigrants, but relatively strong efforts to establish equality of opportunity for, and to prevent discrimination against, black and Asian people who have become or been born full citizens.[96]

The EU cannot readily provide more general, overarching principles to transcend national variations, or harmonize these. Instead, it can ease restrictions in mobility between member states, and make rules through which individuals (including immigrants from outside) can retain their rights while moving from one state to another. But the obligation to admit individuals who have been allowed to enter other member states (e.g., Kurds and Albanians who have claimed asylum on arrival by boat in Italy[97]) may be a factor in each member state tightening its immigration restrictions. In this way it may provoke more restrictive policies in each of them – Fortress Europe.[98]

It is quite consistent with the internal rules of justice between members (citizens) to insist that entry should be on the basis of descent or marriage, or of skills or other resources in short supply (i.e. contributions to the common good); and that numbers should not deplete or congest collective goods. Human rights can illuminate relations between members of a diverse multi-racial society, but not shed much light on how to settle claims for admission to a 'rich men's club' from some of the most needy and disadvantaged in the world.

Finally, the demand for active citizenship may justify an increase in the restrictiveness of immigration policies. If labour-market participation becomes the hallmark of the good citizen who meets his or her civic obligations, and there are limits to the employment opportunities available in the formal sector, then this provides a reason for refusing entry to foreign nationals. The new politics of welfare would, by extension of this logic, become associated with a harder line on immigration, for the sake of mobilizing the existing citizenry in the public interest. There have been indications of such developments in the UK, in the continuing tough policies towards asylum seekers who do not apply at the point of entry, and to Czech and Slovak Romanies who did.

For all these reasons, citizenship cannot shed its associations with exclusive membership, even if it shifts from a national to a transnational (e.g., EU) basis. This causes me to doubt whether the concept of a basic income for all, as the fundamental principle of an alternative programme for social justice, should construct its arguments on the idea of citizenship. The value of equal autonomy for each individual can, of course, be derived from principles of human rights, rather than those of group membership. But the fund from which basic incomes are distributed must be gathered together by a political authority, and it must then decide who is entitled to a share. Legal residents in a country who are not citizens have an equal claim from the standpoints of equal autonomy and equal basic need, and would therefore seem to have as ethically justifiable an entitlement as citizens.[99]

However, this issue would not arise (at least in this form) if every country – for instance, every member state of the EU – had a basic income scheme, and citizens were able to draw this as they moved between member states. In principle there would be no difficulty about the fact that this might vary between countries, so a Portuguese person with a lower basic income might choose to live in Germany, and *vice versa*. Alternatively, there could be a universal basic income for every citizen of the EU, equivalent to the lowest level affordable by the poorest country, and each wealthier nation state could supplement it by a national basic income of its own; perhaps there would be a regional element too, reflecting differences in standards and costs of living in regions of the same country.

In principle, of course, this idea would apply to the whole world as a system of states. If even the poorest gave a minimal income of this kind (or the United Nations distributed a basic income at this very low level to every person in the world) then the equivalent of the potential EU scheme would apply worldwide. But it is doubtful whether this particular way of distributing national resources would be appropriate for countries at every stage of development (although there is interest in the principle in South America and in South Africa[100]). This idea is utopian for the foreseeable future, but it indicates the directions in which welfare provision would have to move to reach some kind of just accommodation between the rights and obligations of members of any territorial political unit, and the human rights of the whole world population.

In summary, the vision of an international order of human rights-respecting states, each giving distributive justice among its member citizens, would still leave many contestable issues about mobility between them, that could not be resolved by a single neat concept of transnational citizenship, or by the principles of human rights themselves. However, there is a danger that the new politics of welfare will move the debate on these issues into the dangerous terrain of nationalism and xenophobia, as I shall argue in the next section.

## Stability, cohesion and reform

To return to the issues of globalization raised in the introductory chapter (pp. 6–11), the rapid increase in the mobility of some factors of production (money, skilled labour) means that corporate executives can make decisions about where to locate their businesses as if the whole world were a single place; it is now possible to make anything anywhere. There are, as we saw, strong arguments that can be advanced from the whole-world perspective that this transformation of the international economy into One Big Market[101] is essentially a step towards global distributive justice, because investment for industrial expansion will tend to flow towards countries where poor peasants can be drawn into more productive and better-paid manufacturing work. But this has a radically destabilizing effect on existing economic structures and social institutions. Schumpeter's forces of 'creative destruction',[102] essential as they may be for long-term development and growth, and for the 'catching up' of less developed economies that Adam Smith foresaw, are highly disruptive of the social formations by which human beings try to protect themselves against risks and vulnerabilities. Hence Polanyi's 'second movement of society',[103] by which they take collective action to try to slow down change, achieve social cohesion, build solidarity and change their institutions in a measured way. Liberal democratic polities aim to do this in the manner that best reconciles individual freedom with social protection, under conditions of radical uncertainty.

Recent events in South East Asia at the time of writing indicate the perils of these processes in the present global economic environment. The success of these economies lay in their adoption of the 'Japanese model' of rapid development, which had served that country so well in the period of reconstruction after the Second World War. This consisted of state control of the financial sector, the allocation of investment in line with national objectives, managed trade and international capital flows, supervised transfer of technology from abroad, and policies for ensuring that the most important sectors of the economy remained in the hands of national firms. In this way, their governments have protected compromises between capital and labour, and national economic management from global market forces.[104] They have subtly resisted pressures to deregulate their economies and make foreign trade more open, helped by their crucial geopolitical location to turn a strategic deaf ear to US criticisms over this. And, as limited democracies or overt autocracies, they have prevented the development of internal coalitions for redistribution through social benefits and services, and kept this form of public spending low.

None of these institutional measures for economic protection has survived the sudden crisis of the final months of 1997. The state-controlled financial sector turns out to have been corrupt in Japan and other countries, and to have made reckless loans in virtually all of them. The drive to expand and win more market share has taken priority over profitability in all, but especially in South Korea, where the huge transnational corporations have overstretched themselves on seemingly limitless supplies of cheap state-bank credit. In some countries – most obscenely Indonesia, where the ex-president's family owns most of the largest corporations – the concentration of ownership has been narrow and corrupt. In many (especially South Korea) wages in the industrial sector have risen very fast, which adds to the shock of sudden mass unemployment, and provokes strong resistance from trade unions to austerity measures. In other words, the myth that these countries' rapid gains in GDP per head was the result of a special combination of 'Asian values' (hard work, thrift, community, respect for authority and family solidarity), and to a coherent set of interlocking political and economic structures, is blown away, revealing an unsuspected fragility in the face of competitive forces, foreign debts of over US\$ 200 billion in South Korea and Indonesia, and serious short- to medium-term problems almost everywhere else.

Yet in the longer term the prospects are very good for almost all these economies, even though some (like Thailand and Indonesia) will take longer to recover from the crisis than others (like Malaysia, with its sound basis for its development strategy). This is because all have the classic elements for rapid industrial expansion – a ready supply of cheap labour from the agricultural sector[105] – and because the inter-national banking system will ride in to rescue them, and international capital will continue to invest in this expansion. Japan will recover in time from the enforced deregulation of its financial and services sectors, and once more become a major source for this investment. South Korea will recover its balance, and embark again upon a more cautious upward path, and the less developed countries will follow suit. Above all China, which will experience a crisis of competitiveness around its determination not to follow the other countries in devaluing its currency, will continue its relentless, rapid growth in national income. In the present situation, China's capacity to control internal population flows, to develop one region at a time by massive industrial expansion and to damp down pressure for rising wages, all give it key advantages over other world economies. But these authoritarian economic powers will eventually come to be in tension with the forces for political liberalization that this development process releases, and when this happens a quite different kind of crisis may engulf it.

In Europe, we are seeing almost a mirror image of these processes of rapid change, as the former communist countries seek membership of the EU. From the perspective of existing member states, the main advantage of an enlargement of potentially 100 million EU citizens is in their opportunities as markets, and sites for profitable industrial expansion. The criteria for entry in the first wave – progress towards political democracy and the creation of market economies – are difficult to apply in a rapidly changing situation, where the Czech Republic is involved in a corruption scandal around the long-serving prime minister Vaclav Klaus, and Slovakia may soon vote to replace its antidemocratic Meciar-led coalition, while Lithuania and Latvia could quite soon produce economic indicators that make them look more plausible candidates than Estonia. From the perspective of the applicant states, the attractions of membership that go beyond access to markets are the infrastructure of a prosperous club with highly developed collective goods, including the possibility of redistribution to their most backward sectors and regions through the Structural Funds. In other words, these formerly debt-ridden (apart from Czechoslovakia) economies, which have endured recession, mass unemployment and rapid price inflation, now see a prospect of stabilizing institutions and protective redistributions that work in their favour – a respite from the pressure of destructive global economic forces raging through their social order.

However, in the longer term it may be the deregulatory aspects of the EU regime that most benefit these economies, given their governments' understandable tardiness in implementing privatization and open market conditions (even the much-trumpeted Czech transformation turns out mainly to have been accomplished with the aid of smoke and mirrors). Despite the talk of 'shock therapies' and 'big bangs' (for instance in the Balcerowitz Plan of 1990 in Poland[106]), these governments have used various means to slow down the pace of change. These include social provision, which has absorbed the stress and contradictions generated in the economic sphere; the proportion of national income spent by the state *increased* in Poland and Hungary between 1989 and 1994, mainly because spending on social security almost doubled.[107] The main feature of this increase has been the enormous expansion of the 'safety net' of social assistance.[108] Now the 'transitional' phase of recession and inflation has passed, and growth is under way again, the deregulatory, market-making requirement of EU membership may be more appropriate to the next stage of their development.

Indeed, it may be that in the longer term (some 10 years after entry) the most successful of these countries will have developmental interests that conflict with those of the older EU members. It is possible to imagine a European scenario in which – through inertia rather than any positive decision – the institutions of the EU still reflect an uneasy compromise between the corporatism and protection of workers' rights of the Continental countries, and the market orientation of the British model. In these circumstances, a country like Poland would probably see the EU as a fetter to its development rather than a springboard. With access to the Baltic and the Black Sea, an economic zone compromising Poland and the Ukraine would have many advantages for rapid growth. Polish capital (partly supplied from the large diaspora in Germany and the USA) could provide the investment, Ukrainian labour, drawing industrial workers from this very low-wage agricultural economy, the workers. Hence there could be in Central Europe a region for rapid industrialization again – as in the Chinese case – with a built-in regulative mechanism between the rural and the industrial zones, in the shape of the border between the two countries.

These are speculations about the medium-term future. In the meantime, the new orthodoxy on welfare reform tries to deal with the effects of these developments in other regions of the world on the internal social relations of First World economies. As we saw in Chapter 3, it seeks to mobilize the energies of national populations through higher formal labour market participation ('full employment'); it promises to deal with the insecurity and vulnerability of less skilled and less mobile individuals in terms of increased 'employability', and a stronger ethic of hard work; and it looks to the sense of civic obligation (and in its absence to the threat of officially imposed deprivation) to supply the motives that actual labour-market wages and conditions cannot offer.

In the second and third chapters of this book, I have argued that the new orthodoxy's programme, and the philosophical arguments used to justify it, do not make sense in the global context of economic change. Both the programme and its justification choose to ignore fundamental issues of distributive justice over roles, responsibilities and resources that are central to tasks of social reproduction. In Chapter 5, I outlined an alternative programme that addresses these issues (of inequalities of power, of exploitation, and of autonomy), and how it can justify its entirely different approach to welfare reform and social provision.

In Chapter 4 I analysed the scope for individual responsibility and commercial provision in the present system in the UK and the USA, and how the new orthodoxy seeks to extend these further. The implications for greater mobility between welfare 'clubs', and more fragmentary strategic action within welfare systems, were spelt out. In this chapter, I have broadened this analysis of mobility and collective action to the consideration of migration and transnational institutions, and how the interaction between national policies and the strategic action of migrant people affects issues of human rights and international social justice.

There is clearly unfinished business in this analysis. I have pointed out a seemingly unresolvable dilemma over the ideals for social justice between members of a national or transnational polity prescribed by human rights, and the rules governing mobility between such political units. Although theoretically a basic income approach to issues of social justice – if applied in every state and region of the world – could supply an important missing coherence to the existing chaotic mish-mash of systems regulating migration and asylum, many questions would remain unresolved for the longer term.

I have also argued, in the introductory section of this chapter, that the new politics of welfare contain some dangerous elements of moral fervour and national self-justification that could be used to generate an authoritarian politics of immigration in First World countries. As 'programmes for national renewal'[109] through labour-market participation, the new orthodoxy's policies largely ignore the issues of justice that arise under conditions of high mobility between countries and regions of the world, especially under pressure of political persecution (as at present in Algeria and Kurdistan). The risk is that the moral mobilization of populations in the name of national renewal and democratic revival (as in New Britain and the people's Europe) could provoke movements that further jeopardize marginal and vulnerable groups within society.

If – as in the 1920s and 1930s – the political institutions of liberal nation states come to be unable to deal effectively with the economic pressures generated by the global expansion of capitalism, then nationalistic authoritarianism is always waiting for the opportunity to step in to 'defend the nation', and to protect it from the twin evils of 'foreign financial interests' and 'degenerate alien influences'. It is ethnic minorities and immigrants who get the blame for the weaknesses of liberal national regimes in the face of global market forces; it is their liberalism that is seen as the source of these weaknesses. Moral authoritarianism, barely concealed in much of the new politics of welfare, creates a fertile cultural environment for the growth of such movements.

We see evidence of this in Asia, with the expulsion of up to a million of the three million immigrants working in Malaysia,[110] and riots in Indonesia against the Chinese minority, with its specialization in shopkeeping and trade.[111] Closer to home, it is Romanies and foreigners who are blamed for the dislocations of the economic transitions in the countries of Central Europe, where young people are mobilized in the name of authoritarian nationalism and its cultural symbols.[112]

Paradoxically, it is not in those countries with the longest liberal traditions that the best defences against these political developments now exist. In the USA there have always been waves of moral authoritarianism that threaten to transform liberalism into something else, as with McCarthyism in the early 1950s.[113] In Britain, the bulwarks against such movements are largely informal, and reside in the popular culture of mistrust of moralizing governments as much as in the political culture of representative democracy. But in Continental Europe, with its interwar experience of Nazism and fascism, the whole institutional structure of national political systems is designed to restrain such movements and the kind of politics they generate. The corporatist engagement of the peak organizations of the 'social partners' in negotiation about the shares of capital, labour and social welfare spending in national income; the structures to focus interactions on long-term growth and investment in the future (such as over-training for industrial work); and the hierarchical structure of income protection, with its focus on high replacement incomes – all these are aimed to restrain conflicts and wasteful competition, and promote harmony, solidarity and cohesion. Conversely, popular mobilizations and enthusiastic ideologies are seen as threats to this stability, and social institutions are designed to avoid a repetition of the authoritarian politics of the interwar period.

In conclusion, therefore, it is this question about the relationship between authoritarian nationalism and the moral mobilization sought through the new politics of welfare which is the most disturbing and unresolved aspect of the present situation. I have argued that the goals of the new orthodoxy are entirely consistent with social justice at the national level, and could be pursued by an alternative programme which would avoid the illiberal aspects of coercion and discrimination in its policy prescriptions. But the absence of any consideration of the issues raised in this chapter means that much the same arguments and enthusiasms can be mustered for less scrupulous ends. For these reasons, the moral underpinnings of the new orthodoxy should be rigorously questioned and criticized – for the sake of liberal values and the human rights of minorities, as much as in the defence of the welfare rights of vulnerable groups. There are fundamental political principles at stake in the new politics of welfare.

## Notes and references

1  B. Jordan and D. Vogel, 'Which Policies Influence Migration Decisions? A Comparative Analysis of Qualitative Interviews with Undocumented Brazilian Immigrants in London and Berlin as a Contribution to Economic Reasoning', *Des Arbeitspapier* 14/97, Centrum für Sozialpolitik, University of Bremen, 1997.

2  E. Hobsbawm, 'The Future of the State', in C.H. de Alcántara (Ed.), *Social Futures, Global Visions*, Oxford: Blackwell/UNRISD, 1996, pp. 55–66.

3  A. de Swaan, *In Care of the State: Health Care, Education and Welfare in Europe and the USA in the Modern Era*, Cambridge: Polity, 1988.

4  B. Anderson, *Imagined Communities*, London: Verso, 1991.

5  K. Polanyi, *The Great Transformation: The Political and Economic Origins of Our Time*, Boston, MA: Beacon Press, 1944, ch. 9.

6  N. Cumming-Bruce, 'Misery for Migrant Millions', *Guardian*, 7 January 1998.

7  A. Hurrell and N. Woods, 'Globalisation and Inequality', *Millennium: Journal of International Studies*, 24 (3), 1995, pp. 447–70.

8  Polanyi, *The Great Transformation*.

9  B. Jordan, *A Theory of Poverty and Social Exclusion*, Cambridge: Polity, 1996, chs 1 and 2.

10  De Swaan, *In Care of the State*, chs 1 and 2.

11  M. Breuer, T. Faist and B. Jordan, 'Collective Action, Migration and Welfare States', *International Sociology*, 10 (4), 1995, pp. 369–86.

12  De Swaan, *In Care of the State*, ch. 2.

13  G.P. Freeman, 'Migration and the Political Economy of the Welfare State', *Annals of the American Academy of Political and Social Science*, 485, 1986, pp. 51–63.

14  T. Faist, 'Immigration, Ctizenship and Nationalism: Internal Internationalization in Germany and Europe', in M. Roche and R. Van Berkel (Eds), *European Citizenship and Social Exclusion*, Aldershot: Ashgate, 1997, pp. 213–26.

15  C. Kindleberger, *Europe's Postwar Growth: The Role of Labour Supply*, Cambridge, MA: Harvard University Press, 1967.

16  T. Hammar, *Democracy and the Nation State: Aliens, Denizens and Citizens in a World of International Migration*, Aldershot: Gower, 1990.

17  Faist, 'Immigration, Citizenship and Nationalism'.

18  Ibid.

19  W.A. Lewis, 'Economic Development with Unlimited Supplies of Labour', *The Manchester School*, 22, 1954, pp. 139–91.

20  M. Okólski, 'Poland's Population and Population Movements: An Overview', in E. Jazwinska and M. Okólski (Eds), *Causes and Consequences of Migration in Central and Eastern Europe*, Migration Research Centre, University of Warsaw, 1996, pp. 19–50.

21  O. Stark, *The Migration of Labour*, Cambridge: Polity, 1991.

22  J.E. Taylor, 'Differential Migration, Networks, Information and Risk', in O. Stark (Ed.), *Research in Human Capital and Development* (*Migration, Human Capital and Development*, vol. 4), Greenwich, CT: JAI Press, 1986.

23  N. Cyrus, 'Menschen ohn Anfenhaltsstatus in der Bundesrepublik Deutschland', Department of Comparative Social and Cultural Anthropology, European University 'Viadrina', Frankfurt (Oder), 1996.

24  D.J. Kyle and Z. Liang, 'Who Controls Undocumented Transnational Migration? The Role of Migration Merchants', paper given at Summer Institute on International Migration (GAAC and SSRC), Berlin, 15–25 July 1997.

25  Channel 4 tv, *Illegal Immigration* (Cutting Edge) 21 October, 1997.

26  Jordan and Vogel, 'Which Policies Influence Migration Decisions?'.

27  Ibid.

28  M. Walzer, *Spheres of Justice*, Oxford: Blackwell, 1983, p. 31.

29 Jordan and Vogel, 'Which Policies Influence Migration Decisions?'.
30 Ibid., pp. 18–20.
31 Ibid., p. 20.
32 B. Turner, *Citizenship and Social Theory*, London: Sage, 1993.
33 De Swaan, *In Care of the State*, p. 49.
34 M. Roche, 'Citizenship and Modernity', *British Journal of Sociology*, 46 (4), 1995, pp. 715–33.
35 Ibid., p. 726.
36 J. Habermas, 'Citizenship and National Identity', in B. van Steenbergen (Ed.), *The Condition of Citizenship*, London: Sage, 1994.
37 E. Meehan, *Citizenship and the European Community*, London: Sage, 1993.
38 R. Bauböck, *Transnational Citizenship: Membership and Rights in International Migration*, Aldershot: Edward Elgar, 1994.
39 J.G. Ruggie, 'At Home Abroad, Abroad at Home: International Liberalisation and Domestic Stability in the New World Economy', *Millennium: Journal of International Studies*, 24 (3), 1995, pp. 507–26, at p. 508.
40 Ibid.
41 T. Salmon, 'Britain and the EU's Democratic Deficit', paper presented at the Thirteenth Lothian Conference: 'A British Leadership for a Federal Europe? Reflecting on the Coming British Presidency of the European Union', London House, 11 December 1997.
42 Ibid.
43 R. Bideleux, 'Civil Association: The British Way Forward in a Federal Europe', paper presented at the Thirteenth Lothian Conference, p. 14.
44 M. Thatcher, *The Path to Power*, London: Harper Collins, 1995, pp. 470–1.
45 M. Forsyth, *Unions of States*, Leicester: Leicester University Press, 1981, p. xi.
46 G. Majone, 'The Rise of the Regulatory State in Europe', *West European Politics*, 17 (3), 1994, pp. 77–101; and 'Regulatory Federalism in the European Community', *Government and Policy*, 10, 1992, pp. 299–316.
47 A.M. Burley and W. Mattli, 'Europe Before the Court: A Political Theory of Legal Integration', *International Organisation*, 47 (1), 1993, pp. 41–76.
48 Bideleux, 'Civil Association', p. 15.
49 M. Oakeshott, *Rationalism in Politics and Other Essays*, London: Methuen, 1962, pp. 40–4.
50 Bideleux, 'Civil Association', p. 25.
51 Ibid., p. 19.
52 F. Scharpf, 'Negative and Positive Integration in the Political Economy of European Welfare States', paper given to a Conference on 'A New Social Contract?', European University Institute, Florence, 8–9 October 1995.
53 T. Salmon, 'Britain and the EU's Democratic Deficit'.
54 Polanyi, *The Great Transformation*.
55 European Community, *Charter of Fundamental Social Rights of Workers*, Brussels, Commission of the European Communities, 1990.
56 S. Leibfried and P. Pierson, 'The Prospects for Social Europe', in A. de Swaan (Ed.), *Social Policy Beyond Borders: The Social Question in Transnational Perspective*, Amsterdam: Amsterdam University Press, 1994, pp. 15–58.
57 Ibid., p. 22.
58 Ibid., p. 23.
59 Ibid., p. 29.
60 Ibid., pp. 30–7.

61 European Commission, *Modernising and Improving Social Protection in the European Union*, COM(97) 102 final, Brussels, Commission of the European Communities, 1997.

62 M. Seeleib-Kaiser, 'The Development and Structure of Social Assistance and Unemployment Insurance in the Federal Republic of Germany and Japan', *Social Policy and Administration*, 29 (3), 1995, pp. 269–93.

63 G. Standing, 'Social Protection in Central and Eastern Europe: A Tale of Slipping Anchors and Torn Safety Nets', in G. Esping-Andersen (Ed.), *Welfare States in Transition: National Adaptations in Global Economies*, London: Sage, 1996, pp. 225–55.

64 J. Handler, 'Work, Poverty and the Future of the Welfare State: Questions About Social Europe by an American Observer', paper given at a Joint Meeting of the Law and Society Association and Research Committee on Sociology of Law, Glasgow University, 10–13 July 1996.

65 K. Hinrichs, 'Demography and Pensions', paper presented at a Conference on the Future of the Welfare State: German and British Perspectives, Humboldt University, Berlin, 17–18 November 1997.

66 J. Andersen, 'The New Left in Denmark', Department of Politics, Economics and Public Administration, Aalborg University, 1991.

67 J. Grahl and P. Teague, 'The Crisis of Economic Citizenship in the EU: Lean Production and the German Model', in M. Roche and R. Von Berkel (Eds), *European Citizenship and Social Exclusion*, Aldershot: Ashgate, 1997, pp. 67–82.

68 D. Soskice, 'Reconciling Markets and Institutions: The German Apprenticeship System', in T. Lynch (Ed.), *Training and the Private Sector*, Chicago, IL: University of Chicago Press, 1994.

69 Grahl and Teague, 'Crisis of Economic Citizenship', p. 69.

70 W. Streeck, *Social Institutions and Economic Performance*, London: Sage, 1993.

71 J. Womack, D. Jones and D. Ross, *The Machine that Changed the World*, New York: Rawson Ass., 1990.

72 A. Sengenberger, *The New Industrial Production*, London: Methuen, 1993.

73 G. Herrigel and C. Sabel, *Craft Production in Crisis: Industrial Restructuring in Germany During the 1990s*, Cambridge, MA: Department of Political Science, MIT, 1994.

74 S. Bergman-Pohl, 'Keynote Address' to the Conference on the Future of the Welfare State.

75 L. Leisering, 'Demography and Pensions', paper presented at the Conference on the Future of the Welfare State.

76 A. Giddens, *Modernity and Self-Identity: Self and Society in the Late Modern Age*, Cambridge: Polity, 1991.

77 Bergman-Pohl, Keynote Address.

78 G. Schmid and J. O'Reilley, 'Future Patterns of Work and Employment', paper presented at the Conference on the Future of the Welfare State.

79 Leibfried and Pierson, 'Prospects for Social Europe'.

80 M. Mitchell and D. Russell, 'Race, Citizenship and "Fortress Europe"', in P. Brown and R. Crompton (Eds), *Economic Restructuring and Social Exclusion*, London, UCL Press, 1994, pp. 136–56.

81 M. Roche, 'Citizenship and Exclusion: Reconstructing the European Union', in Roche and Van Berkel, *European Citizenship and Social Exclusion*, pp. 3–22.

82 W. Kymlicka and W. Norman, 'Return of the Citizen: A Survey of Recent Work in Citizenship Theory', *Ethics*, 104 (2), 1994, pp. 352–81.

83 Turner, *Citizenship and Social Theory*; Roche, 'Citizenship and Modernity'.

84 M. Walzer, 'The Civil Society Argument', in C. Mouffe (Ed.), *Dimensions of Radical Democracy: Pluralism, Citizenship and Community*, London: Routledge, 1992.

85 D. Green, *Reinventing Civil Society: The Rediscovery of Welfare Without Politics*, London: Institute for Economic Affairs, 1993.

86 P. Hirst, *Associative Democracy: New Forms of Economic and Social Governance*, Cambridge: Polity, 1994.

87 B. Jordan, 'Citizenship, Association and Immigration in a European Context: Theoretical Issues', in M. Roche and R. Van Berkel (Eds), *European Citizenship and Social Exclusion*, pp. 261–72.

88 R.D. Putnam, *Making Democracy Work: Civic Traditions in Modern Italy*, Princeton, NJ: Princeton University Press, 1993.

89 D. Gambetta, *Trust: The Making and Breaking of Co-operative Relations*, Oxford: Blackwell, 1988; F. Fukuyama, *Trust: The Social Virtues and the Creation of Prosperity*, London: Hamish Hamilton, 1995.

90 Putnam, *Making Democracy Work*.

91 E. Ostrom, *Governing the Commons: The Evolution of Institutions for Collective Action*, Cambridge: Cambridge University Press, 1990.

92 M. Ignatieff, *The Needs of Strangers*, London: Chatto and Windus/Hogarth Press, 1984.

93 Bauböck, *Transnational Citizenship*.

94 Jordan, 'Citizenship, Association and Immigration', p. 267.

95 J.H. Carens, 'Aliens and Citizens: The Case for Open Borders', *Review of Politics*, 49 (2), 1987, pp. 251–73.

96 I. Forbes and G. Mead, *Measure for Measure: Comparative Analysis of Measures to Combat Racial Discrimination in the Member Countries of the EC*, Sheffield: Department of Employment, 1992.

97 M. Walker and A. Travis, 'Losers in a Game Without Frontiers', *Guardian*, 7 January 1998; I. Traynor and H. Smith, 'EU Passport-Free Regime Buckles', *Guardian*, 6 January 1998.

98 Mitchell and Russell, 'Race, Citizenship and "Fortress Europe"'.

99 Ibid.

100 E.M. Suplicy, 'Guaranteed Minimum Income in Brazil?', *Citizen's Income Bulletin*, 19, 1995, pp. 4–7; J. Baskin, 'A Basic Income for South Africa?', *Weekly Mail and Guardian*, 24 January 1997.

101 Polanyi, *The Great Transformation*.

102 J. Schumpeter, *The Theory of Economic Development* (1911), Cambridge, MA: Harvard University Press, 1936.

103 Polanyi, *The Great Transformation*.

104 M. Bienefeld, 'Karl Polanyi and the Contradictions of the 1980s', in M. Mendell and P. Salée (Eds), *The Legacy of Karl Polanyi*, New York: St Martin's Press, 1991, pp. 15–42.

105 Lewis, 'Economic Development with Unlimited Supplies of Labour'; Kindleberger, *Europe's Postwar Growth*.

106 C.G.A. Bryant and K. Mokrycki (Eds), *The New Great Transformation? Change and Continuity in East-Central Europe*, London: Routledge, 1994.

107 European Bank for Reconstruction and Development, *Transition Report: Economic Transition in Eastern Europe and the Former Soviet Union*, London: EBRD, 1994.

108 S. Golinowska, 'Public Social Expenditures', in *Social Policy and Social Conditions in Poland, 1989–93*, Warsaw: Institute of Labour and Social Affairs, 1994; M. Potucek, 'Current Social Policy Developments in the Czech and Slovak Republics', *Journal of European Social Policy*, 3, 1994, pp. 209–26; Standing, 'Social Protection in Central and Eastern Europe'.

109 Commission on Social Justice, *Social Justice: Strategies for National Renewal*, London: Vintage, 1994.

110 BBC Radio 4, 'Asia File', 24 January 1998.

111 Ibid.

112 European Bank for Reconstruction and Development, *Transition Report*.

113 T. Spragens, Jr, *The Irony of Liberal Reason*, Chicago, IL: Chicago University Press, 1981.

# Bibliography

Andersen, J. (1991) 'The New Left in Denmark', Department of Politics, Economics and Public Administration, Aalborg University.

Anderson, B. (1991) *Imagined Communities*, London: Verso.

Archer, B. (1997) 'Marques out of 10', *Guardian*, 6 October.

Arnold, J. and B. Jordan (1995) 'Beyond Befriending or Past Caring? Probation Values, Training and Social Justice', in B. Williams (Ed.), *Probation Values*, Birmingham's Venture Press, pp. 75–92.

Arrow, K. (1951) *Social Choice and Individual Values*, New York: Wiley.

Bacon and Woodrow Analysis (1993) *Employees and Personal Pensions*, London, Bacon and Woodrow.

Bacon, R. and W. Eltis (1976) *Britain's Economic Problem: Too Few Producers*, London: Macmillan.

Baird, R. (1998) 'Why Not Enough People are Feeling the Benefit', *Guardian* (Jobs and Money), 17 January, pp. 16–17.

Ball, M. (1983) *Housing and Economic Power: The Political Economy of Owner Occupation*, London: Methuen.

Balls, E. (1993) 'Danger: Men Not at Work', in E. Balls and P. Gregg, *Work and Welfare*, London: IPPR.

Bane, M.J. and D. Ellwood (1986) 'Slipping In and Out of Poverty: The Dynamics of Poverty Spells', *Journal of Human Resources*, 2 (1), pp. 1–23.

Barber, B. (1984) *Strong Democracy: Participating Politics for a New Age*, Berkeley, CA: University of California Press.

Barclay, G. (ed.) (1991) A Digest of Information on the Criminal Justice System, London: Home Office.

Barclay, P. (1995) *The Joseph Rowntree Inquiry into Income and Wealth*, York: Joseph Rowntree Trust.

Barker, J. (1995) 'Are Low-Wage Workers a Danger?', *The Times*, 28 July.

Barr, A. (1995) 'Empowering Communities – Beyond Fashionable Rhetoric?', *Community Development Journal*, 30 (2), pp. 121–32.

Barr N. (Ed.) (1994) *Labour Markets and Social Policy in Central and Eastern Europe: The Transition and Beyond*, Oxford: Oxford University Press and the World Bank.

Barry, B. (1995) *Justice as Impartiality*, Oxford: Clarendon Press.

Barry, B. (1991) 'The Continuing Relevance of Socialism', in *Liberty and Justice: Essays in Political Theory, 1*, Oxford: Clarendon Press, pp. 274–90.

Barry, B. (1998) 'Liberalism and Multiculturalism', paper given at the Oxford Political Thought Conference, 8 January.

Barry, N. (1990) 'Markets, Citizenship and the Welfare State: Some Critical Reflections', in R. Plant and N. Barry, *Citizenship and Rights in Thatcher's*

*Britain: Two Views*, London: Institute of Economic Affairs, Health and Welfare Unit.

Baskin, J. (1997) 'A Basic Income for South Africa?', *Weekly Mail and Guardian*, 24 January.

Batten, T.R. (1957) *Communities and their Development: An Introductory Study with Special Reference to the Tropics*, Oxford: Oxford University Press.

Bauböck, R. (1991) 'Migration and Citizenship', *New Community*, 8 (1), pp. 27–48.

Bauböck, R. (1994) *Transnational Citizenship: Membership and Rights in International Migration*, Aldershot: Edward Elgar.

Bauman, Z. (1992) *Intimations of Post-modernity*, London: Routledge.

BBC Radio 4, *Eurofile*, 22 November 1997.

BBC Radio 4, *World at One*, 22 December 1997.

BBC Radio 4, *Asia File*, 24 January 1998.

BBC2 tv, *How Much for Cash?*, 30 October 1997.

Becker, G.S. (1976) *The Economic Approach to Human Behaviour*, Chicago, IL: Chicago University Press.

Bellamy, R. (1998) 'The Politics of Compromise', paper given at the Oxford Political Thought Conference, St Catherine's College, Oxford, 8–10 January.

Benington, J. (1972) 'Community Work as an Instrument of Institutional Change', in *Lessons from Experience*, London: ACW.

Bentham, J. (1843) *Constitutional Code*, in J. Bowring (Ed.), *The Works of Jeremy Bentham*, London: Tait, vol. 9.

Beresford, P. (1996) *Meeting the Challenge: Social Work Education and the Community Care Revolution*, London: NISW.

Bergmann-Pohl, S. (1997) 'Keynote Address' to the Conference on the Future of the Welfare State: British and German Perspectives, Humboldt University, Berlin, 17–18 November.

Beveridge, W. (1909) *Unemployment: A Problem of Industry*, London: Longman Green.

Beveridge, W. (1942) *Social Insurance and Allied Services*, Cmd 6404, London: HMSO.

Beveridge, W. (1944) *Full Employment in a Free Society*, London: Allen and Unwin.

Bideleux, R. (1997) 'Civil Association: The British Way Forward in a Federal Europe', paper presented at the Thirteenth Lothian Conference, 'A British Leadership for a Federal Europe? Reflecting on the Coming British Presidency of the European Union', London House, 11–12 December.

Bienefeld, M. (1991) 'Karl Polanyi and the Contradictions of the 1980s', in M. Mendell and P. Salée (Eds), *The Legacy of Karl Polanyi*, New York: St Martin's Press, pp. 15–42.

Blair, T. (1997) Speech to Labour Party Conference, *Guardian*, 22 October.

Blair, T. (1997) Speech at Durham, 22 December.

Blair, T. (1998) Interview on *Breakfast with Frost*, ITV, 11 January.

Blyth, E. and J. Milner (1993) 'Exclusion from School: A First Step Towards Exclusion From Society?', *Children and Society*, 7 (3), pp. 255–68.

Breuer, M., T. Faist and B. Jordan (1995) 'Collective Action, Migration and Welfare States', *International Sociology*, 10 (4), pp. 369–86.

Brindle, D. (1998) 'Quest for Benefits Fit for 21st Century', *Guardian*, 16 January.

Brown, G. (1997) 'Why Labour is Still Loyal to the Poor', *Guardian*, 2 August.

Bryant, C.G.A. and K. Mokrycki (Eds) (1994) *The New Great Transformation? Change and Continuity in East-Central Europe*, London: Routledge.

Buchanan, J.M. (1965) 'An Economic Theory of Clubs', *Economica*, 32, pp. 1–14.

Buchanan, J.M. (1967) *Public Finance in a Democratic Process*, Chapel Hill, NC: University of North Carolina Press.

Buchanan, J.M. (1968) *The Demand and Supply of Public Goods*, New York: Rand MacNally.

Buchanan, J.M. (1994) *Ethics and Economic Progress*, Norman, OK: University of Oklahoma Press.

Buhr P. and S. Leibfried (1995) '"What a Difference a Day Makes": The Significance for Social Policy of Social Assistance Receipt', in G. Room (Ed.), *Beyond the Threshold: The Measurement and Analysis of Social Exclusion*, Bristol: The Policy Press.

Burley, A.M. and W. Mattli (1993) 'Europe Before the Court: A Political Theory of Legal Integration', *International Organisation*, 47 (1), pp. 41–76.

Calabresi, G. and P. Bobbit (1978) *Tragic Choices*, New York: Norton.

Campbell, B. (1993) *Goliath: Britain's Dangerous Places*, London: Methuen.

Carens, J.H. (1987) 'Aliens and Citizens: The Case for Open Borders', *Review of Politics*, 49 (2), pp. 251–73.

Carvel, J. (1998) 'Labour Revolt on Private Schools Plan', *Guardian*, 7 January.

Carvel, J. (1998) 'Labour Targets Lazy Parents', *Guardian*, 16 January.

Carvel, J. (1998) 'Truant Pupils Blamed for Wave of Street Crime', *Guardian*, 2 January.

*Central Europe Productivity Reporter* (1997), 4th Edition, March, p. 3.

Challis, D. and B. Davies (1985) 'Long-Term Care of the Elderly: The Community Care Scheme, Discussion Paper 386, Canterbury: Personal Social Services Research Unit, University of Kent.

Channel 4 tv (1997) *Illegal Immigration* (Cutting Edge), 21 October.

Checkland, S.G. and E.O.A. (Eds) (1974) *The Poor Law Report of 1834*, Harmondsworth: Penguin.

City of Cologne (1989) *Kolnberg*, Cologne: City of Cologne Council.

Clarke, J. (ed.) (1993) *A Crisis in Care: Challenges to Social Work*, London: Sage.

Cole, G.D.H. (1929) *The Next Ten Years in British Social and Economic Policy*, London: Macmillan.

Commission on Social Justice (1994) *Social Justice: Strategies for National Renewal*, London: Vintage.

Cook, R. (1992) 'Arkansan Travels Well Nationally as Campaign Heads for Test', *Congressional Quarterly Weekly Report*, 11 January, pp. 58–65.

Corrigan, P. and P. Leonard (1978) *Social Work Practice Under Capitalism*, London: Macmillan.

Cumming-Bruce, N. (1998) 'Misery for Migrant Millions', *Guardian*, 7 January.

Currie, E. (1996) *Is America Really Winning the War on Crime, and Should Britain Follow its Example?*, London: National Association for the Care and Resettlement of Offenders.

Cyrus, N. (1996) 'Menschen ohn Anfenhaltsstatus in der Bundesrepublik Deutschland', Department of Comparative Social and Cultural Anthropology, European University 'Viadrina', Frankfurt (Oder).

Dalley, G. (1988) *Ideologies of Caring: Rethinking Community and Collectivism*, Basingstoke: Macmillan.

Danglovà, O. (1997) 'In the Trap of Poverty: Analysis of Poverty-Stricken

Communities in Southern Slovakia', paper given at the Third International Conference on Social Problems, Social History of Poverty in Central Europe, Lodz, Poland, 3–6 December.

Dauges, Y. (1991) *Riots and Rising Expectations in Urban Europe*, LSE Housing Annual Lecture, translated A. Power, London: LSE.

Dean, M. (1991) *Towards a Theory of Liberal Governance*, London: Routledge.

Dean, H. (1994) *Welfare, Law and Citizenship*, London: Routledge.

Dean, H. (Ed.) (1995) *Parents' Duties, Children's Debts: The Limits of Policy Intervention*, Aldershot: Ashgate.

Dean, H. (1995) 'Paying for Children: Procreation and Financial Liability', in H. Dean (Ed.), *Parents' Duties, Children's Debts*, Aldershot: Ashgate.

Dean, H. (1998) 'Undermining Social Citizenship: The Counterproductive Effects of Behavioural Controls in Social Security Administration', paper given to ISSA Second International Research Conference on Social Security, Jerusalem, 25–28 January.

Dean, H. and M. Melrose (1997) 'Manageable Discord: Fraud and Resistance in the Social Security System', *Social Policy and Administration*, 31 (2), pp. 103–18.

Dean, H. and M. Melrose (1998) *Poverty, Riches and Social Citizenship*, Basingstoke: Macmillan.

Dean, H. and P. Taylor-Gooby (1992) *Dependency Culture: The Explosion of a Myth*, Hemel Hempstead: Harvester Wheatsheaf.

Dennis, N. (1993) *Rising Crime and the Dismembered Family*, London: Institute for Economic Affairs.

Department for Education and Employment (1997) *Labour Market Trends, June 1996*, London: Stationery Office.

Department of Social Security (1993) *Equality in State Pension Ages*, London, HMSO.

Department of Social Security (1994) *Households Below Average Income. A Statistical Analysis, 1979–92*, London: HMSO.

Department of Social Security (1997) *Pensions: Consultative Document*, London: Stationery Office, November.

Department of Social Security (1997) *Social Security Statistics, 1997*, London: Stationery Office.

Dex, S. (1988) *The Sexual Division of Work*, Oxford: Blackwell.

Donnison, D. (1991) *A Radical Agenda: After the New Right and the Old Left*, London: Rivers Oram Press.

Donnison, D. (1998) *Politics for a Just Society*, Basingstoke: Macmillan.

Douglas, C.H. (1974) *Economic Democracy* (1919), Sudbury: Bloomfield.

Douthwaite, R. (1996) *Short Circuit*, London: Green Books.

Doyal, L. and I. Gough (1991) *A Theory of Human Need*, Basingstoke: Macmillan.

Dryzek, J. (1990) *Discursive Democracy*, Cambridge: Cambridge University Press.

Duncan, A. and P. Hobson (1995) *Saturn's Children: How the State Devours Liberty, Prosperity and Virtue*, London: Sinclair-Stevenson.

Durbin, E. (1985) *New Jerusalems: The Labour Party and the Economics of Democratic Socialism*, London: Routledge.

Durkheim, E. (1898) 'Individualism and the Intellectuals', *Revue Bleu*, 4th Series (10), pp. 7–13.

Duval Smith, A. (1998) 'Fear Enforces Jungle Law in Cape Town's Badlands', *Guardian*, 13 January.

Düvell, F. and B. Jordan (1998) *Undocumented Immigrant Workers in London*, Interim Report on ESRC Research Project, Exeter: Exeter University.

Dworkin, A. (1998) 'Dear Bill and Hillary', *Guardian*, 29 January.

Dworkin, R. (1985) 'Rights as Trumps', in *A Matter of Principle*, Cambridge, MA: Harvard University Press.

Eichenreich, B. (1998) 'How Bill Screwed Us All', *Guardian*, 24 January.

Elliott, L. (1995) 'Seventies-style Fear and Loathing Makes a Comeback', *Guardian*, 21 August.

Elliott, L. (1995) 'US Reaps the Unhappy Harvest of Deregulation', *Guardian*, 20 February.

Elster, J. (1986) 'Comment on Van der Veen and Van Parijs', *Theory & Society*, 15, pp. 709–22.

Elster, J. (1989) *The Cement of Society: A Study of Social Order*, Cambridge: Cambridge University Press.

Emmaeus, U.K. (1997) *Understanding Emmaeus*, Cambridge: Emmaeus Foundation.

Esping-Andersen, G. (1990) *The Three Worlds of Welfare Capitalism*, Cambridge: Polity.

Esping-Andersen, G. (1996) 'Welfare States Without Work: The Impasse of Labour Shedding and Familialism in Continental European Social Policy' and 'After the Golden Age: Welfare State Dilemmas in a Global Economy', in G. Esping-Andersen (Ed.), *Welfare States in Transition: National Adaptations in Global Economies*, London: Sage, ch. 3.

Etzioni, A. (Ed.) (1969) *The Semi-Professions and their Organisation*, New York: Free Press.

Etzioni, A. (1993) *The Spirit of Community: The Reinvention of American Society*, New York: Touchstone.

European Bank for Reconstruction and Development (1994) *Transition Report: Economic Transition in Eastern Europe and the Former Soviet Union*, London: EBRD.

European Commission (1993) *Employment in Europe*, Luxembourg: Office of the Commission of the European Communities.

European Commission (1997) *Modernising and Improving Social Protection in the European Union*, COM(97) 102 final, Brussels, Commission of the European Communities.

European Community (1990) *Charter of Fundamental Social Rights of Workers*, Brussels: Commission of the European Communities.

Eurostat (Statistical Office of the European Communities) (1996) *Social Portrait of Europe*, Luxembourg: Office for Official Publications of the European Communities.

Evason, E. and R. Woods (1995) 'Poverty, Deregulation of Labour Markets and Benefit Fraud', *Social Policy and Administration*, 29 (1), pp. 40–54.

Faist, T. (1994) 'How to Define a Foreigner? The Symbolic Politics of Immigration in German Partisan Discourse', *West European Politics*, 17 (2), pp. 50–71.

Faist, T. (1997) 'Immigration, Citizenship and Nationalism: Internal Internationalization in Germany and Europe', in M. Roche and R. Van Berkel (Eds), *European Citizenship and Social Exclusion*, Aldershot: Ashgate, pp. 213–26.

Fehér, F., G. Márkus and A. Heller (1983) *Dictatorship Over Needs*, Oxford: Blackwell.

Feige, E.L. (1997) 'Underground Activity and Institutional Change: Productive, Protective Predatory Behaviour in Transition Economies', in J.M. Nelson, C. Tilley and L. Walker (Eds), *Transforming Post-Communist Political Economies*, Washington, DC: National Academy Press, pp. 21–34.

Field, F. (1997) *The Reform of Welfare*, London: Social Market Foundation.

Field, F. (1997) Speech to the Conference on the Future of the Welfare State: British and German Perspectives, Humboldt University, Berlin, 17–18 November.

Filmer, Sir Thomas (1949) *Patriarcha*, in P. Laslett (Ed.), *Filmer's Patriarcha and Other Political Writings*, Oxford: Oxford University Press.

Finer, S.E. (1952) *The Life and Times of Sir Edwin Chadwick*, London: Methuen.

Foldvary, F. (1994) *Public Goods and Private Communities: The Market Provision of Social Services*, Aldershot: Edward Elgar, pp. 30–32.

Forbes, I. and G. Mead (1992) *Measure for Measure: Comparative Analysis of Measures to Combat Racial Discrimination in the Member Countries of the EC*, Sheffield: Department of Employment.

Forrest, R. and A. Murie (1983) 'Residualisation and Council Housing: Aspects of the Changing Social Relations of Housing Tenure', *Journal of Social Policy*, 12 (4), pp. 453–60.

Forsyth, M. (1981) *Unions of States*, Leicester: Leicester University Press.

Foucault, M. (1977) *Discipline and Punish: The Birth of the Prison*, Harmondsworth: Allen Lane.

France, Alan (1997) '"Why Should We Care?" Young People, Citizenship and Questions of Social Responsibility', *Journal of Youth Studies*, 1 (1), pp. 97–111.

Freeden, M. (1993) *Rights*, Milton Keynes: Open University Press.

Freeman, G.P. (1986) 'Migration and the Political Economy of the Welfare State', *Annals of the American Academy of Political and Social Science*, 485, pp. 51–63.

Freie Hansestadt Bremen (1992) 'Regeneration Project Osterholz-Tenever', Application, Urban Pilot Project, Bremen.

Frieske, K. (1997) 'In Search of Social Problems: Poverty, Dependency or Social Marginality', paper given at the Third International Conference on Social Problems, Social History of Poverty in Central Europe, Lodz, Poland, 3–6 December.

Fukuyama, F. (1995) *Trust: The Social Virtues and the Creation of Prosperity*, London: Hamish Hamilton.

Galston, W. (1991) *Liberal Purposes: Goods, Virtues and Duties in the Liberal State*, Cambridge: Cambridge University Press.

Gambetta, D. (1988) *Trust: The Making and Breaking of Co-operative Relations*, Oxford: Blackwell.

Garfinkel, H. (1967) *Studies in Ethnomethodology*, Englewood Cliffs, NJ: Prentice-Hall.

Garner, P. (1994) 'Exclusions from Schools: Towards a New Agenda', paper presented at a conference on 'Changing Educational Structures: Policy and Practice', CEDAR, Warwick University, 15–17 April.

George, V. and P. Wilding (1976) *Ideology and State Welfare*, London: Routledge and Kegan Paul.

Gibbons, J. (1997) 'Relating Outcomes to Objectives in Child Protection Policy', in N. Parton (Ed.), *Child Protection and Family Support*, London: Routledge, pp. 78–91.

Giddens, A. (1991) *Modernity and Self-Identity: Self and Society in the Late Modern Age*, Cambridge: Polity.

Giddens, A. (1993) *The Consequences of Modernity*, Cambridge: Polity Press.

Gingrich, N. (1994) Speech during mid-term elections, *Guardian*, 20 October.

Glendon, M.A. (1991) *Rights Talk: The Impoverishment of Political Discourse*, New York: Free Press.

Glennester, H. (1993) *Paying for Welfare in the 1990s*, London: Heinemann.

Goffman, E. (1972) *Interaction Ritual: Essays on Face-to-Face Behaviour*, Harmondsworth: Penguin.

Golinowska, S. (1994) 'Public Social Expenditures', in *Social Policy and Social Conditions in Poland, 1989–93*, Warsaw: Institute of Labour and Social Affairs.

Goodman, A. and S. Webb (1995) *The Distribution of Expenditure in the United Kingdom*, London: Institute for Fiscal Studies.

Goodwin, B. (1986) *Justice and the Lottery*, Cambridge: Cambridge University Press.

Goodwin, B. (1997) *Using Political Ideas*, 4th edition, Chichester: Wiley.

Gordon, D. (1988) 'The Global Economy: New Edifice or Crumbling Foundations?', *New Left Review*, 168, pp. 24–65.

Gough, I. (1997) Response to Frank Field, Conference on the Future of the Welfare State, Humboldt University, Berlin, 17–18 November.

Grahl, J. and P. Teague (1997) 'The Crisis of Economic Citizenship in the EU: Lean Production and the German Model', in M. Roche and R. Von Berkel (Eds), *European Citizenship and Social Exclusion*, Aldershot: Ashgate, pp. 67–82.

Gray, J. (1983) 'Classical Liberalism, Positional Goods and the Politicisation of Poverty', in A. Ellis and K. Kumar (Eds), *Dilemmas of Liberal Democracies*, London: Tavistock.

Green, A. and H. Steedman (1993) *Educational Provision, Educational Attainment and the Needs of Industry: A Review of Research for Germany, France, Japan, the USA and Britain*, National Institute for Economic and Social Research, Report Services No. 5.

Green, D. (1987) *The New Right*, Brighton: Wheatsheaf.

Green, D. (1993) *Reinventing Civil Society: The Rediscovery of Welfare Without Politics*, London: Institute for Economic Affairs.

Habermas, J. (1987) *The Theory of Communicative Action* (1984), Boston, MA: Beacon Press.

Habermas, J. (1994) 'Citizenship and National Identity', in B. van Steenbergen (Ed.), *The Condition of Citizenship*, London: Sage.

Hadley, R. and R. Clough (1996) *Care in Chaos: Frustration and Challenge in Community Care*, London: Cassell.

Hambleton, R. and H. Thomas (Eds) (1995) *Urban Policy Evaluation: Challenge and Change*, London: Paul Chapman.

Hammar, T. (1990) *Democracy and the Nation State: Aliens, Denizens and Citizens in a World of International Migration*, Aldershot: Gower.

Handler, J. (1996) 'Work, Poverty and the Future of the Welfare State: Questions About Social Europe by an American Observer', paper given at a Joint Meeting of the Law and Society Association and Research Committee on Sociology of Law, Glasgow University, 10–13 July.

Handler, J. and Y. Hasenfeld (1997) *We the Poor People*, New Haven, CT: Yale University Press.

Handy, C. (1989) *The Age of Unreason*, London: Hutchinson.

Hardin, R. (1968) 'The Tragedy of the Commons', *Science*, 162, pp. 1243–8.

Harding, P. and R. Jenkins (1989) *The Myth of the Hidden Economy: Towards a New Understanding of Informal Economic Activity*, Milton Keynes: Open University Press.

Hayek, F.A. (1960) *The Constitution of Liberty*, Chicago, IL: Chicago University Press.

Hayek, F.A. (1976) *The Mirage of Social Justice*, London: Routledge and Kegan Paul.

Hayek, F.A. (1980) *Individualism and the Economic Order*, Chicago, IL: University of Chicago Press.

Hayek, F.A. (1982) *Law, Legislation, Liberty*, London: Routledge and Kegan Paul.

Heady, C. (1997) 'Labour Market Transitions and Social Exclusion', *European Journal of Social Policy*, 7 (2), pp. 119–28.

Held, D. and A. McGrew (1994) 'Globalization and the Liberal Democratic State', *Government and Opposition*, 28 (2), pp. 261–85.

Hencke, D. (1998) 'Benefit Cuts Reap £3.2 billion', *Guardian*, 5 January.

Herrigel, G. and C. Sabel (1994) *Craft Production in Crisis: Industrial Restructuring in Germany During the 1990s*, Cambridge, MA: Department of Political Science, MIT.

Hewitt, P. (1996) T.H. Marshall, Memorial Lecture, in M. Bulmer and A. Rees (Eds), *Citizenship Today*, London: UCL Press, pp. 254–65.

Hilbert, R.A. (1992) *The Classical Roots of Ethnomethodology: Durkheim, Weber and Garfinkel*, Chapel Hill, NC: University of North Carolina Press.

Hillman, M., J. Adams and J. Whitelegg (1991) *One False Move: A Study of Children's Independent Mobility*, London: Policy Studies Institute.

Hills, J. (1993) *The Future of Welfare: A Guide to the Debate*, York: Social Policy Research Unit, Joseph Rowntree Foundation.

Hinrichs, K. (1997) 'Demography and Pensions', paper given at the Conference on the Future of the Welfare State: German and British Perspectives, Humboldt University, Berlin, 17–18 November.

Hirsch, F. (1977) *Social Limits to Growth*, London: Routledge and Kegan Paul.

Hirst, P. (1994) *Associative Democracy: New Forms of Economic and Social Governance*, Cambridge: Polity.

Hirst, P. and G. Thompson (1996) *Globalization in Question: The International Economy and the Possibilities of Governance*, Cambridge: Polity.

Hobhouse, L.T. (1922) *The Elements of Social Justice*, London: Allen and Unwin.

Hobsbawm, E. (1996) 'The Future of the State', in C.H. de Alcántara (Ed.), *Social Futures, Global Visions*, Oxford: Blackwell/UNRISD, pp. 55–66.

Hoggart, S. (1996) 'Is China Trading Places? Why are our plastic bags produced in China and not Telford?, *Guardian*, 28 September.

Hollis, P. (1997) *Jennie Lee, A Life*, Oxford: Oxford University Press.

Home Office (1997) *Prison Statistics 1997*, London: Stationery Office.

Huff Stevens, H. (1994) 'Persistence in Poverty and Welfare: The Dynamics of Poverty Spells: Updating Bane and Ellwood', *American Economic Review*, Papers and Proceedings 84, pp. 34–7.

Hughes, G. and A. Little (1996) 'Radical Communitarianism in Europe: Social

Policy and the Politics of Inclusion in the Work of Jordan and Gorz', Political Studies Association, Proceedings of Annual Conference, 1996, pp. 341–72.

Hughes, G. (1996) 'Communitarianism and Law and Order', *Critical Social Policy*, 16 (4), pp. 17–42.

Hume, D. (1888) *A Treatise of Human Nature* (1745), Ed. L.A. Selby-Bigge, Oxford: Clarendon Press.

Hume, D. (1985) *Essays Moral, Political and Literary* (1742), Oxford: Oxford University Press, pp. 42, 175, 309–10.

Hurrell, A. and N. Woods (1995) 'Globalisation and Inequality', *Millenium: Journal of International Studies*, 24 (3), pp. 447–70.

Hutchinson, F. and B. Burkitt (1997) *The Political Economy of Social Credit and Guild Socialism*, London: Routledge.

Ignatieff, M. (1984) *The Needs of Strangers*, London: Chatto and Windus/Hogarth Press.

Illich, I. (1974) *Deschooling Society*, London: Calder and Boyars.

Illich, I. (1974) *Disabling Professions*, New York and London: Calder and Boyars.

Illich, I. (1975) *Medical Nemesis*, London: Calder and Boyars.

Ingram, A. (1998) 'Models of Integration in Liberal Democracies', paper given at the Oxford Political Thought Conference, 9 January.

International Labour Office (1990) *Yearbook of Labour Statistics, 1989–90*, Geneva: ILO.

International Labour Office (1996) *International Labour Force Statistics, 1996*, Geneva: ILO.

Ivison, D. (1998) 'Excavating the Liberal Public Sphere', paper given at the Oxford Political Thought Conference, St Catherine's College, 9 January.

James, S., B. Jordan and H. Kay (1991) 'Poor People, Council Housing and the Right to Buy', *Journal of Social Policy*, 20 (4), pp. 27–40.

Jargowsky, P.A. and M.J. Bane (1991) 'Ghetto Poverty in the United States, 1970–80', in C. Jeneks and P. Peterson (Eds), *The Urban Underclass*, Washington, DC: Brookings Institute, pp. 235–73.

Jarvis, S. and S.P. Jenkins (1995) 'Do the Poor Stay Poor? New Evidence about Income Dynamics from the British Household Panel Study', ESRC Research Centre on Microsocial Change, Occasional Paper 95-2, Colchester: University of Essex.

Jarvis, S. and S.P. Jenkins (1996) 'Changing Places: Income Mobility and Poverty Dynamics in Britain', ESRC Centre on Microsocial Change, Working Paper 96–19, Colchester: University of Essex.

Jessop, B. (1994) 'The Transition to Post-Fordism and the Schumpeterian Workfare State', in R. Burrows and B. Loader (Eds), *Towards a Post-Fordist Welfare State?*, London: Routledge, pp. 13–37.

Johnson, P. and J. Falkingham (1992) *Ageing and Economic Welfare*, London: Sage.

Johnson, T.J. (1972) *Professions and Power*, London: Macmillan.

Jones, R. (1997) 'Millions Ponder a Return to Serps', *Guardian* (Jobs and Money), 13 December, pp. 6–7.

Jordan, B. (1981) *Automatic Poverty*, London: Routledge and Kegan Paul.

Jordan, B. (1984) *Invitation to Social Work*, Oxford: Martin Robertson.

Jordan, B. (1985) *The State: Authority and Autonomy*, Oxford: Blackwell.

Jordan, B. (1987) *Rethinking Welfare*, Oxford: Blackwell.

Jordan, B. (1989) *The Common Good: Citizenship, Morality and Self-Interest*, Oxford: Blackwell.

Jordan, B. (1990) *Social Work in an Unjust Society*, Hemel Hempstead: Harvester Wheatsheaf.

Jordan, B. (1992) 'Basic Income and the Common Good', in P. Van Parijs (Ed.), *Arguing for Basic Income: Ethical Foundations for a Radical Reform*, London: Verso, pp. 155–78.

Jordan, B. (1994) 'Framing Welfare Claims and the Weapons of the Weak', in G. Drover and P. Kerans (Eds), *New Approaches to Welfare Theory*, Andover: Edward Elgar.

Jordan, B. (1995) 'Are New Right Policies Sustainable? "Back to Basics" and Public Choice', *Journal of Social Policy*, 24 (3), pp. 363–84.

Jordan, B. (1996) 'Basic Income: Is it Too Late?', paper given at Nuffield College Oxford, May.

Jordan, B. (1996) *A Theory of Poverty and Social Exclusion*, Cambridge: Polity.

Jordan, B. (1997) 'Citizenship, Association and Immigration in a European Context: Theoretical Issues', in M. Roche and R. Van Berkel (Eds) *European Citizenship and Social Exclusion*, Aldershot: Ashgate, pp. 261–72.

Jordan, B. (1997) 'Democratic Community and Public Choice', in E.O. Eriksen and J. Loftager (Eds), *The Rationality of the Welfare State*, Oslo: Scandinavian University Press, pp. 76–97.

Jordan, B. (1997) 'Service Users' Involvement in Child Protection and Family Support', in N. Parton (Ed.), *Child Protection and Family Support*, London: Routledge.

Jordan, B. (1998) 'Justice and Reciprocity', *Critical Review of International Social and Political Philosophy*, 1 (1), pp. 63–85.

Jordan, B. and J. Arnold (1995) 'Democracy and Criminal Justice', *Critical Social Policy*, 44 (5), pp. 171–80.

Jordan, B. and A. Travers (1997) 'The Informal Economy: A Case Study of Unrestrained Competition', Exeter: Department of Social Work, University of Exeter.

Jordan, B. and D. Vogel (1997) 'Which Policies Influence Migration Decisions? A Comparative Analysis of Qualitative Interviews with Undocumented Brazilian Immigrants in London and Berlin as a Contribution to Economic Reasoning', *Des Arbeitspapier* 14/97, Centrum für Sozialpolitik, University of Bremen.

Jordan, B., S. James, H. Kay and M. Redley (1992) *Trapped in Poverty? Labour-Market Decisions in Low-Income Households*, London: Routledge.

Jordan, B., M. Redley and S. James (1994) *Putting the Family First: Identity, Decisions, Citizenship*, London: UCL Press.

Kane-Berman, J. (1997) *South Africa's Silent Revolution*, Johannesburg: South African Institute of Race Relations/Southern Book Publishers.

Keane, J. and J. Owens (1986) *After Full Employment*, London: Hutchinson.

Keegan, V. (1998) 'A New Deal – But a Great Gamble', *Guardian*, 1 January.

Kennedy, P. (1996) 'Globalisation and Its Discontents' (Dimbleby Lecture), BBC Radio 4, 30 May.

Kettle, M. (1998) 'White House Wise Guys', *Guardian*, 19 January.

Kindleberger, C. (1967) *Europe's Postwar Growth: The Role of Labour Supply*, Cambridge, MA: Harvard University Press.

Kirklees Metropolitan Authority (1997) 'Working in Communities', Huddersfield: Kirklees Metropolitan Authority.

Kyle, D.J. and Z. Liang (1997) 'Who Controls Undocumented Transnational

Migration? The Role of Migration Merchants', paper given at Summer Institute on International Migration (GAAC and SSRC), Berlin, 15–25 July.

Kymlicka, W. and W. Norman (1994) 'Return of the Citizen: A Survey of Recent Work on Citizenship Theory', *Ethics*, 104 (2), pp. 352–81.

Larmore, C. (1987) *Patterns of Moral Complexity*, Cambridge: Cambridge University Press.

Lash, S. (1994) 'The Making of an Underclass: Neo-Liberalism *versus* Corporatism?', in P. Brown and R. Compton, *Economic Restructuring and Social Exclusion*, London: UCL Press, pp. 157–174.

Laski, H. (1936) *The Rise of Liberalism*, London: Harper.

Leather, S. and B. Jordan (1997) 'Food Poverty: Do Labour's Policies Make Sense?', Exeter: Department of Social Work, University of Exeter.

Leibfried, S. and P. Pierson (1994) 'The Prospects for Social Europe', in A. de Swaan (Ed.), *Social Policy Beyond Borders: The Social Question in Transnational Perspective*, Amsterdam: Amsterdam University Press, pp. 15–58.

Leisering, L. (1997) 'Demography and Pensions', paper presented at the Conference on the Future of the Welfare State: German and British Perspectives, Humboldt University, Berlin, 17–18 November.

de Leonardis, O. (1993) 'New Patterns of Collective Action in "Post Welfare Society"', in G. Drover and P. Kerans (Eds), *New Approaches to Welfare Theory*, Aldershot: Edward Elgar, pp. 177–89.

Lewis, J. (1992) 'Gender and the Development of Welfare Regimes', *Journal of European Social Policy*, 2 (3), pp. 159–71.

Lewis, W.A. (1954) 'Economic Development with Unlimited Supplies of Labour', *The Manchester School*, 22, pp. 139–91.

Liebknecht, W. (1986) quoted in R. Ashton, 'Marx's Friends and Comrades', *Encounter*, February.

Locke, J. (1967) *Two Treatises of Government* (1698), Ed. P. Laslett, Cambridge: Cambridge University Press.

Lustiger-Thaler, H. and E. Shragge (1993) 'Social Movements and Social Welfare: The Political Problem of Needs', in G. Drover and P. Kerans (Eds), *New Approaches to Welfare Theory*, Aldershot: Edward Elgar, pp. 161–76.

Luttwak, E. (1995) 'The Good Bad Guys', *Guardian*, 31 July.

MacAdam, E. (1945) *The Social Servant in the Making*, London: Allen and Unwin.

Macedo, S. (1990) *Liberal Virtues: Citizenship, Virtue and Community*, Oxford: Oxford University Press.

MacIntyre, A. (1981) *After Virtue: An Essay in Moral Theory*, London: Duckworth.

Majone, G. (1992) 'Regulatory Federalism in the European Community', *Government and Policy*, 10, pp. 299–316.

Majone, G. (1994) 'The Rise of the Regulatory State in Europe', *West European Politics*, 17 (3), pp. 77–101.

Malthus, T. (1798) *An Essay on the Principle of Population as it Affects the Future Improvement of Society*, London: J. Johnson.

Mann, K. (1991) *The Making of an English Underclass*, Oxford: Oxford University Press.

Mansbridge, J. (1995) 'Does Participation Make Better Citizens?', *The Good Society*, 5 (2), pp. 1–7.

Marshall, T.H. (1950) *Citizenship and Social Class*, Cambridge: Cambridge University Press.

Marske, C.E. (1991) *Communities of Fate: Readings in the Social Organisation of Risk*, Lanham, VA: University Press of America.

Marx, K. and F. Engels (1976) *The Manifesto of the Communist Party* (1848), in *Collected Works*, London: Lawrence and Wishart, vol. 5.

Mathews, K.G.P. (1982) 'Reward for Currency and the Black Economy in the UK', *Journal of Economic Studies*, 9 (2), pp. 3–22.

Mayo, M. (1994) *Communities and Caring: The Mixed Economy of Welfare*, Basingstoke: Macmillan.

Mazibuko, F. (1996) 'Social Work and Sustainable Development: The Challenges for Practice, Training and Policy in South Africa', paper given to Joint World Congress of IFS and IASSW, Hong Kong, July.

McIntosh, M. (1981) 'Feminism and Social Policy', *Critical Social Policy*, 1 (1).

Mead, L.M. (1989) *Beyond Entitlement: The Social Obligations of Citizenship*, New York: Free Press.

Meehan, E. (1993) *Citizenship and the European Community*, London: Sage.

Mill, J.S. (1912) 'On Liberty' (1889), in *Utilitarianism, Liberty and Representative Government*, London: Dent.

Millar, J. (1997) 'Lone Parents', paper given at a Conference on the Future of the Welfare States: German and British Perspectives, Humboldt University, Berlin, 18–19 November.

Millar, J., K. Cooke and E. McLaughlin (1989) 'The Employment Lottery: Risk and Social Security Benefits', *Policy and Politics*, 17 (1), pp. 75–81.

Miller, D. (1998) 'Prospects for Social Justice', paper given to the Oxford Political Thought Conference, St Catherine's College, 8 January.

Miller, G. (1981) *Cities by Contract*, Cambridge, MA: MIT Press.

Mingione, E. (1993) 'New Urban Poverty and the Crisis in the Citizenship-Welfare System: the Italian Experience', *Antipode*, 25 (3), pp. 206–20.

Mishan, E.J. (1986) *Economic Myths and the Mythology of Economics*, Brighton: Wheatsheaf.

Mishra, R. (1984) *The Welfare States in Crisis: Social Thought and Social Change*, Brighton: Harvester.

Mitchell, M. and D. Russell (1994) 'Race, Citizenship and "Fortress Europe"', in P. Brown and R. Crompton (Eds), *Economic Restructuring and Social Exclusion*, London, UCL Press, pp. 136–56.

Monbiot, G. (1998) 'Sprawling Suburbia', *Guardian*, 7 January.

Morris, L. (1994) *Dangerous Classes: The Underclass and Social Citizenship*, London: Routledge.

Mueller, D.C. (1979) *Public Choice*, Cambridge: Cambridge University Press.

Mueller, D.C. (1989) *Public Choice II*, Cambridge: Cambridge University Press.

Muffels, A., J. Berghman and H-J. Derven (1992) 'A Multi-method Approach to Monitor the Evolution of Poverty', *Journal of European Social Policy*, 2 (3), pp. 193–213.

Mulgan, G. (1991) 'Citizens and Responsibilities', in G. Andrews (Ed.), *Citizenship*, London: Lawrence and Wishart, pp. 37–49.

Murray, C. (1985) *Losing Ground: American Social Policy, 1950–1980*, New York: Basic Books.

Murray, C. (1989) 'The Underclass', *Sunday Times Magazine*, 26 November, pp. 26–45.

Musgrave, R.A. (1959) *The Theory of Public Finance*, New York: McGraw-Hill.

Nichol, C. (1997) 'Patterns of Pay: Results from the 1997 New Earnings Survey', *Labour Market Trends*, Office for National Statistics, November, Table 1, p. 470.

Niskanen, W.A. (1975) 'Bureaucrats and Politicians', *Journal of Law and Economics*, 18, pp. 617–43.

Nozick, R. (1974) *Anarchy, State and Utopia*, Oxford: Blackwell.

Oakeshott, M. (1962) *Rationalism in Politics and Other Essays*, London: Methuen.

Office for National Statistics (1997) *Financial Statistics, 1997*, London: Stationery Office.

Office for National Statistics (1997) *Social Trends, 1997*, London: Stationery Office.

Okólski, M. (1996) 'Poland's Population and Population Movements: An Overview', in E. Jazwinska and M. Okólski (Eds), *Causes and Consequences of Migration in Central and Eastern Europe*, Migration Research Centre, University of Warsaw, pp. 19–50.

Oldfield, A. (1990) *Citizenship and Community: Civic Republicanism in the Modern World*, London: Routledge.

Olson, M. (1965) *The Logic of Collective Action: Public Goods and the Theory of Groups*, Cambridge, MA: Harvard University Press.

Olson, M. (1982) *The Rise and Decline of Nations: Economic Growth, Stagflation and Social Rigidities*, New Haven, CT: Yale University Press.

Orwell, G. (1949) *Nineteen Eighty-Four*, London: Secker and Warburg.

Ostrom, E. (1990) *Governing the Commons: The Evolution of Institutions for Collective Action*, Cambridge: Cambridge University Press.

Pahl, R.E. (1984) *Divisions of Labour*, Oxford: Blackwell.

Parker, H. (1989) *Instead of the Dole: An Enquiry into the Integration of the Tax and Benefits Systems*, London: Routledge.

Parker H. (Ed.) (1995) *Modest-but-adequate Budgets for Four Pensioner Households, October 1994 Prices*, London: Age Concern.

Parker, H. and Sutherland, H. (1995) 'Why a £20 CI is Better than Lowering Income Tax to 20 per cent', *Citizen's Income Bulletin*, 19, pp. 15–18.

Parker, H. and Sutherland, H. (1998) 'How to Get Rid of the Poverty Trap: Basic Income Plus National Minimum Wage', *Citizen's Income Bulletin*, 25 February, pp. 11–14.

Parkinson, M. (1994) 'Economic Competition and Social Exclusion: European Cities towards 2000', paper given at a seminar on the Measurement and Analysis of Social Exclusion. University of Bath, 17–18 June.

Parton, N. (1996) *Social Work, Social Theory and Social Change*, London: Routledge.

Parton, N., D. Thorpe and C. Wattam (1997) *Child Protection, Risk and the Moral Order*, Basingstoke: Macmillan.

Peatfield, Z. (1997) 'Caught on the Edge', *Guardian*, 6 December.

Perkin, H. (1990) *The Rise of Professional Society: England since 1880*, London: Routledge.

Perkin, H. (1996) *The Third Revolution: Professional Society in International Perspective*, London: Routledge.

Phizaklea, A. (1990) *Unpacking the Clothing Industry*, London: Routledge.

Plant, R. (1997) 'Citizenship, Employability and the Labour Market', *Citizen's Income Bulletin*, 24, pp. 2–3.

Plender, J. (1997) 'Shuffle Up the Pension Path', *Financial Times*, 20 November, p. 19.

Plymouth City Council (1997) 'Unitary Plymouth: Plan for Community Development', Consultation Paper, Plymouth.

Polanyi, K. (1944) *The Great Transformation: The Political and Economic Origins of Our Time*, Boston, MA: Beacon Press.

Popkin, S. (1979) *The Rational Peasant: The Political Economy of Rural Vietnam*, Chicago, IL: Chicago University Press.

Popple, K. (1995) *Analysing Community Work: Its Theory and Practice*, Oxford: Oxford University Press.

Potucek, M. (1994) 'Current Social Policy Developments in the Czech and Slovak Republics', *Journal of European Social Policy*, 3, pp. 209–26.

Power, A.E. (1993) *Hovels to High Rise: State Housing in Europe since 1850*, London: Routledge.

Power, A.E. (1997) *Estates on the Edge: The Social Consequences of Mass Housing in Europe*, London: Macmillan.

Psacharopoulos, G. and G. Woodhall (1985) *Education for Development: An Analysis of Investment Choices*, Oxford: Oxford University Press.

Putnam, R.D. (1993) *Making Democracy Work: Civic Traditions in Modern Italy*, Princeton, NJ: Princeton University Press.

Rawls, J. (1971) *A Theory of Justice*, Oxford: Oxford University Press.

Rawls, J. (1989) 'The Domain of the Political and Ideas of the Good', *New York University Law Review*, 64, pp. 234–5.

Rawls, A.W. (1989) 'Language, Self and Social Order: A Reformation of Goffman and Sacks', *Human Studies*, 12, pp. 147–72.

Reich, C. (1964) 'The New Property', *Yale Law Journal*, 73 (5), pp. 473–98.

Reich, R. (1997) 'New Deal and Fair Deal', *Guardian*, 14 July, p. 16.

Reich, R. (1993) *The Work of Nations: Preparing Ourselves for Twenty-First Century Capitalism*, New York: Knopf.

Revenko, A. (1997) 'Poor Strata of Population in Ukraine', paper given at the Third International Conference on Social Problems, Social History of Poverty in Central Europe, Lodz, Poland, 3–6 December.

Roche, M. (1995) 'Citizenship and Modernity', *British Journal of Sociology*, 46 (4), pp. 715–33.

Roche, M. (1997) 'Citizenship and Exclusion: Reconstructing the European Union', in M. Roche and R. Van Berkel, *European Citizenship and Social Exclusion*, Aldershot: Ashgate, pp. 3–22.

Roemer, J.E. (1982) *A General Theory of Exploitation and Class*, part III, Cambridge, MA: Harvard University Press.

Rogers, R. (1995) Reith Lectures, BBC Radio 4, January, March.

Rorty, R. (1980) 'Pragmatism, Relativism and Irrationalism', *Proceedings and Addresses of the American Philosophical Association*, 53, pp. 379–91.

Rowlingson, K., C. Wiley and T. Newburn (1997) *Social Security Fraud*, London: Policy Studies Institute.

Ruggie, J.G. (1995) 'At Home Abroad, Abroad at Home: International Liberalisation and Domestic Stability in the New World Economy', *Millennium: Journal of International Studies*, 24 (3), pp. 507–26.

Ruigrok, W. and T. Van Tulder (1995) *The Logic of International Restructuring*, London: Lawrence and Wishart.

Ryan, A. (1983) 'Mill and Rousseau: Utility and Rights', in G. Duncan (Ed.), *Democratic Theory and Practice*, Cambridge: Cambridge University Press, pp. 56–7.

Sahlins, M. (1974) *Stone Age Economics*, London: Tavistock.

Salmon, T. (1997) 'Britain and the EU's Democratic Deficit', paper given at the

Thirteenth Lothian Conference: 'A British Leadership for a Federal Europe? Reflecting on the Coming British Presidency of the European Union', London House, 11 December.

Salter, T. (1997) 'Being Realistic About Pension Reform', *Citizen's Income Bulletin*, 24, pp. 9–11.

Sandel, M. (1982) *Liberalism and the Limits of Justice*, Cambridge: Cambridge University Press.

Sauvy, A. (1984) *Le Travail Noir et L'Economie de Demain*, Paris: Calman Levy.

Scharpf, F. (1995) 'Negative and Positive Integration in the Political Economy of European Welfare States', paper given to a Conference on 'A New Social Contract?', European University Institute, Florence, 8–9 October.

Scheiber, G.S., J.-P. Poullier and M. Greenwald (1991) 'Health Care Systems in Twenty-four Countries', *Health Affairs*, 10 (3), pp. 22–38.

Schmähl, W. (1997) Comment on a speech by Frank Field at the Conference on the Future of the Welfare State, Humboldt University, Berlin, 17–18 November.

Schmid G. and J. O'Reilly (1997) 'Future Patterns of Work and Employment', paper presented at the Conference on the Future of the Welfare State: British and German Perspectives, Humboldt University, Berlin, 17–18 November.

Schumpeter, J. (1936) *The Theory of Economic Development* (1911), Cambridge, MA: Harvard University Press.

Schumpeter, J. (1947) *Capitalism, Socialism and Democracy* (1943), London: Allen and Unwin.

Scott, J.C. (1990) *Domination and the Arts of Resistance: Hidden Transcripts*, New Haven, CT: Yale University Press.

Seeleib-Kaiser, M. (1995) 'The Development and Structure of Social Assistance and Unemployment Insurance in the Federal Republic of Germany and Japan', *Social Policy and Administration*, 29 (3), pp. 269–93.

Sen, A.K. (1970) *Collective Choice and Social Welfare*, San Francisco: Holden-Day.

Sengenberger, A. (1993) *The New Industrial Production*, London: Methuen.

Silverman, D. (1985) *Qualitative Methodology and Sociology*, Aldershot: Gower.

Smart, B. (1991) *Modern Conditions, Post-modern Controversies*, London: Routledge.

Smith, A. (1937) *The Wealth of Nations* (1776), early draft version, quoted in W.R. Scott, *Adam Smith as a Student and Professor*, Glasgow: Brown, pp. 326–8.

Smith, A. (1948) *The Theory of Moral Sentiments*, in H.W. Schneider (Ed.), *Adam Smith's Moral and Political Philosophy*, New York: Harper.

Smith, A. (1976) *An Inquiry into the Nature and Causes of the Wealth of Nations* (1776), Ed. R.H. Campbell and A.S. Skinner, Oxford: Clarendon Press.

Solow, R. (1990) *The Labour Market as a Social Institution*, Oxford: Blackwell.

Soskice, D. (1994) 'Reconciling Markets and Institutions: The German Apprenticeship System', in T. Lynch (Ed.), *Training and the Private Sector*, Chicago, IL: University of Chicago Press.

South Glamorgan County Council, Children and Families Division (1994) 'Users' Involvement Strategy', Cardiff: South Glamorgan County Council.

Spragens, T. Jr. (1981) *The Irony of Liberal Reason*, Chicago, IL: Chicago University Press.

Spruyt, H. (1995) *The Nation State and Its Competitors*, Princeton, NJ: Princeton University Press.

Standing, G. (1996) 'Social Protection in Central and Eastern Europe: A Tale of

Slipping Anchors and Torn Safety Nets', in G. Esping-Andersen (Ed.), *Welfare States in Transition*, London: Sage, pp. 225–55.

Stark, O. (1991) *The Migration of Labour*, Cambridge: Polity.

Starrett, D.A. (1988) *Foundations of Public Economics*, Cambridge: Cambridge University Press.

Statham, D. (1978) *Radicals in Social Work*, Basingstoke: Macmillan.

Stiglitz, J.E. (1986) *Economics of the Public Sector*, New York: W.W. Norton.

Streeck, W. (1993) *Social Institutions and Economic Performance*, London: Sage.

Suplicy, E.M. (1995) 'Guaranteed Minimum Income in Brazil?', *Citizen's Income Bulletin*, 19, pp. 4–7.

de Swaan, A. (1988) *In Care of the State: Health Care, Education and Welfare in Europe and the USA in the Modern Era*, Cambridge: Polity.

Tawney, R.H. (1921) *The Acquisitive Society*, London: Allen and Unwin.

Taylor, C. (1996) 'The Liberal-Communitarian Debate', in N. Rosenblum (Ed.), *Liberalism and the Moral Life*, Cambridge, MA: Harvard University Press.

Taylor, C. (1989) *The Sources of Self*, Cambridge: Cambridge University Press.

Taylor, J.E. (1986) 'Differential Migration, Networks, Information and Risk', in O. Stark (Ed.), *Research in Human Capital and Development* (*Migration, Human Capital and Development*, vol. 4), Greenwich, CT: JAI Press.

Taylor, M. (1987) *The Possibility of Co-operation*, Cambridge: Cambridge University Press.

Thatcher, M. (1995) *The Path to Power*, London: Harper Collins.

Thomas, J.J. (1992) *Informal Economic Activity*, Hemel Hempstead: Harvester Wheatsheaf.

Thompson, D. (1996) 'Fetishizing the Family: The Construction of the Informal Carer', in H. Jones and J. Millar (Eds), *The Politics of the Family*, Aldershot: Avebury.

Thorpe, D. (1997) 'Policing Minority Child-Rearing Practices in Australia: The Consistency of "Child Abuse"', in N. Parton (Ed.), *Child Protection and Family Support*, London: Routledge, pp. 59–77.

Tiebout, C. (1956) 'A Pure Theory of Local Expenditures', *Journal of Political Economy*, 64, pp. 416–24.

Traynor, I. and H. Smith (1998) 'EU Passport-Free Regime Buckles', *Guardian*, 6 January.

TUC (1983) Labour Party Liaison Committee, *Partners in Rebuilding Britain*, London: Trades Union Congress.

Tullock, G. (1967) *Towards a Mathematics of Politics*, Ann Arbor, MI: University of Michigan Press.

Tully, J. (1980) *A Discourse on Property: John Locke and his Adversaries*, Cambridge: Cambridge University Press.

Tully, J. (1997) *Strange Multiplicity*, Cambridge: Cambridge University Press.

Turner, B. (1993) *Citizenship and Social Theory*, London: Sage.

United Nations (1994) *World Development Report, 1994*, Geneva: United Nations.

US Department of Labor (1989) *Labor Market Problems of Older Workers*, Washington, DC: Department of Labor.

Van Parijs, P. (1992) 'Competing Justifications for Basic Income', in P. Van Parijs (Ed.), *Arguing for Basic Income*, London: Verso, pp. 3–46.

Van Parijs, P. (1992) 'The Second Marriage of Justice and Efficiency', in P. Van Parijs (Ed.), *Arguing for Basic Income: Ethical Foundations for a Radical Reform*, London: Verso, pp. 215–40.

Van Parijs, P. (1995) *Real Freedom for All: What (If Anything) is Wrong with Capitalism?*, Oxford: Oxford University Press.

Vanner, D. (1994) 'Local Economic Strategy and Local Coalition Building', *Local Economy*, 10 (1), pp. 33–47.

Vincent, A. and R. Plant (1984) *Philosophy, Politics and Citizenship: The Life and Thought of the British Idealists*, Oxford: Blackwell.

Voges, W. and G. Rohwer (1992) 'Receiving Social Assistance in Germany: Risk and Duration', *Journal of European Social Policy*, 2 (3), pp. 175–91.

Von Mises, L. (1981) *Socialism*, Indianapolis: Liberty Fund.

Waddan, A. (1997) *The Politics of Social Welfare: The Collapse of the Centre and the Rise of the Right*, Cheltenham: Edward Elgar.

Waldinger, R. and M. Lapp (1995) 'Back to the Sweatshop or Ahead to the Informal Sector?', *International Journal of Urban and Regional Research*, 17 (1), pp. 6–29.

Walker, M. and A. Travis (1998) 'Losers in a Game Without Frontiers', *Guardian*, 7 January.

Walter, T. (1988) *Basic Income: Freedom from Poverty, Freedom to Work*, London: Marion Boyars.

Walzer, M. (1983) *Spheres of Justice*, Oxford: Blackwell.

Walzer, M. (1992) 'The Civil Society Argument', in C. Mouffe (Ed.), *Dimensions of Radical Democracy: Pluralism, Citizenship and Community*, London: Routledge.

Warnes, A.M. (1993) *The Demography of Ageing in the United Kingdom of Great Britain and Northern Ireland*, Malta: International Centre of Ageing, United Nations.

Watson, G. (1997) 'Labour's Welfare Lie', *Guardian*, 24 December.

Weale, A. (1983) *Political Theory and Social Policy*, London: Macmillan.

Webb, S. and B. (1929) *English Poor Law History*, London: Allen and Unwin.

White, M. (1991) *Against Unemployment*, London: Policy Studies Institute.

White, S. (1995) 'Rethinking the Strategy of Equality: An Assessment of the Report of the Commission on Social Justice', *Political Quarterly*, pp. 205–10.

White, S. (1996) 'Reciprocity in the defence of basic income', paper given at Basic Income European Network Conference, Vienna, 12–14 September.

Wicksell, K. (1958) 'A New Principle of Just Taxation' (1896), in R.A. Musgrave and A.T. Peacock (Eds), *Classics in the Theory of Public Finance*, London: Macmillan, pp. 72–116.

Williams, C.C. and J. Windebank (1994) 'Spatial Variations in the Informal Sector: A Review of Evidence from the European Union', *Regional Studies*, 28 (8), pp. 819–25.

Williams, C.C. and J. Windebank (1995) 'Black Market Work in the European Community: Peripheral Work for Peripheral Localities?', *International Journal of Urban and Regional Research*, 17 (1), pp. 6–29.

Williams, F. (1989) *Social Policy: A Critical Introduction: Issues of Race, Gender and Class*, Cambridge: Polity.

Willoughby, W. (1900) *Social Justice*, New York: Knopf.

Wilson, E. (1977) *Women and the Welfare State*, London: Tavistock.

Wilson, W.J. (1989) *The Truly Disadvantaged: The Underclass, the Ghetto and Public Policy*, Chicago, IL: Chicago University Press.

Wilson, W.J. (1997) *When Work Disappears: The World of the New Urban Poor*, London: Vintage.

Windebank, J. and C.C. Williams (1997) 'What is to be Done about the Paid

Informal Sector in the European Union? A Review of Some Policy Options', *International Planning Studies*, 2 (3), pp. 315–27.

Womack, J., D. Jones and D. Ross (1990) *The Machine that Changed the World*, New York: Rawson Ass.

Woodhall, G. (1992) 'Financial Aid: Students', in *Higher Education Encylopedia*, 2, New York: Pergamon Press, pp. 1358–67.

Woollacott, M. (1998) 'Watch That Pension', *Guardian*, 15 January.

Young, H. (1998) 'Vision for Our Future', interview with Tony Blair, *Guardian*, 17 January.

Young, I.M. (1990) *Justice and the Politics of Difference*, Princeton, NJ: Princeton University Press.

# INDEX